Teen Rights:

A Legal Guide for Teens and the Adults in Their Lives

Traci Truly
Attorney at Law

SPHINX® PUBLISHING
AN IMPRINT OF SOURCEBOOKS, INC.®
NAPERVILLE, ILLINOIS
www.SphinxLegal.com

First Edition, 2002
Second Printing, February, 2003
     Published by: **Sphinx® Publishing, An Imprint of Sourcebooks, Inc.®**

Naperville Office
P.O. Box 4410
Naperville, Illinois 60567-4410
630-961-3900
Fax: 630-961-2168
www.sourcebooks.com
www.SphinxLegal.com

This publication is designed to provide accurate and authoritative information in regard to the subject matter covered. It is sold with the understanding that the publisher is not engaged in rendering legal, accounting, or other professional service. If legal advice or other expert assistance is required, the services of a competent professional person should be sought.

From a Declaration of Principles Jointly Adopted by a Committee of the American Bar Association and a Committee of Publishers and Associations

This product is not a substitute for legal advice.

Disclaimer required by Texas statutes.

Library of Congress Cataloging-in-Publication Data
Truly, Traci.
     Teen rights : a legal guide for teens and the adults in their lives / Traci Truly.
        p. cm.
     Includes index.
     ISBN 1-57248-221-4 (pbk. : alk. paper)
     1. Teenagers--Legal status, laws, etc.--United States--Popular works. 2. Minors--United States--Popular works. I. Title.

KF479.Z9 T78 2002
346.7301'35--dc21
                                                            2002075946

Printed and bound in the United States of America.

BG Paperback — 10 9 8 7 6 5 4 3 2

CONTENTS

INTRODUCTION

Teenager's rights is an area of interest to both teens and the adults in their lives. This book will explore several different areas in which teens have rights. School plays a very important role in the lives of every teenager, and we will look at the interaction of teens and their schools, both public and private. Since many teenagers also work, you will find chapters on teens in the workplace. Topics include sexual harassment and discrimination as well as general information about employment laws.

No book about teenagers would be complete without a discussion about the rights of teenagers when they are dealing with their parents. You will find chapters that deal with the issues that most often confront teens and their parents: discipline, birth control, abortion, marriage, and medical care.

Many teens are forced to deal with eating disorders, so we have included some chapters on this issue, its causes, and symptoms. There is also a list of resources in the appendix if you need more information than a book of this type can provide.

Privacy is another big concern of teens. In the section on schools, we have addressed the confidentiality of your school records. You will find information on confidentiality of crime records in the chapter that deals with juvenile crime and on confidentiality of employment records in the chapter about rights and obligations in the workplace. There is an additional, separate chapter about other privacy issues.

Since this is a book about your legal rights, there is also information on how the court system works, how to do legal research, and how to work with a lawyer.

You will notice as you read the book and the specific cases discussed, that different courts sometimes reach different decisions on similar cases.

Many of the rules are decided on a case by case basis and the outcome can vary from one jurisdiction to another. *Jurisdiction* is simply a legal term used to define the geographic areas that a particular court governs. Cases can either be filed in federal court or in state court.

Each state has its own system of state courts. The first level is the trial court; these courts may be called things like district court or superior court. Each state also has a system of appeals courts. Once the highest court of each state, often called the state Supreme Court, has ruled on a case, the losing party at that level can ask the United States Supreme Court to hear the case.

For federal cases, the first court to hear a case is the federal district court, where the case is tried before a single judge. The next step is when the losing party decides to appeal the district judge's ruling. The case then goes to one of the circuit courts of appeals. The next step on the appeals ladder is the United States Supreme Court.

Most cases will be identified as one person or entity versus another. For example, the first case mentioned in this book is called *Hazelwood v. Kuhlmeier*. Not all cases have this same title, though. Some states use different titles for cases involving minors. Sometimes, you will see *In the Matter of* or *In Re* followed by a name or initials. The name or initials belong to the teenager who is involved in the case.

At the end of the chapters, there is an Appendix A. It includes many helpful resources for the topics covered in this book. Not only are they useful for anything you may be dealing with now, they can also help you with writing research papers. If you know of other resources not listed in Appendix A, we would like to hear from you. Contact us at:

info@SphinxLegal.com

SECTION I:

TEENS AND SCHOOL

−1−
THE FIRST AMENDMENT IN SCHOOL

Students do not lose their rights to free speech and free exercise of religion just because they are in school. However, the school district has the right and responsibility to maintain control of the school environment and to maintain discipline. When courts look at cases that involve a school's attempt to regulate or forbid a student's speech or religious expression, they balance the competing rights between the school and the student. In some instances, the student will win. In others, the school will win. This chapter will explore some of the issues that have come up and how the courts have ruled.

THE STUDENT NEWSPAPER
A frequent area of conflict between students and the school administration is the issue of who has the final say about what goes into the school paper. The First Amendment freedom of the press protection does apply to school newspapers. That means that the school must justify any actions it takes that would limit that freedom.

The main case in this area is *Hazelwood School District v. Kuhlmeier*, a United States Supreme Court case that said that the school district *does* have the right to control the contents of a student publication. This case involved a school newspaper that was produced as part of a high school journalism class. The school principal reviewed all of each issue prior to publication.

In the issue that triggered this case, the principal objected to two stories. One was about pregnant students and their experiences. The principal did not like the coverage of sexual activity and birth control. The other story was about the impact of divorce on students.

(continued)

The principal thought that the parents of students who had been quoted should have had an opportunity to respond to what their children had said. Since there was not enough time to rework the stories, some pages were just left out of the paper. Some of the students sued, but the courts decided that school officials could regulate the paper in any reasonable manner and that, in this case, the principal's decisions had been reasonable.

The rules are somewhat different if the publication in question is not produced or sponsored by the school. In some *jurisdictions* (places under a specific court's direction), courts have said that these publications cannot be *censored* at all. The only action, then, that a school can take is to discipline any students involved in the preparation or distribution of the publication. Other courts have said that the school can stop the publication if destruction of school property or physical violence against teachers and fellow students will likely result if the publication goes forward.

The law seems clear that the schools can decide whether or not to accept advertising from particular businesses. This is helpful to the school district as most will not want alcohol, tobacco, or other controversial advertising in the school paper.

OTHER PRINTED MATERIAL

The school district does not have to let students distribute printed material on the campus. And, if the school allows students to pass out literature, they have the right to review the material before it is passed out. The same can be even more true if the material is religious in nature.

It is more of an issue when the materials are religious because, in this situation, the school district must follow the constitutional rules that say that governments cannot do anything that would promote religion. There must be a total separation between the state (our governments) and religion. This applies to schools because schools are considered part of the government.

Bibles

There have been a number of cases brought to court that have to do with passing out religious literature at school. Cases have been decided that say the Gideons, a religious group, cannot come into the classrooms and pass out Bibles. However, in one case, the court said that if the school has allowed the Gideons to use the school premises after school hours, it is not illegal for a Gideon to give a student a Bible in the hall after school. It is legal for schools to allow religious groups to use the school facilities after school hours.

Other cases have allowed an unattended box containing Bibles to be placed in the school building. Students would be allowed to take Bibles from the box without any pressure. Courts say that the Ten Commandments cannot be posted in school, the Bible cannot be used at a school assembly, and the Bible cannot be read at graduation ceremonies. In one case, a court even ruled that it was illegal for a teacher to put religious books in his in-room library and allow students to have access to the books.

In some situations, the rules depend on where you live since courts have reached different decisions on some issues. For example, some courts have said it is illegal for groups of students to gather either before or after school in a classroom and read the Bible together. Other courts have decided that it is *not* illegal. The same difference of opinion exists in cases about students reading the Bible during their free time during school and using the Bible in after-school groups and clubs that use school facilities for their meetings.

Many courts do not allow Bible readings over the intercom and saying the Lord's Prayer in class together. Distribution of Bibles in school, regardless of whether the school or a private entity provides the Bibles, is not allowed in many places either. Furthermore, silent Bible reading by teachers during school hours is not allowed. A school district can even require teachers to keep their Bibles off their desks and out of view.

It is not necessarily unconstitutional to use the Bible as a textbook in school, but the school must take extraordinary care not to present the material in any way that would promote any one religion. The law also says that states cannot prohibit teaching Darwinism and the theory of evolution in school. However, districts are forbidden from teaching creationism.

Witchcraft

The question of whether certain activities and written materials promote witchcraft in school has also received some attention. Some cases involve whether depictions of witches and cauldrons at Halloween unconstitutionally promote the religious practices of *Wicca*, a form of witchcraft. Courts have allowed the decorations to remain in the school.

In one case, **Brown v. Woodland Unified School District**, parents filed a lawsuit against the school district because they objected to the content of the reading instruction program used in their

(continued)

child's elementary school. The program had a section of activities that had the children discuss witches and compose chants. In another section, the students pretended that they were witches or sorcerers and role played the characters in certain situations. The parents claimed this constituted instruction in the practices and rituals of *Wicca*.

The courts disagreed, saying that these activities, constituted only a few sections out of some 10,000 sections in the reading program. The rest of the sections were clearly nonreligious. Therefore, the few sections in question could not be viewed as promoting the rituals of witchcraft and the school could continue using the program.

Use of School Facilities by Outside Groups

If a school allows any religious groups to use its facilities, then it cannot deny any other religious group the right to use the facilities. This is an all or nothing proposition. Either the school district prohibits all religious groups or lets them all in.

VULGARITY AND SLURS

Because students retain the right to free speech, they cannot be punished just because the school does not like what they have said. The school must show that the student's language has an *adverse impact*, such as it was either offensive or that it disrupted the school.

One case (that is also discussed in Chapter 10 on discipline) is of interest here because it addresses the issue of free speech in school.

In the case, **Heller v. Hodgin**, the student, Emily Heller, was disciplined for a verbal argument in the cafeteria after another student cut in line. When Emily told her she had to get out of line, the student who cut-in called Emily a vulgar name that included a racial reference. The court sided with the school because a student's free speech rights in school do not go so far that she can use obscene vulgar language without being disciplined.

APOLOGIES AND FORCED SPEECH

Another side to this coin is whether the school district can force a student to say certain things when the student chooses not to. Sometimes, they can.

In **Kicklighter v. Evans County School District**, Crystal Kicklighter was a student at Claxton High School. She got into an argument with another student before English class started. The teacher heard the argument and told Crystal she could not continue to make "off-color remarks." Crystal told her teacher to "...check the Declaration of Independence," particularly the section on free speech. The teacher told Crystal to find a seat. When she did not, the teacher sent her to the office. The student ended up being required to apologize to the entire English class and serve a five-day suspension. Crystal served the suspension but never apologized.

The principal considered the apology an important part of the discipline imposed, and he ended up having Crystal escorted from the school by the police because she refused to apologize. Ultimately, she left the school permanently and filed this suit.

Crystal came up with an interesting argument for her trial. She said that making her apologize would mean that she felt sorry; feeling sorry was a personal belief and individual thought that should be protected by the First Amendment. However, this court's opinion was that the students in school do not have the same degree of wide freedom that adults have. The judge said that the school district did have the authority to make Crystal apologize.

Another issue Crystal used to try to win her case was a claim that the school district was retaliating against her because she was white and was expecting a child with a fellow student who was black. The judge did agree that dating was an activity that was protected by the constitutional right to free association, but did not find any evidence to support Crystal's claim that the school was punishing her for her choice to date the black student. The judge based his decision partly on the fact that the school could show valid reasons to discipline Crystal that had nothing to do with her pregnancy.

THE FIRST AMENDMENT AND
THE DRESS CODE

As will be discussed in Chapter 2 on dress codes, the First Amendment can come into play in determining whether a school dress code is legal. Clothing that contains a message is protected by the First Amendment under free speech, but schools can still regulate speech. So cases involving clothing are analyzed just like other cases where a student's right to free speech is balanced against the school district's right to maintain control and discipline.

Pyle v. School Committee of South Hadley is a 1996 case from Massachusetts. The school district had a written policy that prohibited clothing that "harasses, intimidates, or demeans an individual or group of individuals because of sex, color, race, religion, handicap, national origin, or sexual orientation." The dress code also prohibited "pictures, slogans, or designs that are obscene, profane, lewd, or vulgar." The court in that case ruled that schools cannot regulate speech, including that contained on clothes, just because it is offensive or vulgar. The school district must show some sort of *disruption* within the school caused by the language. In this case, the student's argument that his right to free speech had been violated was the correct one. Even though his T-shirt contained an obscenity, he should be allowed to wear it.

−2−
DRESS CODES

The issue of dress codes has been a point of contention between students and schools for decades. During the 1960's, students began protesting the schools' attempts to regulate clothing and hair styles. For a while, the students got the upper hand, and the rules were greatly relaxed by school districts. Recently, however, the trend has been in the other direction as schools act to counter violence and gangs. In fact, these rules have come so far that many schools now require uniforms. So let us take a look at some of the rules that apply to school districts in this area.

The law is clear that schools can create reasonable rules regarding student dress and grooming. But the word *reasonable* can mean different things. Ultimately, if a student and her family disagree with the rules set out by the school, a judge or group of appeals court judges will make the final decision as to what is and is not reasonable. In addition to being reasonable, the regulations must be specific enough to give the students fair notice of what violates the dress code.

T-SHIRTS
One of the items of clothing that schools try to regulate is t-shirts. In many instances, these regulations are appropriate because the school does have a responsibility to maintain discipline. Furthermore, courts have agreed that allowing students to come to school with gang insignia, pornography, racial slurs, or other similar sayings or graphics would be disruptive to the functioning of the school.

STYLE OF CLOTHES
The same type of rules apply to the style of clothing. Most judges will find that allowing students to show up looking like they were just in a Britney

Spears or Madonna video will have a disruptive effect on the student body. Schools have been allowed to prohibit short shorts or midriff-baring shirts, as well as styles of clothing that are gang-related.

There does have to be a valid reason behind the regulation, though. Rules that go just to preferences or tastes without a showing of impact on the functioning of the school will not survive a court challenge. Reasons to allow regulation that have been considered valid are:

- teaching hygiene;
- maintaining discipline;
- assuring safety;
- reducing violence; and,
- avoiding distraction and disruption in the classroom.

Some of the cases that have been decided by the courts give us some guidance on whether a particular dress code provision is valid or not. First, let's look at a case that upheld the school's dress code.

In **Bivens v. Albuquerque Public Schools,** Richard Bivens and his mother filed suit against the school district. Richard was suspended for wearing sagging pants, which was a violation of the dress code. He was a freshman at Del Norte High School in Albuquerque. During the very first week of school that year, he was warned by the assistant principal that his sagging pants were out of compliance with the dress code. Richard ignored the warning and kept wearing the pants. He was warned several more times and even suspended for a day or two between August and October of that school year. Richard persisted and finally the school district had enough. In October, he was given a long term suspension and told to return his textbooks. The final suspension prompted the lawsuit.

The school district testified that the dress code provision relating to sagging pants was adopted in response to a growing gang problem at the school. The district agreed with Richard that he was not a gang member and was not trying to get into a gang by wearing the sagging pants. Richard testified that he wore the pants to express himself as a black youth and identify with black culture and, specifically, black urban youth. He claimed in court that this type of expression was permitted because it was part of his right to free speech.

(continued)

The school district presented evidence that many people considered sagging pants to be a sign of gang affiliation and that sagging was a style adopted by many who wanted to get into a gang. Other evidence showed that sagging was just a fashion trend and not considered to be any particular message or form of expression; it was not always gang related.

In the above case, the judge decided that the school's interest in curtailing gang activity and the fact that sagging pants were identifiable as a gang insignia outweighed the student's right to decide what clothes he wanted to wear. (The school district won the right to continue prohibiting sagging pants.)

In another case, however, the school district lost.

In **Stephenson v. Davenport Community School District**, the dress code case related to student tattoos. Brianna Stephenson was an eighth grader when she got the tattoo, a small cross between her thumb and index finger. For almost three years, no one complained about the tattoo. Brianna was a good student with no record of disciplinary problems who regularly made the honor roll.

During her school career, the gang problem within the school district worsened. Students were bringing weapons to class and gang members routinely intimidated other students who were not in a gang. In response, the district passed a rule that said, "Gang related activities such as display of 'colors,' symbols, signals, signs, etc. will not be tolerated on school grounds."

After the regulation was put in place, a school counselor noticed Brianna's tattoo and considered it a gang symbol. The counselor notified the assistant principal, who discussed the tattoo with the police liaison officer at the school. The officer also thought the tattoo was a gang symbol. The school told Brianna and her mother that she would be suspended from school if she did not get rid of the tattoo. The Stephensons complied, spending $500 on a laser removal procedure that left a scar on Brianna's hand. The Stephensons filed suit against the school district, claiming that the rule was too vague to be enforced.

Even though the stated reason behind the rule was to reduce gang activity, just like in the sagging pants case, the judge in

(continued)

Brianna's case invalidated the regulation. The judge pointed out that there are many symbols and phrases that have been adopted by gangs across the country and the school district's rule did not specify what the terms "gang" and "gang activity" meant.

Also, the rule gave the district officials total discretion to decide what qualified as a gang symbol. This meant that the students did not have an effective way of knowing what conduct was off limits. The rule did not offer any guidance to the district officials who would be enforcing the rule, so the school district did not get to keep that version of the rule.

EARRINGS

One of the hottest areas of contention relates to rules that forbid males from wearing earrings while allowing girls to wear them. Next, we will review a couple of cases in this area to get a feel for how courts view this question.

In **Hines v. Caston School Corporation**, Jimmy Hines got suspended from school for refusing to remove his earring and his parents sued the school district. Jimmy was a fourth grader who began wearing a single gold stud earring to school. The principal called Jimmy's parents in and told them that the district had a policy that boys could not wear earrings. Jimmy wore his earring to school anyway and refused to remove it when the principal told him to. Jimmy was then suspended.

His parents sued the district, claiming that Jimmy's fundamental right to "the possession and control of his own person in matters of personal appearance" was violated by the rule. The school district claimed that the rule promoted a positive atmosphere and good discipline. The district also offered evidence that the wearing of earrings by males was not consistent with the community standards of Caston, which is a very conservative area.

The judge agreed with the Hineses that Jimmy had a right to control his own person, but he also decided that the school district had shown a valid reason behind the rule. The judge said that the district had the right, within reason, to "instill discipline" and promote adherence to community standards so the district got to keep its rule.

In the last case, the boy who wanted to wear an earring to school tried to say he had an almost absolute *right* to do so. However, he lost. Furthermore, as the next case shows, earrings on boys are more likely to mean "gang activity" to a judge than earrings on girls.

In ***Olesen v. Board of Education of School District No. 228***, Darryl Olesen, Jr. and his parents challenged the school's ban on earrings on boys, claiming that it violated his right to free speech. He also raised the issue that girls were allowed to wear earrings. The district had a rule that banned gang symbols and activities. Earrings were specifically listed in the school handbook as covered by the ban.

Olesen testified that he wanted to wear the earring as an expression of his individuality and because he thought the earring might be attractive to girls. The district had evidence that Olesen, who used to be a good student, now was failing most of his classes and had excessive absences. He had also been seen at the meetings of a gang that had other members at his school. This particular gang was associated with symbols that included a cross, a pitchfork, and a six pointed star. Olesen's earring had a cross on it.

The judge decided that the school district's rationale of curtailing gang activity was a good one and upheld the rule. On the issue of allowing girls to wear earrings, the judge pointed out that, for boys, the earring could be considered a gang sign while, for girls, it was not.

It is interesting to note that the policy in this case was very similar to the policy in the Stephenson case about the tattoo discussed on page 11 and that the alleged gang symbol in both cases was a cross. In the earring case, the school was allowed to keep the rule. In the tattoo case, the rule was overturned and not allowed.

This is a good illustration of how different judges can reach different results when con-

TEEN TIP

If you are a teen with other types of piercings, such as eyebrow, tongue, or lip, be cautious of your school policy. There are no cases yet, but judges are probably going to treat these cases similarly as ear piercings.

fronted with a similar question. It can also show how important the facts are to a case. In the tattoo case, Brianna was a good student with no gang connections; the school district lost that case. In the Olesen earring case, the student had become a poor student with known gang connections; in that case, the school district won.

POLITICAL OR RELIGIOUS CLOTHING

When confronted with a dress code question, do not forget that the First Amendment free speech protection still applies. So, schools cannot prohibit clothing or hair styles that are intended as political or religious expressions unless the school can show *substantial disruption* to the school as described in Chapter 1. An example of how courts balance these issues can be found in the following 1993 Texas case.

The case of **Alabama & Coushatta Tribes v. Big Sandy School District** was filed by several Native American male students and the Alabama and Coushatta Tribes of Texas. The issue in the case was the dress code provision related to the hair length for male students. This particular type of provision has been the source of a significant percentage of dress code cases that have found their way into the court system.

Here, Big Sandy's dress code required that boys' hair not be longer than the top of a standard shirt collar. The Native American males whose parents filed this suit wore their hair long, a clear violation of the dress code. Some of the students, when threatened with detention, cut their hair. A number of the boys, however, refused to cut their hair. In response, the boys were placed in in-school detention. At Big Sandy, students in detention got their assignments, but did not receive regular instruction so the students fell behind in their school work.

That prompted the tribe and their parents to file suit. At the hearing, an anthropologist, Dr. Hiram Gregory, testified for the students that many southeastern tribes historically wore their hair long as a "symbol of moral and spiritual strength." He went on to discuss how important hair was in that culture, and how cutting hair was equated with removal of a limb, just like losing an arm or a leg. Traditionally, hair was cut only as a sign of mourning.

(continued)

The boys who refused to cut their hair testified that those were, in fact, their beliefs. The judge believed the boys, ruling that they had a "sincerely held belief in the spiritual properties of long hair." This ruling was in spite of the fact that none of the boys' parents believed the same way. The judge went on the rule that the Native American views were clearly religious in nature, and were covered by the protections of the First Amendment freedom of religion clause. The state, and by extension, the school district has the right to pass rules and regulations, and many times this power extends to allow for school dress codes.

However, the dress code cannot unreasonably impact sincerely held religious beliefs. In this case, the school district's stated goals for the dress code were to maintain discipline and respect for authority and project a favorable public image. After looking at all of the factors, the judge decided that the school district could find another way to meet those objectives without forcing the Native American students to violate their religious beliefs and cut their hair. The boys won their case and were allowed to return to their regular classes with their hair long.

APPROVED DRESS CODES

Some kinds of dress code rules that have been approved are:

- ◆ no cleats or metal heel plates;
- ◆ no shorts; and,
- ◆ no hats or headwraps. (One headwrap case involved a student who was wearing traditional African headgear to celebrate her African heritage.)

Rules that prohibit girls from wearing pants or any student from wearing clothing with a professional sports team logo have even been invalidated by some courts. It seems clear under the present laws that schools can require all of the students to wear uniforms and many schools have adopted these rules.

–3–
SCHOOL PRAYER

One of the most controversial, and most often *litigated* (brought to court) issues is school prayer. There are hundreds of cases that have been to court about this issue.

STUDENT-LED PRAYER

One of the most hotly contested issues is that of student-led prayer. It has long been clear that prayers led by school officials, either at school or at extracurricular activities, is unconstitutional. Schools cannot bring in outside clergy to give prayers. This particular issue was decided in a case that involved a school district's use of a minister to say a prayer at graduations. The question then became one of whether the district could get around these rulings by having students read the prayers.

The most recent United States Supreme Court ruling in this area came in the year 2000 and is discussed below.

In the case **Santa Fe Independent School District v. Doe**, the school district had a policy that allowed the students to elect a student chaplain for each year. That student was then responsible for giving the opening prayer or invocation at school activities like football games. The prayer was delivered over the public address system.

Two families, one Catholic and one Mormon, challenged this practice and sued the school district. The families claimed that the policy violated the constitutional provision that banned government from establishing religion. While the suit was making its way through the system, the school district changed its policy. The new policy had the students first conduct an election to decide whether or not "invocations" should be delivered at games. If the student body decided to have invocations, then a second election would pick the person to deliver the invocations for that school year.

(continued)

The district court, the court that first heard the trial of the case, said that they could have a student deliver a message before games, but it had to be "nonsectarian, nonproselytizing prayer." This meant that the prayer could not be specifically tailored to one religion. For example, it could not be a Christian or Muslim prayer. Furthermore, the prayer could not be designed to convert the listeners to any denomination or religion.

The families appealed the case to the Fifth Circuit Court of Appeals, and that court invalidated the whole policy. The school district appealed to the Supreme Court. The Supreme Court agreed with the appeals court that the school policy was unconstitutional. The justices felt that the policy was clearly designed to promote school prayer.

They were not impressed by the district's adoption of the two election method to decide whether or not there would be prayer before football games, pointing out that an election in which the majority decision controlled only served to guarantee that the minority viewpoint would never be heard. In effect, the school was promoting one religion.

This issue will undoubtedly continue to end up in the court system. There are many groups that want to find a way to get official, organized prayer into the school systems and other groups that are just as determined to keep it from happening. As schools develop policies, there will be cases to see whether the particular policies are legal.

Students can form groups on their own for religious purposes. The groups cannot meet during school hours. Whether they can meet on school property or not depends on the policies of the individual school district. Students are, however, always free to pray silently on their own.

PRIVATE SCHOOL PRAYER

The rules are different at private schools. Because they are not agents of the government, they are free to promote religion and use the Bible or other religious texts in any way they choose. Private schools can have organized prayer or other religious observances. Furthermore, the private, contractual relationship between the school and its students means that the school has a greater degree of control over what the students are allowed to say or publish in the school paper. Conversely, students' free speech rights are more restricted. This is because the law views the admissions contract as a voluntary limit agreed to by the student and his or her family.

–4–
COMPULSORY ATTENDANCE LAWS, PRIVATE SCHOOLS, AND HOME SCHOOLS

All states have laws that make attending school mandatory. Some states will allow students to drop out prior to reaching age 18, others will not. Some states make attendance at school a condition of having a driver's license. There are, however, different ways of fulfilling this obligation. The most obvious is to attend the public schools in your town or city.

There are many reasons that students and their parents may not want to use the public school system. Some are concerned about the crime rate in some schools. Others are concerned about the quality of the education in the public schools. There are also individuals who object on philosophical or religious grounds to the curriculum used in the public schools. So, whatever their reasons, they look for alternatives.

While it is permissible for the state to require children of certain specified ages to be educated and to place parents under a duty to educate their children, the state cannot require that this education take place in a public school. The two primary alternatives to public school are private schools and home schools. It is permissible for states to regulate to some degree both private and home schools. This is so that the state has some way of insuring that its children are receiving similar educations in the basic subjects, regardless of where they attend school.

THE LAWS ON SKIPPING SCHOOL

A student's failure to comply with the state compulsory attendance law (skipping school) will result in a *truancy* proceeding. You become *truant* when you have too many unexcused absences from school. The school district sets the policy for what constitutes an excused absence. Illness is commonly considered to be a valid excuse, and students can be withdrawn from school if they are suffering from extended illnesses.

TEEN TIP

If you are suspended from school, those absences do not have to be treated as excused. If your school policy treats them as unexcused, a lengthy suspension can keep you from getting credit for that semester and even cause you to have to repeat a grade.

NOTE: *Students can also be exempt from attendance at school based on their religious beliefs.*

The truancy laws vary from state to state. A book of this type cannot include an in-depth analysis of the truancy laws of each state; therefore, if you find yourself in court on a truancy case, you should contact an attorney. You can also research the laws yourself. In Appendix B, you will find a listing for the compulsory attendance laws for your state. This would be the starting point for your research.

Generally, there are two aspects to truancy laws. First, most states punish parents for failing to send their children to school. Second, the laws also try to force the student to go to school.

Holding Parents Responsible

From the parents' perspective, the statutes fall into two categories. Some statutes will only provide for fines for the parents. But, there are other states that charge the parents with a crime, for which punishment can include time in jail, in truancy cases.

For example, Indiana has a statute that allows parents to be charged with *felony educational neglect* in more severe cases. The exact laws will vary between the states, but generally, the state will have to prove that the parent did not comply with the state compulsory attendance law and that the student missed school.

These cases become very difficult from the parents' point of view when older teenagers are involved. The way the laws of many states work, teenagers reach a point—usually when they are seventeen—where their parents' ability, both legally and practically, make it impossible for them to force the teen to do anything—including go to school. However, the laws also make the parent responsible for the actions of the teen until they are eighteen.

This "in between" year creates lots of problems for parents who have rebellious teenagers. For instance, in the truancy situation, the parent cannot force their seventeen year old child to attend school but the truancy court can still punish the parent for failing to get the child to school.

This is particularly a problem when the child is no longer living with either of the parents. Since the parents may not be able to force the teen to move back home, they are sometimes forced to report the teen as a runaway to avoid liability in the truancy court. Runaways are dealt with in the juvenile justice system and a teen can end up on probation or in some placement outside his or her home as a result of being classified as a runaway.

In addition to criminal proceedings against the parent, the state can also involve the child welfare department and take the children away from the parents just like they do in child abuse cases.

NOTE: *A substantial percentage of the reported truancy cases against parents involve parents who have chosen to home school their children. The laws and issues related to home schooling are covered under home schooling, on page 24.*

While the whole point of the laws relating to parents in truancy matters is to punish the parents for not complying with the law, the laws that apply to the student are really designed just to force the student to go to school and are not really criminal in nature. However, the case may be handled just like other juvenile criminal cases. In fact, students who skip school regularly can find themselves declared a delinquent child by the juvenile court and sent to a juvenile placement facility. There are cases, however, that say that a student cannot be treated as a delinquent unless the state can prove that the parents did not know about the absences and did not consent to them.

In the Matter of B.M., a 1998 Texas case, a student was first sent to the justice of the peace court because he had too many unexcused absences. Under the Texas statute, justice of the peace courts are the courts that first hear truancy cases; the justice court is not a juvenile court and does not have the authority to send a student into a placement like the Texas Youth Commission.

The justice of the peace ordered the student to pay a $75 fine and to attend school without any more unexcused absences. The student did not pay the fine, so the justice of the peace transferred the case to the juvenile court.

JUVENILE COURT

Once the case is transferred to a juvenile court, the juvenile court conducts a hearing to decide whether the student has failed to comply with the court orders from the justice court. For example, in Texas, if the judge finds that the student did violate the court order, then the judge can order the student to be committed to the Texas Youth Commission. This is the most serious punishment available in Texas for juveniles charged with crimes. It is the juvenile version of adults going to prison.

Other punishment possibilities can include being placed on juvenile probation. This involves numerous court-imposed rules like regular reporting to a probation officer, payment of monthly probation fees, performance of community service, and often a very restrictive curfew (for instance, having to be home by 5:00 p.m. unless you are with your parents).

Attorneys

Because truancy violations can result in students being confined in a juvenile detention facility, the student is entitled to have a court-appointed attorney if they cannot afford to hire one on their own. This right does not "kick-in" until the student's case gets to a court that has the authority to send him or her to a facility. For example, in the Texas case, the student did not have the right to an attorney in the proceedings in the justice of the peace court because that judge did not have the authority to send the student to detention. However, once his case was transferred to the juvenile court, he did get the right to a court- appointed attorney.

In the Interest of J.E.S., a Colorado student got into trouble for not going to school. The school attendance officer asked the district court for an order forcing the student to attend school. The court granted this request and warned J.E.S. that he could be held in contempt of court if he ignored the order.

Sure enough, J.E.S. ended up back in court on contempt proceedings because he missed more school. The judge ordered him to perform ten hours of community service, which he did. However, he still was not going to school regularly. When the judge asked him why he continued to miss school, he answered, "I'm lazy. I don't want to." The judge gave the student another chance, ordering him to attend school and have a doctor's excuse for any future absences.

(continued)

Undaunted, J.E.S. missed some more school with unexcused absences. This time, the judge told him he had to go to summer school. Toward the end of the summer, the court had another hearing. J.E.S. had not even tried to enroll in summer school, much less actually go. This time, the judge sentenced him to forty-five days in the detention center. J.E.S. appealed the judge's decision but lost and had to spend the time locked up in the detention center.

While truancy may not seem like much of a big deal to a teenager, it can be very expensive to both parents and students. Parents can be fined and have to pay attorney's fees. Students can be locked up.

REGULATING WHAT IS TAUGHT

The curriculum in private and home schools is not regulated to the extent it is regulated in public school systems. For example, it is well known that public schools cannot teach or otherwise promote religion. Private and home schools are not under that requirement, and religion-based studies are frequently found in those settings. This means that all of the cases relating to prayer in schools and the celebrating of religious holidays apply only to public schools and not to private or home schools.

The flip side to this coin is that students in private schools and home schools do not always have the same rights as those students in public schools. The legal basis for this distinction is that the public school is considered part of the government. Therefore it must follow all of the rules and protections that apply to protect citizens from improper conduct by our government.

Private schools are not agencies of the government, but instead are protected by the constitutional right of *free association*. This right says that the government cannot control or limit its citizens' right to associate with whomever they choose. This means that students' rights and duties are determined by the contract between the school and its students. Thus, the private schools can have much more rigid—and perhaps more liberal—policies and procedures to control admittance, conduct, discipline, and expulsion.

Students have fewer rights in private school, and generally have just those rights that are given the student by the institution. You will see mentions of these differences throughout this book whenever schools are discussed.

HOME SCHOOLING, SPECIFICALLY

Another method of education, and one of the fastest growing trends in education, is home schooling. This is obviously the type of school that is subject to the least amount of government regulation. Home schooled students also have the fewest rights of all students. The rights of a home schooler are only those of any child in the parent-child situation. The parents are in charge, as in other settings. Punishment in the home school is like any other type of parental punishment; corporal punishment is permitted as long as it does not become physical abuse. There is no *due process* for the student and no *constitutional protections* for free speech and from searches. These refer to the rules that protect a person's legal rights.

States are allowed to regulate home schools to insure that education is actually occurring. For instance, you may be required to register a home school with your local superintendent. The state is allowed to check up on the home school. The state can require parents who home school to file an outline of the courses being taught and to document the time spent on each subject.

Home schooling is not a *fundamental right*, that is, a right guaranteed by the constitution. Therefore, there is no requirement that states permit home schooling. In fact, some courts have ruled that a state can keep parents from home schooling their children by determining that home schooling does not comply with the compulsory attendance law.

PARENT TIP

If you are a parent who is home schooling or a teen who attends school at home, you need to keep in mind that you must have adequate records to prove what is being taught in the home school. It is best to use some sort of professional curriculum, a number of which are available on the open market. Additionally, there are numerous home school associations.

In the case of **Null v. Board of Education of County of Jackson**, a 1993 West Virginia case, the court denied a mother the right to continue home schooling her son. While West Virginia had a specific law that permitted home schooling, there was an additional
(continued)

regulation that said if a student's test scores in any single year for English, grammar, reading, social studies, science, and mathematics fell below the fortieth percentile, the parent had one year to remedy the problem. If, after the remedial year, the test results remained below that level, the parent was no longer entitled to home school.

Brent Null attended public school for kindergarten, first grade, and second grade. In the second grade, Brent scored in the sixty-second percentile on a national, standardized test. After the end of the second grade, Brent's mother began home schooling him. At the end of Brent's first year of home schooling, he was only in the seventeenth percentile. The school told his mother that she had one year to get Brent's scores back above the fortieth percentile level. After that second year of home schooling, Brent's scores only got up to the thirty-eighth percentile. At that point, the school declared Brent ineligible for home schooling and his mother filed suit.

In making a decision, the judge balanced the parent's rights to control the upbringing of her son against the state's interest in the education of its children. The judge ruled that the West Virginia rules were reasonable and allowed the school to require Brent to return to public school.

Some states have laws that require home schools to use certified instructors as teachers. This type of law could be used to effectively keep most parents from home schooling unless they went through some sort of formal certification process. Some of these requirements have been taken to court, and courts have ruled that such a requirement violates the free exercise of religion clause of the First Amendment to the Constitution. Some parents' religious beliefs prohibit the use of such instructors. However, other courts have ruled differently, finding that the parent's right to free exercise of religion was not violated. In those states, home schools must be taught by a certified instructor.

In **People v. DeJonge**, a 1993 Michigan case, the court reviewed the state law that home schools use certified instructors. The DeJonges home schooled their two children using a program administered by the Church of Christian Liberty and Academy of Arlington Heights, Illinois. However, neither of the DeJonges was a certified teacher and their local school district filed charges against

(continued)

them for violating the compulsory attendance law. They were convicted, fined, ordered to get certified instructors, and they appealed.

The Michigan Supreme Court decided that the DeJonges' opposition to the certification requirement was a religious belief that they sincerely held and that the certification requirement put a burden on their exercise of their religion. The court ended up finding the certification requirement unconstitutional.

However, in a 1986 case, the North Dakota Supreme Court reached the opposite conclusion.

In that case, a group of Seventh Day Adventist parents were convicted of violating the state compulsory education law because they were home schooling their children without using certified instructors. The court ruled that the state's interest was more important than the fact that a burden was placed on the parents' religious beliefs. The parents lost, and their convictions were upheld.

The state can visit home schools as a general rule to be certain that the students are getting an equivalent education, but only as long as the visits are infrequent and not overly intrusive.

If the parents are divorced, the law may require both parents to agree before home schooling is permitted. In some states, if the custody order does not address the issue and the state law allows home schooling, the parent with custody of the children can decide to home school. One situation in which home schooling is almost always allowed is when a student is disabled and the disability keeps him or her from being able to attend school.

CHARTER SCHOOLS

A new trend in education is the *charter school*. Charter schools are a hybrid creation of the various state legislatures, combining characteristics of both public and private schools. They are an attempt to improve the educational opportunities for students who are at greater risk of dropping out of school. The idea is that the charter school will be smaller and better able to tailor the programs to the individual needs of the students because they are exempt from some of the administrative requirements that apply to public schools. In that respect, they are somewhat like private schools. But in almost all other respects, they are like public schools.

Charter schools are formed when an individual or group applies to the local school board for a charter to run a school. The school is funded with public funds. For that reason, the constitutional rules and protections that apply to public schools apply to charter schools. That also means that charter schools cannot be *segregated*, or limited to students of a particular race or religion, and cannot discriminate in any way. Charter schools cannot promote religion or violate a student's right to due process for disciplinary proceedings. Due process and discipline will be discussed in Chapter 10.

For purposes of this book, the chapters on school issues for public school students apply the same way for charter school students.

CHANGING LAWS

Your state legislature and the federal government often change the rules and regulations in the area of schooling. Since the requirements for private and home schools vary from state to state, it is important to know what the law is in your state. A detailed listing of all of the applicable laws is beyond the scope of this book, but you will find a listing in Appendix B of the ages for compulsory attendance in your state and the statute number. This will provide a starting point for you if you want to research some of these issues on your own.

PARENT TIP

You can get information about the schooling laws from your local school district administration or you can consult with an attorney who is familiar with school law.

–5–
SEARCHES IN SCHOOL

One issue that frequently comes up in the school setting is the right of school officials and police officers to search students, lockers, cars, and possessions. Whether this is legal or not depends on who is doing the searching and what the circumstances are.

The Fourth Amendment to the U.S. Constitution says that we are all protected from unreasonable searches and seizures by government officials. Adults and students, when they are out of school, cannot be searched by the police unless *probable cause* exists for the search. In many instances, the police are required to get a judge to issue a search warrant before they can search someone or their property.

Probable cause is a phrase with a legal definition: facts that would lead a reasonably intelligent and prudent person to believe that an accused person has committed a crime. Over the years, there have been hundreds and hundreds of cases where courts have decided whether probable cause exists in a particular case. (A detailed analysis of what probable cause is and when it exists is far beyond the scope of this book. The facts of each case also have a great deal to do with whether or not there is probable cause for a search.)

TEEN TIP

If, as a teenager, you are stopped by the police, searched, and then arrested and charged with a crime based on what is found in the search, you or your parents will need to hire an attorney to represent you in the criminal case. The lawyer will discuss the probable cause issue with you if necessary.

SEARCHING POSSESSIONS

But what if you are in school and the principal wants to search you or your locker or backpack? Do the same rules apply? Does the principal have to go to a judge and get a search warrant? Do you have to agree to the search?

A school official, such as a principle, can search without a warrant as long as they have a *reasonable suspicion* that a violation of either the law or school rules has occurred. That is a much easier standard for the school to meet than probable cause because it requires only a few facts that may mean a crime has occurred. In the cases that have gone to court, judges have balanced the rights of the student, including the student's right to privacy, against the rights of the school to control what happens on campus and their duty to protect the other students and faculty. However, the courts have ruled that the search must also be reasonable in scope in relation to the facts that caused the search in the first place.

This means that, as long as the search is reasonable, it is legal. Factors that go into determining whether or not a search is reasonable are things like the student's age, sex, history, and school record; the nature of the infraction; the reason for conducting the search; the student's consent or refusal to consent to the search; the involvement of outside police officers; and the type of search conducted.

Schools cannot generally conduct mass searches of all of the students or even just a big group of students, although there are some exceptions as you will see next.

Courts that have reviewed these issues have found some of the following factors to be enough for reasonable suspicion: possession of rolling papers of the type commonly used for marijuana, drug paraphernalia visible through a car window, an obvious smell of marijuana, bulging pockets, or observation of illegal activities.

For example, let's assume for the moment that Susan is a student at your high school. A fellow student reports to the principal that Susan is smoking in the restroom. The principal, Mrs. Sanders, comes into the restroom and sees Susan smoking a cigarette. Mrs. Sanders asks Susan for permission to search her purse, which is on the floor beside her, and Susan refuses. Mrs. Sanders searches Susan's purse anyway.

In addition to a package of cigarettes, marijuana, rolling papers, and some empty bags are found. Mrs. Sanders calls the police and Susan is arrested. She is also expelled from school because the student conduct handbook states that students caught with drugs on campus may be expelled.

Is what happened to Susan legal? The answer is yes. These facts are very similar to those in the most important case relating to searches in school. This is the case of *New Jersey v. T.L.O.* and was decided by the United States Supreme Court in 1985. Because the search was legal, the fact that drugs were found in Susan's purse can be used against Susan in a criminal case. And, whether or not the search was legal for criminal court purposes, the findings of a school search can always be used against the student in school disciplinary proceedings.

For example, let's assume that your school has a police officer permanently assigned to your campus and that the school principal asks that officer to assist in the search. And let's also assume that Susan has finished her cigarette by the time the principal and the officer get to the restroom. When they see her for the first time, Susan is walking out the door of the restroom with her purse in her hand. She tells the officer that she had to go to the bathroom and is now headed to class. The principal asks Susan if she and the officer can search her purse. Susan refuses.

Because the police officer will be helping to conduct the search, this may mean that the search is no longer being conducted by school officials. How much of a difference this makes will depend where you live. Some courts have said that the participation of a police officer means that there must be probable cause to search. Reasonable suspicion is only enough when the the school officials are searching alone in these courts.

In the case of **Patman v. State**, a police officer was assigned to the local high school. The school secretary told the officer that Patman was late getting to school and that he smelled of marijuana. The officer followed him down the hall and stopped him. The officer also noticed a strong odor of marijuana.

The officer decided to frisk Patman to check for weapons. When he did, he felt some small bags in the student's pocket. The officer reached into the pocket and pulled out bags of marijuana. Although in this case the court ruled that the search was legal, they also said that because it was a police officer who performed the search, he had to have probable cause to make the search legal.

Different states can come out differently on similar issues. A court in a different state reached a different result with regard to a police officer search.

TEEN TIP

If a police officer is participating in a search, and you know that you have in your possession (either on your person or in something that belongs to you) an item that is illegal for you to have, you should *consider* refusing to consent to the search. If you agree to let the school official or police officer search you, then it does not matter whether they had either reasonable suspicion or probable cause. Because you have agreed to be searched, you have lost your right to complain about this issue.

As you make this decision, however, you should be aware that you can be disciplined by the school based just on your refusal to consent to the search. Ultimately, this means that you should not refuse to consent to a search just because you want to give the principal or vice principal a hard time. Save this refusal for a time when you need to avoid being criminally prosecuted. This is particularly true if you are old enough under the laws of your state to be prosecuted as an adult and might end up with a criminal conviction.

In the case *In Re Josue T.*, the court decided that the police officer only needed reasonable suspicion to search because the officer was really just assisting the school officials in the search. In that case, several students who had ridden to school together were questioned about drug use.

When the school official who was doing the questioning got to Josue, the official noticed that Josue was evasive. The school official smelled marijuana. He took the student to the office, and was joined by the police officer assigned to the school.

The school official noticed a bulge in the student's pants pocket and asked the student to empty his pocket. Josue refused, and then the police officer took the student's hand out of his pocket and found a gun.

The court said this search was legal because the search was initiated by the school official and the officer just became involved when a safety concern arose.

In our hypothetical situation on page 30, Susan was wise to refuse to agree to the search. Now, if she is searched anyway, the marijuana is found in her purse, and she is charged with a crime, she and her lawyer may be able to keep the prosecutors from using the fact that marijuana was found in her purse against her. Susan may still face discipline from the school for refusing to consent to the search. However, she may have kept herself from having a criminal conviction on her record (if she is over eighteen) or from being sent to a juvenile detention facility.

The type of search conducted may also be important. Because drugs and weapons are such serious problems and represent such a real danger to the safety of the school and its students, courts are more likely to try to find a way to permit those searches. On the other hand, a court might look less favorably on a full strip search by a school official to find missing money.

STRIP SEARCHES

Strip searches, themselves, are not *automatically* illegal. Courts will look at all of the circumstances surrounding the search in determining its legality. In many instances, a court will find that the privacy rights of the student are greater than the school's right to search, and not permit a strip search. From the point of view of the school, it is always better to allow law enforcement personnel to conduct a strip search. They should also be reserved for serious threats to the safety of other students.

LOCKER SEARCHES

Searches that involve any sort of personal search of the body of the student involve a greater privacy right for the student, but they may still be legal. Lockers come with a much lesser privacy right for students.

In the Pennsylvania case of **Commonwealth v. Cass**, a student was prosecuted for drugs that were found in his locker. On the day the drugs were found, the principal announced to the student body that a safety inspection would be done and they all had to remain in their classrooms. The "safety inspection" was really a search of all of the school lockers. In addition to school officials, two police officers and a drug dog participated in the search. The drug dog pointed to Cass' locker, it was searched, and the drugs found. In reaching its decision, the court analyzed the case in four segments.

(continued)

First, the judge looked at the degree of privacy that applied to a student locker, and found, as have most courts, that the expectation of privacy in your locker is minimal. Second, the judges looked at how extensive the intrusion was, and decided that it was also minimal. The third step was to decide whether the reason for the search was sufficient. Because the school had experienced an increasing drug problem, the judges felt that the principal's stated purpose of deterring drug use was appropriate.

The fourth step was to rule that the means that the school used was a practical solution to the drug use problem. That meant that the school district won the case because the court decided that the principal had acted appropriately.

Now, let's review another case that illustrates the tendencies of courts to find that locker searches are valid.

In **In Re Adam**, the student was spotted in the stairwell of the school building smoking cigarettes with another student. This, of course, was a violation of school rules. The teacher who found them thought he smelled the odor of marijuana, and asked the boys what they were smoking. The boys denied using marijuana. They were taken to the principal, who had them empty their pockets.

No drugs were found and the principal admitted in court that he did not smell marijuana on the boys. When the principal did not find anything on the boy's person, he searched his locker. He found a pipe with the residue of marijuana in a book bag in the locker. The court decided that, based on all of the facts, the principal had reasonable suspicion to search the locker.

Drug Dogs

Many school districts use drug dogs to search lockers for illegal drugs or other contraband. In most instances, this is permissible and the student has no right to complain. The reasoning behind this is that courts have viewed lockers as shared by the student and the school and not as an exclusive possession belonging to the student. Therefore, the student does not have the same expectation of privacy in a shared locker as in, for example, his or her pockets.

STUDENT'S RIGHT TO AN ATTORNEY

Another closely related issue is the right of a student to an attorney during questioning and the allowable uses of statements given by students in such settings. As with searches, the answer depends on who is doing the questioning. If the principal calls you into his or her office and asks you questions—even questions about conduct that is criminal—you do not have a right to an attorney.

The principal does not have to give you the famous *Miranda warnings* either. We are all familiar with these warnings from television: you have the right to an attorney and anything you say can be used against you. But just because the principal does

TEEN TIP

Once you are placed under arrest by a police officer, you do have a right to an attorney and the police have to tell you about this right. As soon as you ask for an attorney, they should stop questioning you immediately. The officer may ask you to waive your right, and you should not do that until you talk to your parents and an attorney.

As a general rule, any time the police are involved or you are being questioned about activities that could get you charged with a crime, you should ask to call your parents or an attorney before you answer any questions.

not have to give you the warning does not mean that your statements cannot be used against you. They *can* be used in disciplinary proceedings in the school, and they *can* be used in a criminal investigation.

Once again, however, the presence of a police officer changes everything. In the school settings, it is very common for a school official to contact the police and report that a student has violated the law. The officer comes in and places the student under arrest. Then, the principal or vice-principal and the officer question the student. Although it happens frequently, it is *not* legal.

From the school district point of view, it is better to allow at least the preliminary questioning of a student to be done by a school official, outside the presence of law enforcement officers, if it can be done safely.

RANDOM SEARCHES

Whether a search is reasonable often depends on what is being searched and on how much of an expectation of privacy the student has. Remember that you have a much greater expectation of privacy in searches of your person than you do for searches of your locker. Another factor is what information triggered the decision to search. Random searches with no suspicion of the individual students searched are more questionable than searches based on actual observations by the school official. As you will see, it also may depend on where you live and which court hears your case.

Now, let's review some cases to see how real situations come out in court.

> A case that addressed the issue of drug dog searches in 1999 was ***B.C. v. Plumas Unified School District***. In that case, the principal and assistant principal of Quincy High School in Plumas County, California conducted a random search that was not based on any particular suspicion or report of drug use and possession. Instead, the officials called all of the students in one classroom out into the hall. On their way out the door, the students all had to pass by a police officer and the drug dog. The dog reacted to B.C., one of the students. The students had to pass by the dog again on the way back into the room. Once again, the dog reacted to the same student, but no drugs were found at the school that day.
>
> The United States Supreme Court had ruled that using a drug dog to conduct a sniff test is not the kind of search that is controlled by the Fourth Amendment, which would require probable cause or a search warrant. The Fourth Amendment says that we are protected from unreasonable searches and seizures. This usually comes into play when police officers search a person, car or house for evidence of crimes. The meaning of the Supreme Court ruling is that, at least in this instance, using drug dogs is not a "search."

There are differing opinions among the various federal courts of appeals as to whether the rules are different when the drug dog is used to sniff a person. Some courts treat the sniff of a person just like a luggage sniff and allow it. Other courts say that it is a search and the regular rules for searches apply.

In B.C.'s case, the court decided that, because there was no evidence that Quincy High was suffering from an immediate drug crisis, the search was unreasonable. The judges indicated that the outcome might have been different had there been a documented, significant existing drug problem at the school.

Backpacks or Purses

Many students have backpacks or purses with them at school, and these items are often searched by school officials.

In one case, **DesRoches v. Caprio**, all of the students in a class were searched when a pair of tennis shoes that had been left in the classroom over the lunch period were stolen. DesRoches refused to consent to the search and was suspended for ten days. The court decided that, based on the information the school officials obtained from the other students during their investigation, the officials had developed enough of an individualized suspicion to merit a search of DesRoches.

Pat-Downs

Of course, the most intrusive search is that of the student's person. In many instances, courts will find that the facts warrant such a search.

In **C.S. v. State**, C.S. was on juvenile probation. One of the conditions of his probation was that he was not allowed to have guns in his possession. At school one day, another student reported C.S. to the campus police officer for misconduct. The officer got C.S. out of class to talk to him in the hall. As part of that process, the officer performed a pat down search and found a gun in his pants pocket. When C.S. tried to keep the results out of court in his criminal proceeding by claiming that the search had been improper, the judge decided that the officer's safety concerns justified the search and the student lost his case.

In another case, **In Re F.B.**, a knife was found when F.B. was searched as part of a search that was required on that day for every student to enter the school building. The search was done at the only entry point to the school and every student was subjected to the search. The courts allowed the school to conduct searches of all students as a precondition for entering the building.

Drug Testing

One final area related to searches at school and random searches is the question of requiring *urinalysis* (drug test through urine) for all students as a condition of participating in extracurricular activities. The Supreme Court has ruled that those students can be required to undergo random urine tests. This has been found to be true whether the activity is athletics or another kind of extracurricular activity.

There have been attempts by a few school districts to implement widespread drug testing. It is unlikely that the courts would allow a school district to require drug testing for all students as a condition of admission to school. However, a district might be permitted to require drug tests of individuals if the requirement was based on a specific suspicion of that student, particularly if the student participates in any extracurricular activities. The reasoning behind this seems to be that, while students are entitled to an education, the extras are a privilege and not a right. Schools have a much greater ability to restrict and control things that are a privilege than they do things that are constitutionally guaranteed student rights.

PRIVATE SCHOOLS

There are not many cases that have gone to court involving searches of students in private schools. Those cases that have been decided indicate that private school students do not enjoy the same constitutional protections on searches as do public school students. This means that private school officials can probably conduct just about any kind of search they choose to without breaking the law.

−6−

CONFIDENTIALITY OF SCHOOL RECORDS

Federal laws protect the *confidentiality* of school records. The primary law in this area is the *Family Educational Rights and Privacy Act of 1974*, frequently referred to as *FERPA*. This law applies to all schools that receive federal funds, so it may apply to many private schools as well as public schools. When students are still under eighteen, their parents have a right to access the school records. The word *parents* is defined by this law to also include foster parents or other persons acting in the role of parent for the student. Once the student reaches age eighteen or is enrolled in a post-secondary school (college, trade school, etc.), then the parents no longer have a right to access the records. At that point, the access right belongs only to the student—even if the parents pay tuition.

In schools with a police officer present, the records created by the law enforcement unit are not confidential. They are public records, not educational records, and release of these records is treated the same way as release of all other law enforcement records.

For example, assume that Sam assaulted John at school. The campus has a police officer assigned to it, and the officer witnessed the fight. After it was over, the officer wrote a report about the fight. The report included Sam's and John's full names and address and a description of the fight. The fight was also witnessed by the assistant principal of the school, and he wrote a report about the fight. Without the police officer present, the assistant principal questions Sam, who admits that he started the fight. The local newspaper reporter has heard about the fight at school, and wants to write a story about it. Can she use the reports for her story?

PUBLIC RECORD

The report written by the police officer is a public record and the reporter will be allowed to see it. The assistant principal's report, however, is a school record and must remain confidential. This is true even if the assistant principal's report is given to the police officer, something that is permissible because schools are allowed to give information to and cooperate with law enforcement. In that situation, the police must make certain that only the law enforcement records, and not the school records, are released to the reporter.

After you have left a school, those records remain confidential. That way, even if you are fortunate enough to become a professional athlete or famous actress, your school records will not be public.

Name, Address and Phone Number

There are, however, some parts of your records that can be disclosed without your consent. Federal regulations allow "directory information" to be disclosed. This is information such as your name, address, phone number, photograph, e-mail address, date of birth, place of birth, major field of study, grade level, dates of attendance, enrollment status, participation in officially recognized activities and sports, and the height and weight of athletes. There is an exception on *dates of attendance.* The public has access to the overall period of enrollment at a school, but *not* the daily attendance records.

Educational Record

Additionally, there are other situations in which your entire educational record may be disclosed without your knowledge or consent. Your records may be disclosed to:

- ◆ other school officials with a legitimate need for the records;
- ◆ other schools in which you seek to enroll;
- ◆ juvenile justice officials;
- ◆ accreditation officials; and,
- ◆ courts under a subpoena or court order.

Now, let's take a look at a specific set of facts. Amy has been assaulted at school by a group of other students. Naturally, she is very upset by what happened, and has been seeing the school counselor. The counselor has records and notes of Amy's visits with her. The students who committed the assault think they will be charged with crimes for their actions. Their parents know that Amy will testify against the boys and would like to see Amy's records. They hope she has told the school counselor something that will help them keep their children from getting in trouble. Do they get to see the records? The answer is no. The records are part of Amy's education records and they may not be disclosed to the other students or their parents.

Now, change the facts slightly. Let's assume that Amy told her school counselor that she was being sexually abused by her father. The counselor's records, as educational records, would seem to be confidential. But state laws require the counselor to report child abuse to either the police or the child protective services department. This means that the school counselor cannot keep what Amy has told her confidential.

Grades

Another area related to confidentiality has gotten a great deal of publicity recently. It involves the application of these federal privacy laws to a student's grades. There is a reported case from New York in 1980 that allowed a school to release the names and test scores of a class of seventy-five third graders with the only requirement being that the results be released in a "scrambled "order. However, there is a case before the Supreme Court that could keep courts from reaching that same decision in the future.

In the case of **Falvo v. Owasso Public Schools**, a mother sued the Owasso school district over their policy of allowing students to grade each other's work and then call out the grade to the teacher. The mother, Kristja Falvo, said that this policy violated her son's right to privacy because his grades were being disclosed to the other students. The lower court found in favor of the school district and the parties ended up appealing the case all the way up to the Supreme Court. The United States Supreme Court announced its decision in the case on February 19, 2002, and found in favor of the school district.

The Supreme Court felt that extending the privacy laws all the way to specific assignments was too intrusive and not what Congress intended to do when they passed FERPA. The justices said in their opinion, "Correcting a classmate's work can be as much a part of the assignment as taking the test itself." The Court did not think that

(continued)

Congress intended to extend the law so far that a teacher who put a smiley face on a student's paper had violated federal law if another student happened to see the smiley face. The unanimous decision means that students can grade each other's papers and, even if a student is embarrassed by having his scores announced or is ridiculed by his classmates, he cannot sue for invasion of privacy.

Now, let's review some more real cases to see how courts treat the release of school records. How they treat it depends on the specific facts of a case.

In one case, **Jensen v. Reeves**, a judge ruled that releasing a student's records did not violate FERPA. The student, known only as C.J., was an elementary school student with a long disciplinary history, beginning in the first grade. Among his many transgressions, C.J. was accused of harassment. After investigating, C.J. had to spend a week having lunch in the principal's office. The principal notified the parents of the children C.J. harassed about the discipline imposed on C.J.

C.J. kept on having trouble in school, and his parents retained a psychologist to evaluate him. The psychologist was in private practice and not affiliated with the school in any way. Various school officials cooperated with the psychologist by completing evaluation forms for him. Unfortunately, C.J. kept on getting into trouble, and he got suspended for one and one half days for hitting two other students.

After the suspension, C.J. ran into trouble on the playground. The principal talked to all of the students involved in the playground incident, including C.J., and decided to suspend C.J. for ten days, or until his parents cooperated and came in for a formal meeting.

Instead of coming in for the meeting, C.J.'s parents filed suit. Of course, one of the issues was whether or not C.J. had received his *due process* when he was suspended. The judge ruled that the conversations with all of the children constituted sufficient notice and opportunity for C.J. to respond and upheld the suspension.

One of the other issues the parents raised was whether C.J.'s privacy rights under FERPA were violated by the school when the principal notified the parents of other children that C.J. had been

(continued)

disciplined for harassing their children. The judge said that inform-
ing the parents of the results of their complaint did *not* mean any
educational records had been released.

In an emergency, courts allow the release of confidential information
as well, but the school may get to decide what is or is not an emergency.

In another case, **Jain v. State**, a court decided that it was permissible for a school to disclose otherwise confidential information in
an emergency. This case involved a college student at the University
of Iowa who was over eighteen. (Remember that FERPA's privacy
right belongs to the student and not the parents when the student is
over eighteen or enrolled in a post-secondary institution.) Jain's parents were no longer automatically entitled to his records.

Jain had emotional problems at school and had several interactions with the school. He was disciplined a few times and also talked
to school officials because he had been threatening to commit suicide.
His parents were never notified about any of his problems or about
the suicide threats.

Several months passed, and ultimately Jain did, in fact, kill himself
in his dorm room at school. His parents sued the university, claiming
that they should have been told of their son's emotional problems.
They relied on a provision that gives schools the discretion to release
records in an emergency.

The parents lost the case, because the judge decided that a school
cannot be sued for failing to use its discretion and release records.
However, in the opinion, the judge pointed out that, had the school
chosen to release the records, it would not have been a violation of
the law.

Courts have also ruled that this law is designed to correct systematic
problems with the release of information by a school. Therefore, that it
takes more than one mistake by the school in releasing school records to
create a violation of the FERPA law.

One case talks about what kinds of records are considered student
records covered by this law. In this case, a high school student was charged
with violating the civil rights of one of his teachers and with malicious
destruction of school property. This student got mad at a teacher, and

wrote obscenities and racial slurs on the teacher's chalkboard. Later, he did the same thing on a wall in the corridor. As part of the investigation of the criminal case, the assistant principal gave copies of the student's homework and school papers to the authorities and they used the handwriting on the papers to tie the student to the vandalism.

The student tried to keep the papers from being used in court against him in his criminal case by claiming that they were confidential student records and their release to the police violated FERPA. The judge did not agree, stating that students do not have an expectation of privacy in their handwriting because it is frequently displayed in public. More importantly, the court said that homework assignments and papers were not student records and were not kept confidential by FERPA.

It is interesting to note the differences in the way this court ruled and the decision made by the court in *Falvo*, discussed on page 41.

Psychiatric Records

Another issue that has been to court is that of a parent's ability to access the records of the school psychologist. This is an important area because students often tell the school psychologist things that they would not want revealed. One case that addressed this issue came from Pennsylvania, where the state had additional regulations about the confidentiality of school records.

Parents Against Abuse in Schools v. Williamsport Area School District, involved a number of students who had been abused by a teacher. In the course of the investigation, the school counselor talked to the children who had been victims of the abuse. The district and the parents had a deal that the school doctor would not be doing any therapy, just talking to the students to investigate the truth of the allegations against the teacher. This court decided that, even if an exception for releasing psychological records applied, a student could still get their own records reviewed by appropriate professionals. FERPA allowed release of the records to the parents because the students were all under eighteen.

On occasion, a criminal defendant will try to get access to the victim's school records to use in court. Courts have generally decided that FERPA does not prevent access to the records.

In one case, **State v. Birdsall**, Birdsall was charged with murdering a fourteen-year-old junior high school student, and he wanted to get a copy of his victim's school records. The judge decided that there would be some instances when the victim's behavior might be relevant in the criminal trial (for example, instances involving aggressiveness or assaults committed by the student).

The criminal defendant did not get to have all of the records; the appeals court ruled that the trial judge in the criminal case should review the school records privately. If relevant information was found to be in the records, then the law would allow those portions of the records to be legally turned over to the defendant.

Another appeals court reached a similar decision.

Zaal v. State is the case of a grandfather who was accused of sexually molesting his granddaughter. The grandfather's defense in his criminal case was going to be that he and his son, the girl's father, had a bad relationship and that the son and granddaughter were framing him when nothing improper had actually happened. The courts said that the records should be reviewed privately and any relevant parts could be released to the grandfather.

SUBPOENA

Schools can also release records without violating the law if the records have been subpoenaed by a court. A *subpoena* is a court document that requires either that the person who gets the subpoena appear in court or that, as in this example, records in a person's possession be turned over to the court. Of course, the records can only be released in compliance with the subpoena; the district cannot release the orders to anyone else they want to just because the records were subpoenaed.

TEEN TIP

You and your parents cannot, however, use the subpoena as a way to challenge a grade you have received. The only exception to this is if you can show that the grade you got was incorrect because of a clerical or mathematical error.

FERPA, itself, does not allow individuals to sue the institution for releasing records in violation of the law. Under FERPA, only the Secretary of Education can bring suit for violations of FERPA. In the past, some federal courts have allowed individuals to sue the school under the regular civil rights statute for FERPA violations; other jurisdictions have said that there is no way an individual can sue the school for improperly releasing records. However, the U.S. Supreme Court ruled in June of 2002 that only the Education Department can sue for FERPA violations. If your records have been improperly released by an educational institution, you will need to consult an attorney to see whether your state's courts allow individuals to sue or not.

In addition to FERPA, there may be state laws that address the issue of whether or not your records can be released and under what circumstances. State laws cannot supersede FERPA and allow records to be released when not permitted under federal law, but the state laws may apply to parts of your records that are not considered education records.

−7−

SEXUAL HARASSMENT AND DISCRIMINATION IN SCHOOL

It is illegal for any school that receives federal funds to have opportunities that are available to one gender and not the other, or to allow students to be sexually harassed once the school knows the harassment is occurring. One of the issues in this area relates to opportunities to participate in school sports; others include what kind of conduct between students and between school employees and students is permissible.

HARASSMENT BY AN OFFICIAL

We will first address the issue of sexual harassment in the school setting. Basically, the law considers sexual harassment to be a form of educational discrimination and lawsuits are filed under the same federal law, Title IX, that is used to equalize the sports opportunities for women. As with workplace sexual harassment, there are two ways for harassment to occur. In one way, a teacher or other school official offers a specific trade-off in exchange for sexual contact with the student. For example, it is improper for the teacher to condition a student's grade or ability to graduate on sexual intercourse with the teacher.

A second way a student may suffer from sexual harassment is if the school creates a *hostile environment*. There is no hard and fast rule about what does and does not constitute a hostile environment. The existence of a hostile environment depends on the facts of each case, and, ultimately, the courts decide what is and is not a hostile environment. We can, however, get some guidance from cases that have been decided already by the courts.

One of the leading cases in this area is **Franklin v. Gwinett County Public Schools**, a 1992 United States Supreme Court case that originated in Gwinnett County, Georgia. Christine

(continued)

Franklin filed the original lawsuit that alleged that, when she was a student at Gwinnett High School, a teacher and coach named Andrew Hill continually sexually harassed her. Christine said that among the things Coach Hill did were to engage her in sexually explicit conversations; to ask her if she would consider having sex with an older man; and, to forcibly kiss her on the mouth. The harassment escalated to the point that, on three occasions, Coach Hill got Christine out of other classes, took her to an isolated area of the school, and raped her.

The school district was aware of the allegations and even conducted an investigation. Christine also claimed that the district discouraged her from filing charges against the coach. Ultimately, he was allowed to make a deal with the district and resign in exchange for all of the proceedings against him being dropped.

The trial court and appeals court both ruled that the case against the school district should be dismissed. The Supreme Court disagreed, and this case became the precedent that allows students who have been sexually harassed by teachers to sue for and recover money damages from the school district under Title IX of the Education Amendments of 1972.

NOTE: *The full text of Title IX can be found at Title 20 of the United States Code (U.S.C.) Sections (Sec.)1681-1688. This refers to the set of books that contain federal laws passed by Congress.*

Whether the student is actually able to win the case depends on the facts of each case. Different courts have come up with somewhat different standards to create liability for the school district, but the primary focus of all of the standards is a failure of the district to act on knowledge of the harassment.

Let's look at a few real life cases to see how judges look at claims of sexual harassment by a teacher.

Nelson v. Almont Community Schools comes from Michigan, and was decided in 1996. Tad Nelson was a 17 year old junior at Almont High School. In 1993, Tad took an overdose of drugs. His parents searched his room, hoping to learn what drugs he had taken. In the process, they found notes and letters from Tad's

(continued)

English teacher, Mrs. Schohl. It seems that Tad and Mrs. Schohl had developed a personal relationship. They went out to dinner together and to concerts and movies. Although they had hugged and kissed, they did not have sexual intercourse.

At one point, after a chaperone complained about the way they slow danced at a school dance, the principal investigated. He questioned both the teacher and the student and they denied having any sort of improper relationship. At that point, the principal dropped the investigation.

Later, Tad decided he wanted to end the relationship with his teacher. Mrs. Schohl seemed to have had difficulty accepting his decision and pressured him to continue seeing her. It was during this time that Tad made his suicide attempt. This prompted a new investigation by the principal, who learned that several teachers had seen the student and Mrs. Schohl out together.

The judge decided that these facts were enough to state a valid claim, and it would be up to a jury to decide whether or not the school district had acted appropriately in handling this case.

We can also learn from the outcome of another 1996 case.

In **Abeyta v. Chama Valley Independent School District No. 19**, a twelve-year-old girl sued the Chama Valley district because her sixth grade teacher called her a prostitute. The problem began when the teacher confiscated a note the girl had written to a boy in her class, telling him that she liked him. The teacher read the note aloud to the class, then asked the class if they thought the girl was a prostitute. They laughed. At recess and lunchtime, the students teased and taunted the girl, also calling her a prostitute.

The teacher continued referring to the student that way for another month and a half. At that point, she withdrew from that school and she and her family filed suit. The judges who heard this case did not think this was enough to qualify as sexual harassment, and the student lost her case.

The more severe the actions, the greater the chance that the student can win the case. But the final decision will depend on how a judge, and maybe a jury, feels about what has happened. Of course, most school districts have written policies and procedures prohibiting sexual relationships between students and district employees.

In some instances, depending on the age of the student, sexual contact between a teacher or coach or other school official and a student may also be a criminal offense. Each state has laws that deal with sexual contact between adults and children. There is a huge difference in how a relationship between a thirty-year-old teacher and an eighteen-year-old student will be treated and that of the same teacher with a thirteen-year-old student.

> **TEEN TIP**
>
> You and your family should always make the school officials aware of any improper conduct between students and teachers so that the district has a chance to act. If you do not give them an opportunity to respond and resolve the problem, then you cannot come back and sue them later.

In most instances, the teacher who engages in a relationship with the thirteen-year-old will be guilty of *statutory rape*. The phrase statutory rape means that, as far as the law and legal system are concerned, any sexual contact is *automatically* rape. Minors under a certain age (this age is set by the laws of your state) are legally incapable of consenting to sex and the willingness of the student is not a factor in determining whether the adult is guilty of rape.

If you are approached sexually by a school official, you should firmly refuse the advance and immediately report the incident to your parents and to the school district. The principal of the school should be informed. If the principal is the one who made the advances, then complain to his supervisors in the administration. You should keep working your way up the chain of command until you get a satisfactory response.

> **PARENT TIP**
>
> These types of lawsuits are very complicated and you should not try to represent yourself once you reach the point of filing a suit in court.

You can also file a complaint with the Office of Civil Rights in the U.S. Department of Education.

If the school district does nothing to stop the harassment, then you and your parents should consider consulting an attorney. If you meet the legal standards discussed above, you may have a right to get money from the school district.

STUDENT-TO-STUDENT HARASSMENT

Frequently, it is not a school official who is guilty of harassment. It is another student. If certain criteria are met, student-to-student harassment can also qualify as illegal sexual harassment and the district can be sued. The federal Department of Education has published a list of some factors that should be considered in determining whether a particular set of facts is, in fact, sexual harassment:

- ◆ the degree to which the conduct affected one or more students' education;
- ◆ the type, frequency, and duration of the conduct;
- ◆ the relationship between the harasser and the victim;
- ◆ the number of people involved; and,
- ◆ the age and sex of the harasser and victim.

Now, let's look at some examples taken from real cases.

One of the leading cases in the student-to-student harassment area is **Davis v. Monroe County**, a case that began in Virginia and resulted in a ruling in 1999 by the Supreme Court. In this case, a mother filed suit against the school district seeking damages on behalf of her fifth grade daughter, LaShonda Davis. Mrs. Davis claimed that, over a period of several months, LaShonda was sexually harassed by a fellow student who was identified in the case only as G.F. Allegedly G.F. touched LaShonda's breasts and attempted to touch her genitals on numerous occasions.

LaShonda reported the harassment each time to her mother and to her teacher. The principal was also informed. In fact, LaShonda and a group of girls who all claimed to have been harassed by the same boy tried to talk to the principal, but were refused. At one point, in a conversation with the mother, the principal stated, "I guess I'll have to threaten him a little harder."

(continued)

G.F. was never disciplined by the school; in fact, it was three months before the teacher would let LaShonda change seats in the classroom so that she no longer had to sit by G.F.

TEEN TIP

If you are interested in more information about the Department of Education guidelines on sexual harassment, the full title of this publication is "Sexual Harassment Guidance: Harassment of Students by School Employees, Other Students, or Third Parties" and its full text may be found either at Volume 62 of the Federal Register, Page 12,033 or on the Internet through the Department's website (www.ed.gov). This publication is published by the Office of Civil Rights, so you should go to that section of the website.

This case set the standard for holding school districts liable for sexual harassment by other students. It allowed awarding money to the victims because districts are not permitted to be "deliberately indifferent" to claims of sexual harassment by one of its students. In order to win one of these cases, a victim must prove that the school district knew of the problem and then failed to act appropriately to fix it.

Not all cases in which there is some sort of offensive contact, even if it is sexual in nature, will qualify as sexual harassment.

In the case of **Manfredi v. Mount Vernon Board of Education**, the mother of a seven-year-old second grader filed suit against the school district. Her daughter was repeatedly bothered by another student in the class. He did things like hit her, tease her, spit on her, and push her to the ground. Her mother complained repeatedly to the teacher and to the principal. At one point, the mother and the principal met with the boy's parents. The boy was never disciplined by the school.

The judge, in the written opinion, stated that these incidents "amounted to nothing more than mean-spirited teasing that troublesome little boys sometimes inflict on little girls." One other incident occurred at school: the boy touched the girl's vagina through her clothing. The judge who heard this case did not believe that this incident was severe enough to qualify as sexual harassment.

The cases we have reviewed so far deal with conduct that has occurred on school property between teachers and students and between students only.

But what if the conduct between the teacher and a student occurs off campus? And what if the relationship between the adult and the child does not develop as a result of the fact that the adult is a teacher? It may still be a set of facts that will support a lawsuit against the school district.

In the case of **Patricia H. v. Berkeley Unified School District**, Patricia H. was the mother of two daughters, ages ten and twelve. Patricia was involved in a romantic relationship with Charles Hamilton, who happened to be a band director in the Berkeley school system. Although neither of the girls was in band, Hamilton did teach band in the schools they attended. Hamilton allegedly sexually molested one of the girls on a vacation in Lake Tahoe and the other girl in her room at home. None of the sexual contact between Hamilton and the girls occurred on school property or at school activities.

The mother claimed that the mere presence of Hamilton in the school created such a hostile environment that the girls would be deprived of the full enjoyment of their education. The judges on the court of appeals agreed that it was possible, because of the "severity of the molestation, and the grave disparity in age and power between the girls and Hamilton," that a hostile environment could exist at the school that would rise to the level of discrimination and allow the family to recover damages from the district.

This means that the situation at school was so bad that the students do not really benefit from being in school. If a court decides that a hostile environment exists, then the district may have to pay the student and parents money.

Let's assume for now that you have been a victim of sexual harassment and you report it to the school district. The second part of any successful lawsuit is proving in court that the district *knew* of the sexual harassment and *failed* to act to remedy the problem. The question of whether or not the district acted reasonably is one that will be decided by the judge or jury in a trial. The final outcome will depend on the facts of each case.

TEEN TIP

If you are a victim of student-to-student harassment, it is very important that you or your parents report the conduct to the school officials. You should at least report it to the school principal. Once the school becomes aware of harassment, the officials are obligated to investigate and to take reasonable steps to protect you from continued harassment.

If they fail to act, you may be able to sue them for money. The reporting step is critical, however, to this process. The school district cannot be held liable in court, if they were not notified about the harassment.

The school district does not have to expel every student who is guilty of sexual harassment, but the school district does have to take some sort of action once it becomes aware of the problem. The standard is that the district's actions cannot be unreasonable and they cannot just refuse to respond. Nor can they just continue to use a response they know is not working. An example of this strategy is found in the following case.

In **Vance v. Spencer County School District**, the student, Alma McGowen, was harassed repeatedly over a period of several years by fellow students. Among the incidents that Alma reported to the school assistant principal were that she had been asked if she were gay; been called a whore; been stabbed in the hand with a pen; had her buttocks grabbed; and, been asked, as a sixth grader, by a high school student to describe oral sex.

In the most dramatic incident, Alma was cornered in the restroom by a group of boys who backed her up against the wall. They held her down, while calling her crude names, and yanked off her shirt. One of the boys said that he was going to have sex with her. Finally, another student intervened and ended the assault.

After each of these incidents, the students involved were called in to the office. Several times, the boys later taunted Alma by telling her that they had been "talked to" but that nothing else would happen to them. And nothing did.

The judges ruled that the school, even though it had taken some action, did not do enough. When they could see that talking to the boys was not working, they should have used other disciplinary methods to protect Alma from her tormentors.

YOU AS THE ACCUSED

Up to this point, we have looked at cases from the perspective of the victim. But what if you are a student or the parent of a student who has been accused of sexual harassment? There are two areas of potential trouble for you when this happens. First, you must consider the possibility of disciplinary proceedings at school. Second, you may be facing criminal charges, as well.

The range of school discipline that may apply will depend on what you have done and, to some extent, on the written policies and procedures that apply in your district. As with any other infraction, the more serious the conduct, the more serious the consequences. At the lesser end, the matter may not go any further than a conversation with your teacher or the principal or vice principal. However, you could also get the most severe discipline, including expulsion from school.

If your behavior included unwanted sexual contact with another student, you can also be charged with *sexual assault*. Sexual offenses are generally classified as *felonies*, and can have very significant consequences for you. If you are old enough (somewhere around 14 for most states), it is possible that you could be charged as an adult. If convicted, you will have a felony conviction that will follow you for the rest of your life, impacting your ability to rent an apartment, go to college, and find a job. You could even go to prison. Convicted felons cannot vote or own a firearm. And, depending on the laws in your state, you could be forced to register as a sex offender. This is true even if you are prosecuted as a juvenile.

A sexual assault charge is a very serious matter, and you should think carefully before you make sexual comments to or about other students. You should also be absolutely certain that you do not make unwanted sexual advances. What seems like harmless joking around and teasing to you (typical teenage behavior in other words) may end up being judged in court by an adult system that does not see such behavior as funny.

TEEN TIP

If you are arrested, you should not talk to the police without first consulting with an attorney. In fact, if you are accused of sexual harassment or any other crime, you and your parents should consult an attorney at the earliest possible time.

If you are called in to the office and accused of any form of sexual harassment, you need to remember that whatever you tell the school officials can be used to prosecute you in criminal court. Also, if there is not a police officer present for the questioning and you are not placed under arrest, you do not have the right to have an attorney and you will not be warned about the possible criminal consequences of giving a statement.

Remember that any contacts you have with law enforcement, even if it is just being questioned at school by the police officer assigned to the school, may create a type of police record that could be treated as a public record rather than a private educational record.

For more information on criminal prosecutions, please read Chapters 39 and 41 on juvenile criminal proceedings and searches. There is more information about the confidentiality of records in Chapter 6.

—8—
DISCRIMINATION IN ATHLETICS

Over the past thirty years, there have been many changes in school athletics as a result of the passage of a federal law commonly known as Title IX. (This law is formally known as Title IX of the Educational Amendments of 1972.) This law prohibits discrimination in schools based on gender and has forced schools to have equal opportunities in athletics for both males and females. As with most federal laws that deal with education, this law applies to schools that receive federal funding and not necessarily to private schools. It will, however, apply to private schools that get any sort of federal funding.

Over the years, there have been many cases in the court system on this issue. The cases cover a wide range of topics, from requiring that Little League baseball allow girls to participate, to requiring schools to add sports teams for girls. Some cases have involved girls attempting to make the college football team. We will look at some of the cases that have been decided in this area to provide an overview of the law. However, a book of this type cannot possibly cover all factual situations and all sports. The only way to know the law applicable to your particular situation is to either do additional legal research yourself to see if you can find cases that are similar to yours, or to consult an attorney who specializes in school or civil rights law.

CONTACT SPORTS
Most courts have ruled that schools cannot simply exclude girls from all contact sports and try to justify the exclusion as necessary to prevent injury to the girls. Those courts have said that the law requires that the school either allow girls to be on the boys' team or establish separate teams for both boys and girls.

In the case of **Lantz v. Ambach**, a sixteen-year-old girl in Yonkers, New York wanted to play football. Her school did not have a girls' team and they would not let her play on the boys' team. The reason for that decision was a New York Department of Education regulation that said boys and girls could not be on the same team in basketball, boxing, football, ice hockey, rugby, and wrestling.

The girl's parents sued in court and won. The judge said that the New York rule excluded all girls from the boys' teams in those sports just because they were girls without taking into consideration the fact that some girls are strong enough and athletic enough to play on the boys' teams. The judge said courts cannot order the school to put the girl on the boys' football team, but they can order the school to permit the girls to compete for a spot on the boys' team on equal terms with the boys.

In another football case, **Darrin v. Gould**, two sisters were allowed to play on their school team in practice. The school district officials and the football coach agreed that the girls were holding their own in practice and were as competitive as the boys.

Other than the fact that they were girls, they met all of the eligibility requirements to play on the team in games, but the Washington Interscholastic Activities Association (WIAA), the governing body for school sports in Washington, had a rule that prohibited girls on the boys' football team. The girls' parents filed suit to force the WIAA to let girls play. The court agreed with the girls, and said that the athletic association could not prevent girls from playing just because they were girls.

As you would expect, the growing popularity of soccer has prompted litigation about girls on the boys' soccer team. As with the football cases, the courts have ruled that schools cannot exclude girls from the boys' soccer team, where there is no girls' team, based strictly on gender.

Wrestling is another contact sport that has been the subject of litigation. Courts have ruled that, where schools do not have a girls' wrestling team, the girls must be allowed to try out for the boys' team. This has been a controversial decision, and many schools have argued that, because of the nature of the holds applied in wrestling, the rules should be different. That means there may be additional cases brought to court about wrestling teams as schools work to resolve this problem.

NON-CONTACT SPORTS

Baseball teams have also been the subject of litigation. Schools cannot deny girls the right to be on the boys' baseball team unless they also have a comparable program for girls, usually a softball team. If the school has both baseball and softball teams, the teams must be treated the same. This means that the facilities for the teams have to be equal.

In one case, a school district tried to solve its Title IX problem by keeping the boys from using some of the existing facilities, but not upgrading the girls' facilities. The courts decided that imposing disadvantages on boys by keeping them from using facilities already built for them to avoid upgrading the girls' facilities violated the law.

Cases involving track have also made it to the court system. In one case, a girl was kept off the school's only cross country team based strictly on her gender. The court invalidated that rule, and said that the district had to consider her individual qualifications for the team and not just automatically exclude all girls.

BOYS SEEKING TO BE ON GIRLS' TEAMS

The rules are not as clear where the situation is reversed and boys seek to be on girls' teams. In one case, the school was allowed to keep boys off the girls' tennis team even though they had been allowed on the year before. This court said that excluding boys was a permissible way of correcting past discrimination and equalizing the opportunities for boys and girls. A court in California reached the same conclusion and used the same reasoning in a volleyball case. However, a different court in Rhode Island said that boys could not be kept off the girls' volleyball team if there was not a boys' team.

Field hockey is traditionally a girls' sport, but there are some reported cases where boys have sought to play on the field hockey team. The courts have generally allowed them to play, but the outcomes have depended on the facts of the cases. The courts seem to reach their decision by looking at the overall opportunities for both boys and girls at the school. If the opportunities are greatly in favor of the girls, the boys have been put on the team. If the opportunities have historically favored the boys, then the courts generally allow the school to exclude the boys.

This is only an issue when there are not separate teams for each gender in the sport in question. In schools where there are two teams, the courts will allow the school to restrict the boys' team in that sport to boys and the girls' team to girls.

–9–
STUDENTS WITH DISABILITIES

There are hundreds and hundreds of reported cases dealing with students with disabilities, and this is an area that lends itself to conflict between parents and schools. A detailed analysis of every aspect of this area of the law would take an entire book of its own, so this will, by necessity, be only an overview. If you are a student with a disability or the parent of such a student, you should discuss any questions about your particular situation with an attorney.

The primary law in this area is the *Individuals with Disabilities Education Act*, also called *IDEA*. The purpose of this law is to insure that students with disabilities get the free public education to which they are entitled and to be sure that their rights and the rights of their parents are protected in the process. It is also designed to help states and schools in providing education to disabled students.

The agency responsible for overseeing administration of this law is the Office of Special Education and Rehabilitative Services, part of the federal Department of Education. Each state is responsible for developing its own programs to meet the needs of disabled students, but IDEA sets up the minimum standards the states must meet.

IDEA has several different aspects. In addition to guaranteeing all students, including those with disabilities, a free public education, IDEA also sets up procedural protections for both students and their parents and provides a mechanism for funding to states to offset the cost of the programs.

DEFINING DISABILITY
The first issue to consider is what qualifies a student as "disabled." The law sets up several categories of disabilities:
- mental retardation;
- hearing impairments;

◆ speech or language impairments;

◆ visual impairments;

◆ serious emotional disturbance;

◆ orthopedic impairments;

◆ autism;

◆ traumatic brain injury; and,

◆ other learning disabilities.

There are some students that will clearly fall within these guidelines–blindness, deafness, or severe retardation are obviously covered. But there is also room for argument in a list like that. Children who are not severely disabled question whether their disability falls within the protection and coverage of IDEA. It should come as no surprise that there are quite a few cases that address this issue, and each student's situation must be evaluated on a case by case basis.

For example, children with chronic asthma, allergies, migraines, and sinusitis have been ruled to be disabled within the meaning of this law. However, Acquired Immune Deficiency Syndrome (AIDS) does not qualify as a disability by itself; the student's condition must have deteriorated so that their ability to learn has been affected. Questions often arise about whether students with attention deficit disorder qualify for special education under IDEA. The answer to those questions is that it depends. The student can qualify if his or her ability to learn or academic performance is negatively affected, but not if he or she just has socialization problems.

EVALUATING THE CHILD'S NEEDS

Once the initial question of whether a child is disabled has been answered, the next step is to do an evaluation of the child's needs and create a plan to meet those needs. Generally, the school will do this evaluation, but the parents may, under some circumstances, have the right to get an independent evaluation at the school's expense.

The plan that is created is called an *Individual Education Plan*, or *IEP*. It must provide for the student's education in what is called "the least restrictive environment." This provision is what is frequently called *mainstreaming*. If there is a way for the student to function in a regular classroom, then the student must be placed there. This is true even if it means that the school must provide some additional assistance to the student. The student does not have to stay in the regular classroom all of the time in order for the plan to follow the law. The student may be removed from the class in order to receive services like speech therapy or physical therapy.

Courts decide whether a particular plan qualifies by looking at two aspects. First, they evaluate whether the student's educational needs can be met in a regular classroom with additional aids provided by the school. If this is not possible, then the court looks to see whether the student has been mainstreamed to the maximum extent possible while still meeting the needs of the student. Various court cases have established some factors that go into this decision. One question is whether the student's needs can be met better in the regular classroom or in special education.

Another factor is the nonacademic benefits the disabled child gets from interactions with nondisabled students. The effect the presence of a disabled child will have on the teacher and other students can also be considered. A final issue is the cost to the school of mainstreaming the disabled student.

Once the student is placed, the state must be sure the student is receiving an appropriate education. This has been defined as an educational environment that allows the student to make academic progress. The student has to be receiving a meaningful benefit from his or her education.

PROVIDING SERVICES IN SCHOOL
The IEP must also set out which services have to be provided by the school and which ones do not. The law sets out a list of services that schools are compelled to provide. These are generally classified as developmental, corrective, or other supportive services. Things that are included are:

- transportation;
- speech pathology;
- audiology;
- psychological services;
- physical and occupational therapy;
- recreation;
- therapeutic recreation;
- social work services;
- counseling services;
- rehabilitation counseling; and,
- medical services.

NOTE: *The medical services category is defined as including diagnosis and evaluation, but not a full-time physician for the student. The school does not have to provide medical treatment, so the amount of physical and occupational therapy provided is limited.*

The law requires that the IEP contain certain things:

- a statement of the present levels of the child's performance;
- a statement of annual goals, including short-term instructional objectives;
- a statement of the specific educational services to be provided to the child, and the extent to which the child will be allowed to participate in regular educational programs;
- a statement for the needed transition services for students beginning no later than age sixteen, which must be done on at least an annual basis;
- the date the services will begin and the anticipated date they will end; and,
- a list of objective criteria and evaluation procedures to determine whether or not the educational objectives are being met.

If the parents do not like the district's decision, they have a right to a formal hearing. State law determines which agency is responsible for conducting this hearing. If the parents are still not happy with the outcome, then they have the right to take the school district to court. The law specifically gives parents that right so that they do not have to overcome the *immunity* from lawsuits that schools normally have over the way they provide education to their students.

As a general rule, schools and other parts of the government cannot be sued. However, there are some exceptions to this rule; the exceptions are created by laws the government has passed, which set up certain situations in which they can be sued.

There is a provision that permits public schools to pay for private schools in some conditions. Before the parents can force the school to pay, they must prove that the public school placement was totally inappropriate and did not meet the educational needs of their child.

NOTE: *The school's obligation to provide a free education ends when the child turns twenty-one.*

PARTICIPATING IN EXTRACURRICULAR ACTIVITIES

One final area to consider is the role of the disabled student in extracurricular activities. There is no constitutional right to participate in athletics or other extracurricular activities. That means that the rules that most interscholastic associations have that limit the age of the participants and the number of semesters of eligibility are legal. A student that has remained in high school for longer than the usual term just because he or she is disabled cannot force the school or the association to allow him or her to compete in athletics. This is also true if there are age requirements and the student is too old under those rules because he or she repeated early grades, like first and second grade, due to a learning disability.

However, IDEA does offer some protection to disabled students who want to participate. If the student's individual plan calls for the student to participate in athletics as a motivational tool, at least one case has held that the student has a federally guaranteed right to participate in interscholastic sports. In that situation, the student has a right to due process and the school must evaluate individually each student's case to see if an age requirement waiver is appropriate. The right to due process is similar to the due process issues we have previously discussed, and has to do with the procedures the school must follow to be sure that the rights of the students are protected. If the age requirement is waived, that means that students that would be too old to participate under the regular rules are allowed to participate in the activities for which the age requirement is waived (done away with).

The federal guarantee does not mean that the student has an absolute right to be the starting quarterback for the football team. The school just has to find some way to accommodate the student's participation.

–10–
SCHOOL DISCIPLINE

The disciplinary options available to school officials are an area of intense interest to students and their parents. The following discussion will apply primarily to public school students. This is because private schools have such wide latitude in student discipline. Attendance at a private school is not considered a right; rather, it is a privilege. The relationship between the school and its students is controlled by the policies of the school as set out by the contract between the school and the students and their parents.

Public school students can be disciplined in a variety of ways for all sorts of conduct. The general rule is that teachers and administrators can do whatever is reasonably necessary to discipline students. This means something different in different states and situations. In school, behavior is regulated by the school district; however, there are also instances in which conduct that occurs away from school can also result in disciplinary proceedings *in* school. The discipline options range from minor punishment, like detention, to placement in an alternative school, and even all the way to suspension or expulsion from school.

WRITTEN RULES

Most schools have a set of written rules for student conduct. This conduct code should be provided to all students and their parents in written form. The tendency for most students and parents is to just toss this handbook aside without ever reading it; however, you should really review this information with your parents so that you know what all the rules are. Sometimes, what seems like a minor violation of the rules can have serious consequences that go way beyond a few days in detention hall. Remember, these rules apply not just on the school campus but also at all school-sponsored activities.

One of the best examples of this is the unwitting student who gets bored in an assembly. Instead of paying attention, he or she gets out a pen and writes his or her name on the arm of the chair. It is made of wood and the wood is soft. It makes a permanent mark on the arm. The school principal finds the student's name scratched onto the chair. The school has a zero tolerance policy on graffiti and vandalism. Instead of dealing with the matter internally, the principal turns the matter over to the police and juvenile authorities.

The student is arrested, charged, and subsequently convicted. He or she is over seventeen, so is treated as an adult. Unfortunately, he or she learns from a lawyer that graffiti in school is a felony offense. Not only does this student acquire a felony record for a very minor incident, he or she may now be ineligible for college scholarships and aid. Because he or she was bored and pressed too hard with a pen writing, he or she has run afoul of the new federal law that makes people with felonies ineligible for federal school loans and grants.

Also, many students do not realize how easy it can be to get summoned to the office because of innocent doodling on their notebook. In many schools, gang activity has been a serious problem and the police have assigned experienced gang unit officers to the school. It is possible for a student with no gang contacts to get labeled by zealous officers as a gang member because they noticed "suspicious gang symbols" on the student's notebook. At that point, any rule-breaking by that student will be taken very seriously because they are now believed to be a gang member.

SCHOOL POLICE OFFICER

Many students are under the impression that it is not a big deal to be pulled in by the school police officer. What you may not realize is that, if your school is computerized, the police officer creates an official record of his or her contact with you. That becomes an official law enforcement record just as though you had been questioned by the police outside of school. This is the type of record that can follow you forever, and perhaps find its way to prospective colleges and employers, so it is best if your record is not filled with repeated law enforcement contacts. This is especially true if you are in a school where the school officials routinely call in the police rather than handle things within the school.

JUVENILE DETENTION

There are many instances in which conduct that used to be cause for a visit to the principal's office and nothing more can now result in a trip to juvenile detention and criminal charges being filed. An easy example of this situation is the fight between two students at school. In your parents' day, the guilty parties would be called in to the assistant principal's office and punished in some way—perhaps a few smacks or days in detention. If the students were known trouble makers, they might be suspended for a few days.

That same school fight, even though it does not involve weapons of any sort, now frequently results in the combatants being arrested. If they are under seventeen, they will be sent to juvenile detention. Their parents will have to hire an attorney and the students will end up classified as a juvenile delinquent and having to serve at least a term of probation. Too many trips through the juvenile justice system can result in being placed in a juvenile justice institution. That is all in addition to whatever punishment the school doles out—perhaps a stay in alternative school or even expulsion from school. If the student is over seventeen, he or she may end up with an adult criminal record of some sort. That is why it is important to know the rules of your school, and abide by them as much as possible.

CRIME AND PUNISHMENT

Now, we will look at some different types of conduct and the types of school punishment available. The general rule is that any violation of school rules can give rise to student discipline. Things like fighting or other disruptive behavior can be disciplined, and can in certain circumstances, result in suspension or expulsion. So can things like possession of weapons or drugs or alcohol on campus. You can be disciplined for failing to obey instructions. Being abusive or threatening toward a staff member or another student on the campus can also get you expelled. In some instances, the same thing can happen even if the threat occurred *off* campus.

Drugs or Alcohol before School

There are other instances in which the off campus behavior of students can be punished by the school. There are cases that say that schools can keep students from going to certain businesses or merchants while on the way to and from school. Students who come to school under the influence of drugs or alcohol can be disciplined even though the alcohol or drugs were consumed off campus.

Internet Use away from School

A big area of off-campus behavior that sometimes violates school rules and subjects students to discipline involves the use of the Internet. Clearly, student use of the Internet that occurs on the school campus can be regulated by the school. Whether school discipline is appropriate for off-campus Internet activity depends on the ability of the off-campus activity to interfere with the operation of the school. For example, a student who posted instructions on how to hack into the school computers was once disciplined at school even though he posted the instructions from home.

Another court authorized the school to expel a student who created, from his home, a website that contained derogatory comments about a teacher, including a list of reasons "Why she should die." This student designed a picture of the teacher with her head severed and another with her face morphing into that of Adolph Hitler. The site also included a request for money to help the student hire a hit man. Obviously, this type of conduct poses a very serious and real threat to the teacher and to the safe operation of the schools.

But what if the student had stopped with just making insulting remarks about the teacher? In that case, it will be difficult for the school to show that school will be disrupted, even if a lot of students at that school visit the website. Therefore, the student's First Amendment rights win out and he cannot be punished for what he says.

It is impossible to set out a specific line that separates off-campus conduct that can be punished at school from that which cannot. For example, a court in Washington refused to allow a school to suspend a student for creating a website from home that included mock obituaries. The difference in this case was that the court did not think the school had shown that a threat was intended. Another court has ruled that a home page that included criticism of the school was not enough to warrant suspension of the student even though several students saw the page and it was discussed by numerous students at school.

The bottom line, then, is that you should be careful about what you do with the Internet, even from home. Any type of activity that can be construed as a threat or as likely to disrupt the function of the school can get you a punishment. You may find out the hard way that something that you intended to be humorous ends up getting you in trouble with the school officials. Especially in today's climate, with all of the concerns about violence in schools and school shootings, you should be cautious.

Changing Grades

One *disciplinary* method that causes controversy is the changing of a student's grade. If the student can show that the grade was changed just for disciplinary purposes and not academic purposes, then the student might win. If the grade is changed for academic reasons, for example if the student skipped class, then this is usually permissible. It will also make a difference if the school has a written policy that warns that grade reduction is a possible penalty.

In one case, a group of students at a band program played some guitar pieces that the students knew were prohibited. Written school policy stated that grade reduction was a possible discipline method. The court upheld the grade reductions in this case, even though it kept the students from graduating with honors.

Alternative Schools

Another method of discipline is the use of *alternative schools*. The specific use of alternative schools will be determined by local district policy. One common way to end up in alternative school is to violate a criminal law and end up in the juvenile system. In many school districts, this triggers a trip to alternative school.

DUE PROCESS

Any time you are suspended or expelled, the law says you are entitled to *due process*. Due process is a legal term, found often in criminal cases. It has a different meaning in school discipline cases; it has been determined by courts to mean that you have a right to have the school formally tell you what rules they say you have violated and you get to have a hearing with the school officials where you and the school tell your sides of the story before you can be suspended for more than ten days or expelled. Basically, what this means is once the school district tells the student what they believe has occurred and gives the student an opportunity to respond, the student has received their *due process* and can be disciplined. The exception is that longer suspensions and expulsions require a formal hearing.

Let's look at some examples taken from real cases and see what kinds of conduct can get you suspended and what counts as due process. The first case deals with issues related to what students said at school. Discipline in this area is significant because it requires balancing the school's right to control the school against the student's constitutional right to free speech. As a student, you do not give up your constitutional rights at school, but sometimes the school's power is greater than your rights.

In **Heller v. Hogdin**, a student was suspended after a verbal dispute with another student. Emily Heller was a high school senior who got into trouble in the school cafeteria when a sophomore student cut into line in the "seniors only" serving area. Emily told the student to get out of line. That student responded by calling Emily an obscene name. Emily got mad, and yelled back at the student, in the process repeating the obscenity. Emily was taken to the office by the assistant principal. On the way to the office, Emily and the administrator discussed the incident and Emily was told she would be suspended for five days for the obscenity. School rules stated that use of obscenities was a violation of school rules.

Later, both Emily and her mother had several conversations with school officials. Emily filed the suit claiming that she had been denied her due process rights prior to being suspended. The judge disagreed, saying that Emily had plenty of opportunities to tell her side of the story to the school. The judge pointed out that the hearing on a suspension of that length does not have to be a formal hearing, and that the conversation Emily had with the assistant principal on the way to the office was sufficient.

In another instance, **Breeding v. Driscoll**, two different students filed suit in the same case against their school. The first student, T.P., got into a fight with another student. T.P. was so out of control that she kept trying to attack the other student even after the faculty intervened and she had to be physically carried to the office. She continued to shout obscenities and tried to run away from the office. The police were summoned and T.P. was taken to the police station. T.P. and her mother discussed the incident later that day with the principal and T.P. was suspended.

Approximately a week later, the assistant principal was told by a student that another student, C.B., was going to make a drug sale later that day and that the drugs were hidden in C.B.'s coat. The administrators called C.B. out of class and asked him to empty his pockets. Two packets of what appeared to be marijuana were found. Several days later, the school had a conference with C.B., his parents, and his aunt, who also happened to be a lawyer. The principal decided to suspend C.B. for nine days and then send him to alternative school. In this case, the judge decided that both students had received due process and upheld their suspensions.

Sometimes, the discipline can be not for spoken words, but for written ones.

In **Donivan v. Ritchie**, a group of students created a nine page document they called "The S*** List." The document contained a list of students by name followed by statements about the student that ranged from insulting to sexually explicit. Although the list was created away from school, it was brought to school by Donovan and two other boys. The boys admitted to photocopying the list, but told the principal they could not be disciplined because they did the photocopying away from school. The principal did not agree with their assessment and told them they would be suspended.

The school sent a letter to all of the students involved in creating the list, scheduling a meeting with them and their parents. After the meeting, Donovan and his mother met with the principal, who told them Donovan was indefinitely suspended. A few days later, the principal notified Donovan and his mother that the suspension would be for ten days. The judge sided with the school and let the suspension stand.

DRUGS AND ALCOHOL POLICIES

Another frequent area of discipline relates to violations of the alcohol and substance abuse policies of school districts.

In the case of **In the Interest of T.H.**, a student was suspended for ten days for violating the school's alcohol policy. T.H., who was six-teen, and two other boys consumed beer that they obtained off cam-pus and drank off campus. Then they went to the high school foot-ball game. The ticket taker detained them because she smelled alcohol. The police kept T.H. until his parents came to get him. The matter was referred to the school for discipline. The principal talked to T.H., who admitted to drinking. Later that day, T.H.'s parents were notified of his suspension. This school's policy was that stu-dents could not get any credit for things missed during the suspen-sion. The court let the suspension stand, even though it meant that T.H., who had been an all B student, would fail for the semester.

Drug sales, even if they occur off campus, can also result in discipline.

In *Giles v. Brookville Area School District*, a student was expelled for the last three months of one school year and all of the next one. The student and another student agreed, while at school, that Giles would sell, and the other boy would buy, marijuana. The drugs were delivered to the boy's home and Giles was paid forty dollars. The purchaser resold the drugs to other students who were caught smoking on campus. Giles was identified as the original source of the marijuana. Giles was expelled after a hearing before the school board. The judge sided with the school and let the suspension stand.

SUING THE SCHOOL FOR BEING DISCIPLINED

Federal courts and most state courts have rules that allow parties to be fined for filing a suit that does not have any merit.

TEEN TIP

If you have been the subject of disciplinary action and are considering filing a lawsuit, you should first consult with an attorney.

In *Smith v. Severn*, a student was suspended for three days for disrupting a school assembly with a chain saw and a live boa constrictor. The principal met with the student and his mother and told them the student was suspended. Then, after the meeting, the school sent a note giving the parents an opportunity to have a hearing before the school board, which the student accepted. A hearing before the board was held, and the suspension was upheld. There was evidence that the student's grades suffered as a result of the suspension.

The student lost his case at trial and appealed to the Seventh Circuit Court of Appeals. In the closing paragraph to the opinion, the judges noted that this was a "wholly unremarkable disciplinary action of a modest suspension which was preceded by entirely appropriate constitutional safeguards." The judges said that this case

(continued)

was *frivolous* (without merit) and that, if the school district had asked for fines against the student and his family for filing a frivolous lawsuit, they would have been awarded.

NOTE: *Not every case should be taken to court, and you should be sure that you have something legitimate to complain about before you file a lawsuit.*

CORPORAL PUNISHMENT

Another controversial aspect to school discipline is the use of *corporal punishment*. Corporal punishment means any type of discipline that involves physical contact between the school official administering the punishment and the student.

Some states permit corporal punishment while other states have statutes that forbid it. In jurisdictions where it is allowed, it must always be *reasonable* and not excessive. The final decision as to whether a particular occurrence is reasonable is made by a judge or jury in a trial. To be reasonable, it should follow a warning about the conduct and the student should be given an opportunity to tell his or her side of the story. You are not entitled to a formal hearing before corporal punishment is administered.

How the punishment is administered is also a factor. There is a difference between paddling a student with a wooden paddle and the actions, for example, of a school principal in the next case.

> **TEEN TIP**
>
> Since these cases can be hard for a student to win, you should consult an attorney early in the disciplinary process if you are considering a lawsuit.

In **P.B. v. Koch**, the principal thought he overheard some students making derogatory remarks about him. He became angry and choked, slapped, and punched the three students. The students won this case, with the judge saying that there was no way the principal could have thought what he did was proper.

As you have seen, the due process concept is often interpreted to favor the school, and the shortest of conversations between an assistant principal and student will qualify.

CRIMES AT SCHOOL

If you get into trouble at school, the school principal has two options. One is to handle the problem internally, impose discipline on the student at school, and not turn it over to the police. The other option is to deal with problems by just handing the matter over to the juvenile authorities. The choice belongs to the school and students have no ability to complain if they do not like the choice made by the school.

That means that you need to be careful about the way you behave at school and at school activities. Getting into a fight can result in more than just trouble at school; you may also find yourself facing juvenile delinquency proceedings in juvenile court, or *assault* or *disorderly conduct* charges in adult criminal court. You should also avoid grafitti and vandalism; those acts also have consequences that extend beyond the schoolhouse door.

Students of both genders need to be careful in how they handle themselves in the dating arena. Unwanted advances that include some sort of physical contact can, depending on the facts, also be treated as a crime. The best rule of thumb here is to keep your hands to yourself unless you are absolutely sure the other person does not object to the contact. (See Chapter 7 on harassment.)

This is particularly true if the contact between the students is sexual. If you engage in sexual activity and the other person has not consented, you can find yourself facing a rape charge. If convicted, you could end up registering as a sex offender for the rest of your life. Also, always remember that if there is a significant age difference between you and your partner, and you are the one who is older, you could be charged with rape just because the younger person is deemed to be legally too young to have consented.

If you are accused of a crime at school, you will want to carefully review the information on searches in school, Chapter 5. If you are questioned at school, you can always ask to talk to an attorney before you answer any questions. You may not always be legally entitled to have an attorney when you are asked questions at school, but it never hurts to ask.

There is more information on your right to an attorney and on working with an attorney in Chapter 38. You also need to remember that, if you are questioned at school about activities at school that can also be considered crimes under the laws of your state, you can be charged criminally based on things you tell the school officials.

Depending on what you have done wrong and on the laws of your state, your parents may also be financially responsible for your actions. This is particularly true when you have damaged school property. For more information on this topic, please see the section in the book on parental liability, Chapter 15.

–11–
EXPULSION FROM PRIVATE SCHOOL

The rules that apply to expulsion from private school are very different from those that apply to expulsion from public school. Public schools are treated like other parts of the government, because they are funded by public tax money. That means that they are held to higher standards. The courts have also recognized that students have a right to a public education. Therefore, the student's rights must be protected before his or her right to attend public school can be limited. This is the due process concept discussed before in Chapter 10 on school discipline.

Private school students, however, do not have those same protections. There is no constitutional or other legal right to a private school education. A private school has the protection of the constitutional right to freedom of association, and they do not have to admit students unless they choose to. Once the student is admitted, the rules are set by the school in the admission contract and the school catalog.

The law treats this relationship as a contract between the school and the student's parents and the terms of the contract control. That means that the conditions under which a student can be expelled from a private school are contractual as well.

TEEN TIP

If you are facing expulsion or have already been expelled from a private school, you will need to either research the laws of your state or consult an attorney to help you determine whether you can sue the school for expelling you or force the school to let you remain enrolled.

We have discussed in Chapter 10 the processes that apply to being expelled from public school; those rules do not apply to private schools. In private schools, expulsion rules are determined by the contract between the school and the parents, and the laws that deal with contracts in that state.

We can get some guidance from looking at some cases that have already gone to court. You would normally expect that it would be the conduct of the student that triggered an expulsion. But there is a case that allowed a private school to expel a student based on the conduct of his parents.

In 1993, in **Allen v. Casper,** the Allens' two children were enrolled in Bethlehem Christian School. Both children had previously attended other schools and this was their first year at Bethlehem. The school had a written policy that said, "The school reserves the right to refuse admittance, suspend, or expel any student who does not cooperate with policies established in this book. The high standard and Biblical principles that our school holds apply to after school hours as well. If any parent or student refuses to follow those standards, then they place their privilege of attending B.C.S. in jeopardy."

The parents were given a copy of this policy as part of the admissions process. Parents also had to sign an agreement that they would uphold the student handbook, encourage their children to cooperate with the teachers, and not go around complaining to other parents if they were unhappy. Instead, they were supposed to take the matter to the school board.

The Allens did become unhappy with the way the school handled a problem with their daughter, who was six. The girl claimed that two other students, who were also six, had pulled her dress up and put their hands on her panties. The parents complained to the school, and the principal talked with the two students. The principal felt, based on the ages of the students involved, that they did not realize they had done anything wrong. He told them not to touch students that way again or he would have to spank them.

The following month, the daughter complained again about one of the boys doing the same thing to her. The principal called in the boy's parents and had a conference with them. With the parents' consent, the principal spanked the boy.

(continued)

Mrs. Allen called the school demanding to know how the situation was handled. The principal told her that it was school policy to discuss disciplinary action only with the parents of the child who was disciplined. The Allens did not like this answer, so they met with the minister of the church with which the school was affiliated.

The school handbook required that parents go to the school board if they wanted to discuss a decision made by the principal, but the Allens never took this step. The minister asked the principal to tell the Allens how the child involved in the second incident with their daughter was disciplined, and he complied.

The following month, the girl told her mother that another child had spit on her while they were out on the playground. Mrs. Allen called the teacher, who told her that the other student had a dental problem that caused him to spray saliva when he talked and that he had not spit on her daughter intentionally. Mrs. Allen did not like the answer, so she angrily demanded to talk to the principal. The principal told Mrs. Allen that he could call the child's parents.

Mrs. Allen called back the next day to see what the parents had said, and was furious when the principal told her that he had not been able to reach the other parents. Mrs. Allen called the principal "unChristian" and accused him of working with the devil. At this point, the school decided that it had had enough of the Allens and told them they would have to find another school for their children. The school stated that the Allen's tuition payment would be refunded.

The Allens filed this lawsuit against the school, claiming that the school had unlawfully dismissed their children. The courts disagreed, and said that the school had the right, under its contract with the parents, to expel students if the parents failed to follow the student handbook.

SUING FOR MONEY

If parents believe that their child has been wrongfully expelled from a private school, they can sue for money, but they likely cannot sue to force the school to keep the child as a student.

In *Bloch v. Hillel Torah North Suburban Day School*, a student was expelled from the school at mid term. The school said it was for excessive absences and tardiness. The parents said it was because the school did not like the actions of the student's mother in leading a movement to battle head lice at the school. The parents tried to say that the school had to keep their daughter as a student because that school was the only one in the area that could meet their religious needs. They also said the admissions contract was for the entire eight years of grades the school offered; the school said the contract was for one school year at a time.

The court decided in favor of the school on the issue of keeping the child enrolled in school, saying that it was just too difficult and impractical to order parties to maintain such a personal relationship as that of educating a child when one of the parties does not want to remain in that relationship. The appeals court judges said the parents' only remedy was to sue for money damages, which they could get if they convinced either the trial judge or a jury that the school had breached the contract between the parties by expelling the student.

DECIDING FACTORS IN COURT

When deciding whether a school has violated its contract with the parents, the judge cannot make his or her decision based on whether he or she thinks the student should have been expelled or disciplined. Judges will only look at whether the school complied with the terms of the contract and applied the rules fairly and reasonably.

Types of conduct for which students have been legitimately expelled include:

- fighting at school;
- lying to school officials;
- alcohol or drug consumption;
- hazing; and,
- other violations of specific school rules.

Let's look at how one judge in a real case looked at these issues.

In **Spell v. Bible Baptist Church, Inc.**, Spell was expelled from school. Several students at the school had a beach party at a rented apartment. They left the apartment damaged and littered with beer cans, liquor bottles, pornographic magazines, vomit, and other litter. The students were confronted about the incident, and expelled. Spell's parents filed suit against the school. They claimed he had been expelled unfairly and in breach of the parents' contract with the school.

The court disagreed, ruling that the school had clearly proved that drinking alcohol and immoral conduct were violations of the school's policies, and further that school policy stated that these offenses were cause for expulsion from the school.

Additionally, students can be expelled for failing to maintain their academic performance.

For example, in **Rich v. Kentucky Country Day, Inc.**, the courts allowed a school to deny enrollment to a student based on his academic performance the previous year.

Finally, it is clear that students can be expelled for academic dishonesty. Cheating and plagiarism are generally specifically prohibited by a school's rules and violation of the rules will almost always justify expulsion from a private school.

PARENT TIP

If a student is expelled, the parents are still responsible for payment of the tuition and other fees. Unless the contract with the school provides for a refund in the event the student is expelled, the entire contract amount remains owed to the school. However, you may be able to negotiate this issue with the school.

PRIVATE SCHOOL CONTRACT VERSUS PUBLIC SCHOOL NOTICE

Remember that the rules for private schools are different from those that apply to public schools. The public school can expel students only after giving them notice of the reason for which they are being expelled and an opportunity to respond to the allegation. The private school only has to comply with the terms of its contract with the parents and you only get the rights that are contained in that contract. Things like the student handbook or code of conduct will be considered a part of the contract.

–12–

DROPPING OUT
AND THE GED

Every state has some form of compulsory attendance law, but the ages during which students are required to be in school vary from state to state. For a list of ages for your state, please see Appendix B.

If you stay in high school and successfully complete all of the requirements, you will be awarded a diploma. If you drop out, you will not be able to get a diploma. Your only option at that point is to pass the test to get a *Graduate Equivalency Degree*, or GED.

Some states will make you stay in school either until you

> **TEEN TIP**
>
> If you are considering dropping out of school, you will need to determine whether the law of your state *allows* you to do so.

turn eighteen or graduate from high school. Other states will let you leave at a younger age, but you may have to have permission from the school district. Some states have requirements that you must meet before you drop out, for instance that you be studying for the GED or have a full time job that you must keep in order to support yourself.

There are some states that make staying in school a requirement before underage teens can get a marriage license. If you are married and want to remain in school, you will be allowed to do so. It is illegal for

> **TEEN TIP**
>
> If you are married, you may not be required to remain in school. Once again, this varies from state to state.

schools to keep married students, pregnant students, and students who already have children from attending. Once you reach age twenty-one, however, you are no longer eligible to attend public school.

Staying in school may also be a condition of getting and keeping a driver's license. That is not the case in all states, so it is important to know the law of your state before you make a decision to leave school.

If you find yourself in trouble with the juvenile authorities, you will almost always be required as a condition of your probation to stay in school. If you are sent to a juvenile detention facility, you will still have to attend school. You will take the same sort of classes you would be taking if you were still in regular school. You may also have the option to get your GED while you are in the placement. If you get into trouble as an adult and you have not finished high school, many judges will make you get your GED as a condition of probation.

If you plan on attending college, you will need to either have a high school diploma or GED to meet the admission requirements of most colleges. Many employers will require that you have one or the other as well.

–13–
SUING THE SCHOOL

There may be times when a student or her parents would like to sue the school district for actions by school administrators, teachers, or other students. The overall general rule is that schools and their employees enjoy a certain degree of immunity from lawsuits. As with most areas of the law, there are exceptions and distinctions. This means that the answer in a particular situation depends on the facts of that situation.

Whether it is a public school or a private school can make a difference. Also, as the different courts around the country rule on cases that come before them, the law may change. There is no way for a book like this to give you a hard and fast rule that will apply in every fact situation.

One situation in which parents and students would like to file a suit to recover money damages from a school is when a student is a victim of a crime on campus. The student's ability to sue depends on the facts. If an outsider assaults a student while the student is walking home from school, the school is unlikely to have any liability.

> **TEEN TIP**
>
> Before you decide to pursue a claim against a school district, district employee, or private school in any of these areas, you and your parents should discuss your set of facts with an attorney.

Contrast that to a sexual assault by a teacher with a previous criminal record against a student on school grounds. Courts are more likely to impose liability in this situation against the school district for failing to protect the student. As an example, let's review the following case.

In a 1995 Georgia case, **Holbrook v. Executive Conference Center**, the student nearly drowned in the swimming pool at a hotel where the student was staying on a school band trip. The student's family sued, claiming that the school was *negligent*, or careless, in its supervision of the students and that contributed to the near drowning. The court said that the school district could not be sued under these circumstances because of the general rule that prohibits lawsuits against governments and schools.

IMMUNITIES

Sovereign immunity is a legal doctrine that says that governments in many instances have immunity and cannot be sued. Because a public school is considered part of the government, this protection applies to them and there are some things for which the school just cannot be sued. This is an issue you will need to discuss with an attorney before you file a lawsuit against a school district.

This doctrine will not apply to private schools, but there is another type of immunity that may protect the private school from being sued. This is the doctrine of *charitable immunity*, which holds that charities are exempt from being sued for torts. A *tort* is any civil wrongdoing other than a breach of contract. Not all courts recognize the charitable immunity, so you will need to discuss this issue with an attorney or research the laws of your state to determine which position your state courts take. If your state does not have charitable immunity, then the school will be treated just like any person for the purpose of determining liability. If you are in a state that has charitable immunity, it extends to cover injuries of those other than students.

In **Gray v. St. Cecilia's School**, a mother who was hurt on the premises of her son's parochial school could not sue the school to recover money for her injuries because of this doctrine. The court ruled that she benefitted from the school's works, so she could not sue.

Even in states that recognize charitable immunity, your particular private school may not qualify for this protection. Schools that are not legally organized as a charity can be held liable as can schools whose charters do not restrict them to charitable activities. However, the fact that a school makes money, for example from its football program, does not necessarily keep them from being considered a charitable operation. Of course, not all private schools are set up as charitable organizations, so the charitable immunity protections do not apply to those schools at all.

DISTRICT LIABILITY

Another area of interest is whether school districts can be made to pay for actions by other students. This is a developing area of the law, and the changes are likely the result of changes in public attitudes and some of the dramatic school shooting incidents. Historically, courts have said that there is not a constitutional duty for schools to protect students from the acts of other students. But by the same token, the school cannot create a dangerous environment. Furthermore, when they know there is a problem, they cannot ignore it.

Finally, students who are injured as a result of participation in athletics have tried to recover money from their school district. This is another area in which the chance of success depends on where you live because different courts have made different decisions about the extent of school liability. The school district has to provide its athletes safe equipment and appropriate instruction and supervision. Students, however, also assume some responsibility because there is a risk of injury that is inherent in sports participation.

Let's look at some cases taken from real life. Some courts have decided that a school can be liable to students for injuries they receive as athletic participants.

In *Leahy v. School Board of Hernando County*, a 1984 Florida case, the school district was held liable for injuries sustained by a freshman football player. In that case, there were not enough helmets for all of the players, and several freshman participated in practice without helmets. During a drill that required a player to hit a lineman with his hands and then roll onto the ground, one of the players without a helmet was injured when his hands slipped and he hurt his face on the lineman's face mask. The coaches were supervising, but the players without helmets were not given any special instructions or consideration.

The appeals court ruled for the student, saying that the school had a duty to provide equipment to all of the athletes and should have treated the athletes without helmets differently from the ones with helmets.

In another case, **Everett v. Bucky Warren, Inc.**, a court ruled that a school could be liable when a student was hurt as the result of an unsafe hockey helmet that had been selected by the coach.

Contrast that to the decision reached in the following case.

In **Hunt v. Skaneateles Central School District**, a football player was hurt during a varsity football scrimmage. That player lost his case because the judge said he knew that football carried a risk of injury and the player accepted the risk that he would get hurt when he signed up for football.

There have also been differences of opinion in cases that claim player injuries resulted from improper coaching decisions.

In **Jarreau v. Orleans parish School Board**, a 1994 Louisiana case, a football player hurt his wrist in a game early in the season. The coaching staff knew he was hurt, but allowed him to continue to practice and play. At the end of the season, the trainer suggested he get medical attention for his wrist. When he went to the doctor, he learned that he had a disabling wrist injury.

His parents sued the school district, claiming the school should have sent the player for medical attention earlier. The court agreed, saying that the student had continued to complain of pain but the coach pressured him to play when he should have been given medical attention by the school.

In another case, **Palmer v. Mount Vernon Tp. High School District**, the student was a basketball player. At practice, he tried on another player's protective eye wear. When the coach told him to take it off, the player assumed he was not allowed to wear protective eye gear. The court in that case said he could not sue the school because the school did not have to warn the student about what protective gear he could and could not wear.

Unfair Competition

Another issue comes about when students want to sue because of something unfair about the competition.

In **School Board of Broward County v. Beharrie**, a student sued after he was injured in a soccer game when a student on the other team committed a foul. Just before the student was hurt, the opposing team's coach yelled to the player who committed the foul to "take him" and "waste him." The student did not win his case against the opposing school because he could not prove the coach's action caused his injury.

NOTE: *Courts have also refused to hold schools liable for injuries caused when football players of different weights are injured when they play against each other.*

Because this area of the law is determined so much by court decisions, you should consult an attorney if you are considering a lawsuit against either a public or private school.

SECTION II:

TEENS AND HOME

−14−
BECOMING AN ADULT

Each state determines the age at which children become adults. This is called the *age of majority*. In most states, that age is eighteen but Alabama sets the age at nineteen for single people and eighteen for those who are married. Nebraska also has a slightly different rule. If you live in Pennsylvania, you will want to check your state laws carefully because their system is unique in many respects. The process of becoming a legal adult is called *emancipation*. You can find more specific information for your state in Appendix B.

Reaching a certain age is not the only way to reach legal adulthood. In most states, but not all, marriage will allow teenagers who have not reached the age of majority to be treated as an adult; so will joining the military.

It is also possible to be considered an adult for some purposes and not for others. For example, a teenager who gets married at sixteen may be an adult for most purposes but still not be considered an adult for purposes of the underage drinking laws.

TEENS SEEKING EMANCIPATION

Many states also have a court procedure that permits teenagers who are not yet eighteen, but are living on their own, to be treated as a legal adult. The laws vary from state to state, but generally allow teenagers who have reached a certain age and who are living on their own and are supporting themselves to go to court and have a judge sign an order that emancipates them. The ages vary from state to state and so do the requirements. You will need to either look up the laws for your state or contact an attorney to help you with the emancipation proceeding. In some states, your parents will have to consent, but not in others.

NOTE: *There are some states that do not have an emancipation statute, but have an informal procedure by which minors can be deemed to be adults.*

PARENTS SEEKING EMANCIPATION

In some instances, it is not the teenager who is going to court to seek an emancipation. It is the parents. This is permitted under the laws of some, but not all, states. Parents can seek to avoid liability when they are no longer in control of their teenager.

For example, a parent might seek an emancipation if they are unable to force their teenager to go to school. The purpose is for the parent to avoid prosecution for violating the compulsory attendance at school law. (see Chapter 4.) The parent may also be trying to get out of the legal obligation to pay child support.

LIMITED RIGHTS

State laws may limit the adult rights that the emancipated minor gets. This is called an *emancipation for limited purposes*. In other instances, an emancipated minor gets all of the rights of an adult. This is called an *emancipation for general purposes*. Some states have provisions for only one of the types of emancipation while other states allow both.

PROCEDURE

For the most part, in order for a minor to be emancipated, there will have to be a court order. Just because a minor lives apart from his or her parents and supports himself or herself, does not mean he or she is legally emancipated. Furthermore, the minor's parents may still be liable for his or her support. They can be required to pay debts he or she incurs while she is living on her own. Once a judge signs an order emancipating a minor, the minor's parents are no longer responsible for the minor or the minor's expenses.

In some states, there are some exceptions to this rule that relate to liability for automobile accidents. Those states have specific laws that either both of the parents or the parent who signed the consent for the teenager to get his or her driver's license remain liable for driving-related damages caused by the teen.

"DIVORCING" YOUR PARENTS

In the past, there have been cases where teens went to court to "divorce" their parents. Of course, the lawsuit is not a true divorce proceeding, but it involves a child going to court to terminate his or her parents' rights to him. Termination legally ends the parent-child relationship between the parent and the child forever; it is as though they were never related to each other. (This is the same as when a parent wants to terminate parental rights, except that here, the child rather than the parent is requesting it.)

The most famous case in this area is *Kingsley v. Kingsley*, a 1993 Florida case in which an eleven- year- old child filed a petition to terminate his mother's rights to him so that his foster parents could adopt him. Prior to the final trial, the foster father, the child welfare department, and an attorney appointed by the court to represent the child also filed petitions to terminate the mother's parental rights. The judge ended up terminating the mother's rights and allowing the adoption.

The mother appealed the case. The appeals court ruled that the child should not have been allowed to file his own petition to terminate his mother's rights. The adoption was upheld, though, because of the other petition for termination filed by the child's appointed attorney.

Not all states permit children to sue on their own for termination of parental rights. A case like this will be much too difficult to do without an attorney. If you are considering such an extreme move, you will need to consult an attorney to see if this procedure is possible under the laws of your state. As an alternative, you and your family might consider family therapy or another form of therapy.

If the reason you want to divorce your parents has anything to do with abuse or neglect, you should report the situation to either the police or the child welfare department in your town or city.

NOTE: *If it is the parents that are seeking to end the parent-child relationship, the teenager really has no way to stop that. If this is happening to you, seek professional help.*

THE IN-BETWEEN YEAR

In some states, the laws are set up in such a way that the final transition from child to adult can be very difficult for both parents and teens. Because states have different legal ages for different purposes, a teenager's seventeenth year has some special challenges associated with it. The teen is not completely an adult and no longer completely a child. The parent still has responsibility for the teen but a more limited ability to exercise control. This can lead to a sort of legal limbo; it is not completely clear how the rights and obligations are balanced. Unfortunately, there are no easy answers to this dilemma.

A frequent area of conflict centers around school attendance. Many states still require a teenager to be in school at age seventeen. But those same state laws may not give the parent any recourse to force the child to go to school. The same can be true if the child refuses to come home. Let's look at an example of how this works, using Texas laws.

For instance, the Texas compulsory attendance law says that everyone under eighteen must be in school, with certain exceptions. Paul is seventeen and does not meet any of the exceptions. He has missed numerous days of school and the school is about to initiate truancy proceedings. Paul has also refused to come home and is living with an older friend who has an apartment. Paul does not have a job and has not been paying for his own living expenses. Paul's parents have tried repeatedly to get him to come home.

Texas law allows parents to be fined for violations of the truancy law, and the school officials are going to file a complaint against Paul's parents and against Paul. Paul's parents want to avoid being fined and make Paul return home. What are their options?

Unfortunately for Paul's parents, they do not have many choices. Because Paul is under eighteen, his parents are still subject to the truancy law. They would not be if Paul were legally an adult, but he is not. He is not married, and there is not a court order of emancipation. Just because Paul is living on his own does not make him a legal adult; he has to go to court and have an emancipation order signed by a judge for that to happen.

If Paul were younger, his parents could report him as a runaway because he refuses to come home. The police would pick Paul up and make him come home. Being absent from a parent's home without the parent's consent does make a child a runaway, but the juvenile justice code defines a child as someone under seventeen. For the purposes of that law, Paul is not a child and the police will not make him come home. So the parents have no effective way to force his return home.

Paul's parents would like to have Paul declared an adult by filing an emancipation petition, but Texas law does not allow parents to file. Only the minor child can seek his own emancipation and there is no informal procedure for being emancipated. Paul's parents are still responsible for him and for his actions even though they have no right to control his conduct.

From Paul's perspective, he does not qualify to file an emancipation petition because he is not working and not self-sufficient. If he were, however, he could ask a judge to declare him an adult. Paul could avoid the truancy case by withdrawing from school and taking the GED, which would qualify him under an exception to the compulsory attendance law.

As you can see, this is a difficult situation, especially for Paul's parents. The problems cannot help but spill over and affect the relationship between Paul and his parents. It has made the transition to adulthood even more difficult.

−15−

TEENS' RIGHTS VERSUS THE RIGHTS OF OTHERS

All areas of the law involve the balancing of the rights of one person against the rights of another. There are many instances in which parents' rights over their children are superior to the rights of the children. In other instances, the rights of the children are given a higher priority than the rights of the parents. For instance, you will note in Chapter 16 on discipline, the parents' rights to discipline their children are greater than the child's right to determine his own conduct.

A child's right to control his own body can be trumped by a parent's right to spank the child. But when the discipline rises to the level of abuse, then the child's right to safety is greater than the parent's right to discipline.

YOUR BODY

Normally, a teenager has control over his own body and his rights in that regard are superior to others' rights in most instances. You will recall from the chapter on searches in school that sometimes, the schools' right to search can be stronger than the student's right to control his body. Another situation in which the teen's right to control his body comes in second is when tattoos and body piercing are involved. Most states have laws that require a minor to have parental consent before getting either a tattoo or a body piercing. Some states make exceptions for ear piercing, while others do not.

SPEECH

Both children and parents have their constitutional rights to free speech. But a parent has the right to control what a child says. For example, the child's free speech right to use curse words is not violated by a parent's reasonable punishment for that behavior. Children have a constitutionally protected right to the free exercise of religion, but their parents' right to control the religious upbringing of their children means that parents can keep children from participating in activities of which the parents do not approve, even if the activities are religious in nature.

PARENTAL OBLIGATIONS AND RIGHTS

Once you reach legal adulthood under the laws of your state, then your rights to control your own life become paramount. Your parents' legal right to discipline you and to control your upbringing end when you become an adult. Their legal obligation to provide financial support for you also ends at that time.

Of course, there may be other ways that parents have some say over the lives of their young adult children. Providing financial support conditioned on certain behavior by the child is one way. The parent's control is not based on their legal rights, but on the fact that the parent possess something the adult child wants: money.

SCHOOL

This same analysis applies to the balancing of your rights versus the rights of the school district on issues that arise related to your education. Your parents have the right to make decisions about your education, but while you are at school, the school has the greater right to control the environment. As you may have noticed in the chapters on First Amendment rights and discipline in school, there are times when your rights get more protection from the law than the school district's rights. But in other instances, your rights are secondary to the school's rights to maintain order.

Your parents' rights to control your upbringing and make educational decisions for you can also be limited by the school's rules. In some disputes between parents and schools, the school's rules control and the parents can either obey the rules or put the child into another school. The rise of home schooling is due in part to parents' unwillingness to go along with the educational decisions of the public school system where their children are concerned.

WORKPLACE

Similar analogies exist in the workplace. As a worker, you retain your constitutional rights. But there are times when the employer's rights are superior. For instance, your right to free speech does not extend so far that you can sexually harass other employees. The other employee's rights to be free from harassment and the employer's right to control the work environment are superior to your rights and you can be fired by the employer and sued by your fellow employee if you engage in sexual harassment.

If you are not a legal adult, your parents can decide for you whether or not you can have a job. They can also impose rules on which places you can work and which places you cannot. Sometimes, the law has restrictions on the kinds of job a teenager can have. Depending on the laws of your state, your parents may have the right to keep the money you earn at your job. In other states, the law may give you the right to keep your earnings.

The reason for the difference in laws is that some state legislatures have balanced the rights of the parents and teenagers to prefer the parent and other states have chosen to prefer the teenager.

YOUR ACTIONS

Actions between teens are also subject to that same balancing act. Your right to control your own actions does not go so far as to allow you to go around hitting other people without cause. In that case, the other person's rights are more protected.

But, if the other person hits you first, the law of self defense may give you the right to hit back. In that scenario, your right to defend yourself is greater than the instigator's right to not be hit.

FRIENDS

Sometimes, the authorities have the right to interfere with your constitutional right to decide with whom you want to associate. Your right to pick your friends can be limited by a court order not to associate with certain people if you get into trouble and end up on juvenile probation. Laws designed to curb gang activity may mean that you cannot do certain things that you would otherwise be entitled to do. But, if the laws go too far in the opinion of the court system, then your rights may be superior; that would mean that the law cannot be enforced.

There is no way for a book to tell you how each and every situation will come out. The answers depend on the facts of each case and the particular laws that apply to the situation. This is a guideline only. If you have questions about a particular incident or situation, you will need to either research the laws of your state or consult an attorney.

–16–
DISCIPLINE BY PARENTS

At one time or another, every family experiences conflict between parents and teenagers. Frequently, the conflict is over control, with teens and parents each wanting control. Parents and teens do not always agree on what is best for the teenager. Sometimes, parents feel that teens need to be disciplined and teens feel that they should be making their own decisions.

Whether discipline is severe enough to be considered abusive is a question that is answered on a case by case basis. Of course, there are some things that will always be considered abuse. Parents, unfortunately, have used things like burning with cigarettes and hitting with coiled extension cords as a punishment method; these things are abusive and can result in parents being criminally charged with child abuse.

> ## TEEN TIP
>
> Until you reach the age of legal adulthood, your parents still have the right to discipline you. However, you have the right to be free from abuse. That means that your parents' discipline must be reasonable. Absent abuse, courts will not second guess your parents' discipline decisions.

But does *any* kind of physical punishment equal child abuse? Not necessarily. In fact, some states have laws that specifically authorize the use of physical punishment. It is really a matter of degree. One swat with an open hand on a child's backside is not generally child abuse. A beating with a fist that leaves bruises or breaks bones is.

Parents have other methods of discipline available to them. Grounding and withholding privileges clearly fall within acceptable limits. Like any-

TEEN TIP

If you are a child who is being abused, you should report what is happening to you. Either tell your school counselor or teacher, family doctor, minister, or another adult you trust. You can also call the authorities yourself. Check Appendix A for child abuse reporting hot lines.

thing, they can be taken to extremes and become abusive. Never letting a child leave the house, even to go to school, is not acceptable. While withholding privileges is permissible, withholding food for a significant period of time is not.

If your parents are abusing you and you are not yet a legal adult, the authorities can help you to get out of the abusive situation. You can be placed with one of your relatives or placed in foster care. If one of your parents is abusing you and the other one is not, you will probably be sent to live with the non-abusive parent.

If there is violence in your family, you should call the police. There are many programs available to help the abuser and his or her victims. Courts can force the abuser to go to counseling and order the abuser to stay away from the family.

We most commonly hear about men as abusers and women as their victims, but women can be abusers and men can be their victims. While men are not as likely to report the abuse, there is help available for them and women who abuse need help just as much as male abusers.

PARENT TIP

If you are a parent who is accused of child abuse, you should hire an attorney to represent you just as soon as possible.

–17–
WHEN PARENTS DIVORCE

Unfortunately, an experience many teens share is the break-up of the family when their parents divorce. When this happens, decisions have to be made about where the minor children will live and how the parents will divide their duties and obligations as parents. In many cases, the parents can resolve these issues themselves. When that happens, the divorce process is much less costly for everyone in both emotional and financial terms.

But settlement is not always possible. When the parents cannot agree, they turn to the courts to make the decision for them. This decision making process occurs as part of a contested child custody case. The judge looks at factors like the financial stability of each of the parents, the degree of past involvement with the parenting of the children, the emotional stability of each of the parents, the needs of the children, and the relative abilities of the parents to meet those needs. As children get older, their desires also carry increased weight with the judge.

DECIDING WITH WHICH PARENT TO LIVE

With older children, parents sometimes put pressure on the children to make a decision about where they want to live. Most of the time, this is done with the best of intentions and parents do not realize the difficulty it causes for the child to choose one parent over the other. Of course, there are also situations in which the child has a strong preference about where he or she wants to live.

Sometimes, you will be given the opportunity to let the judge know how you feel about the custody decisions. This will happen in one of three ways.

In some places, the judge will order that a *social study* be done in custody cases. The name of this report may be different in your state, but it works in basically the same fashion wherever you are. This means that a licensed social worker will interview your parents and any other people who have knowledge of your family situation. The social worker then files a report in court that recommends to the judge which parent should get primary custody.

TEEN TIP

If you are being asked to decide where you want to live and you do not have a preference one way or the other or you would rather not give an opinion, then you should not be afraid to be honest about not choosing.

If one of your parents is abusive or you are afraid of them for some other reason, then you should either let your other parent or another trusted adult know how you feel and what is happening.

As a part of working on the report, the social worker may talk to the children about what they want. If you are involved in this process, this is your opportunity to tell the judge whatever it is you want him or her to know. If one of your parents is abusive or there are problems at home, you should be honest about the situation. The social worker and the judge cannot make good decisions if they do not have all of the information.

Sometimes, the judge will *talk to the children in chambers,* which is the legal terminology for talking to you in the judge's office. Once again, you should answer the judge's questions as completely and as honestly as you can. Sometimes, your parent's lawyers will be in the office when the judge talks to you; sometimes, it will just be you and the judge.

The final way, and the most difficult for the children, is to be called as a *witness to testify in court.* If you have to testify in court, you will be asked questions by the attorneys. Your parents will also probably be in the courtroom. If you will be testifying, you should have an opportunity to talk to the attorney for whichever parent is having you testify. You can ask that attorney questions about what to expect in court.

DEALING WITH COURT PROCEDURE

When dealing with court proceedings, you should take the process seriously. Be polite and respectful at all times and be as accurate as you can be when answering questions and giving information.

However, you will not always have an opportunity to give your opinion. In many cases, the decision is made by the judge after a trial or by the parents in a settlement without consulting the child. You do not have an automatic right to participate, although many states have laws that let you sign an *affidavit* (sworn statement) selecting the parent with whom you want to live.

GUARDIAN *AD LITEM*

In some courts and in some cases, the judge may appoint an attorney to represent your interests. This attorney is called an *ad litem*. You should talk to him or her and give any information that might be relevant to the custody issue. He or she should also be available to answer whatever questions you have about the process. While this attorney does represent you and your interests, the *ad litem's* role is somewhat different from that of an attorney hired to represent someone.

In a regular attorney-client relationship, the attorney's job is to do what the client instructs them to do, as long as it is legal. Your attorney *ad litem* does not necessarily have to do what you want them to. His or her job is to help the judge decide what is in your best interest. Sometimes that corresponds with what you want and sometimes it does not. The attorney *ad litem* will have to tell the judge what he or she thinks is in your best interest. If this is something other than what you want, you can ask that attorney to tell the judge that you want something different as a part of their report. (In contested cases, the final decision will be made by either a jury or the judge.)

CUSTODY ORDER

As part of the *custody order*, the judge will decide which parent has primary custody. This is the parent that you will live with. The order will also set up a schedule for you to visit the other parent. Many states have a standard schedule that they use for most cases, and it is usually some sort of alternating weekends and split holiday arrangement.

As a teenager, you may not always want to go to visit the other parent all the time. The laws of each state are different, and it may be that you have to go whether you want to or not if your *noncustodial* parent insists. Other courts and jurisdictions give some leeway to older teens (sixteen and over) and are not as strict about the visitation requirement.

Factors to Decide Custody

If your parents cannot agree on custody arrangements and a court decides where you will live, many different factors go into this decision. Some states have a list of factors the judge is supposed to use to make the decision while other states do not. In some states, the law may allow your parents to request that a jury, instead of a judge, decide where you will live. Sometimes, it may be totally up to the judge.

Whether your state has a specific list of factors or not, the same general areas will be used to make the custody decision. These are things like:

◆ your age;
◆ the relationship you have with each of your parents;
◆ your preferences;
◆ the living arrangements that are in place at the time the final decision is made by the judge and how long those arrangements have been in place;
◆ the ability of each of your parents to adequately care for you and supervise you; and,
◆ the overall situation in each home.

Things like alcohol and drug abuse by one of your parents can make the other parent more likely to get custody. If one of your parents has been violent, toward anyone but especially a member of the family, that factor should be considered by the judge before giving custody, or even visitation, to that parent.

Two factors that cannot be considered are race and religion. If the parents are of different races or religions, the judge cannot choose to place you with one parent over the other based on that parent's race or religious preference.

A factor that is not supposed to be used is the gender of the parents. Under old laws, the mother was given a legal presumption that she was the best parent to have custody. In those days, it was very difficult for fathers to get custody of their children, especially when the children were very young. Those laws have now been changed so that each parent starts out with an equal chance to get custody. As a practical matter, many parents agree that the children will live primarily with the mother, but more and more fathers have primary custody of their children.

One case that illustrates the use of these factors is **Wilson v. Upell**, a 1982 Michigan case. In this case, the child was born out of wedlock and lived with the mother while the case was working its way through the system. The father filed a parentage suit and asked for custody. The mother also wanted custody. The trial court judge decided that both parents were basically good parents who loved the child and provided adequate care for her. They both had steady jobs. Although the child had been with the mother, the judge gave custody to the father. The factors that decided the case against the mother were her two hospitalizations since the birth of the child, one of which was for misuse of prescription drugs, the live-in relationship the mother had with a man she subsequently married, and the fact that the mother had moved four times since the baby's birth. The appeals court agreed with the trial judge, and the father won custody.

Many states have laws that say that the parents should have *joint custody* in most cases. Joint custody does not necessarily mean that you spend half of your time with each parent. It generally means that your parents share equally in the decisions about things like your education, discipline, and medical care. Even in joint custody, in most cases you will live mostly with one parent and have visitation with the other.

Another issue that may come up in a custody case is the *sexual orientation* of the parents. The simple fact that a parent is gay or lesbian does not generally keep them from getting custody of their children. However, in a contested case where a judge or jury will be deciding where a child will live, it is almost always more difficult for the gay or lesbian parent to win the case.

If one of the parents is living with someone, that factor can play a part in who gets custody and in the visitation arrangements. The judge will have to consider that this person will have a lot of contact with you. If that person is not appropriate for you to be around, then the parent who lives with them will not get custody and may have restrictions placed on their visitation.

For example, if your mother moves in with a man who is a convicted sex offender, a judge will not want you to live with your mother and will not want you to be alone with that man during visitation. In that scenario, the judge might only let your mother have supervised visits.

If your parents are still legally married to each other and living with someone else, some judges may consider this a negative factor. It will not disqualify that parent from custody, but it will just be one thing that the judge considers when making a decision. If your parents are divorced, and there is nothing about the person with whom your parent lives that would be harmful to you, the fact that they are living together and are not married will not make that much difference.

In some states, parents have the option of getting a *legal separation.* This means they are not divorcing, but are not able to continue living together. In other states, legal separation can be a required first step in the divorce process. In either case, when the parents are no longer living together and decide to formalize the arrangements with a legal separation, decisions about custody, visitation, and child support must still be made. The factors and processes are similar to those in a divorce setting, and all that we have discussed in the divorce context will also apply to separations.

CHILD SUPPORT

The parent that does not have custody will have to pay the other parent *child support.* This amount will be some percentage of the parent's income, and the percentage may be determined by state law. If it is not, then the judge will set the percentage.

Even in states that have a percentage, the judge can consider other things to see if the support should be set either above or below the guidelines. These factors include things like any special needs that the child has, such as unusual medical problems or disabilities or special educational needs, to go above the guidelines. If the parent has some sort of disability that keeps them from working, that can affect the amount of child support. If the parent makes a lot of money, then the judge can set child support higher than the guideline. Another factor is whether the parent has other children they are legally obligated to support.

One case that looked at how the child support guidelines are applied is the case of ***Tilley v. Tilley***, a 1997 Kentucky case. In that case, the parents originally entered into an agreement for the father to pay $250 per month. Four years later, the mother filed a motion to increase the child support, claiming that the $250 being paid was well under the amount of child support that should be paid when the state guidelines were applied to the father's income. The courts agreed with the mother that the big difference between the amount

(continued)

of child support she was getting and the amount she should get under the guidelines entitled her to an increase. The father had to begin paying $702 a month in child support.

The child support is not designed to cover all of the costs of child rearing. It is simply designed to offset a portion of the costs. Noncustodial parents may or may not be ordered to pay for extras like sports activities and extracurricular activities at school. In many instances, the custodial parent will have to pay for the extras without getting any additional child support.

Once a parent had been ordered by a court to pay child support, they can be put in jail if they refuse to pay. In most states, failing to pay child support does not mean that the parent loses their rights to visitation with the child. By the same token, not having visitation with your child does not entitle a parent to quit paying child support.

GRANDPARENTS' RIGHTS

There may be some situations in which your grandparents may ask for court-ordered visitation with you. This will generally occur when your parents are not allowing you to have contact with your grandparents for some reason. Unless they go to court and get an order, grandparents do not have an automatic right to see their grandchildren.

There is a recent United States Supreme Court case, **Troxel v. Granville**, that talked about this issue. That case says that, for the most part, the decision the parent makes about visitation between grandparents and their grandchildren stands. Unless the grandparent can convince a judge that the parent is somehow unfit to make this decision, they probably will not be able to get court-ordered visitation with their grandchildren.

As a teenager, however, you are old enough to contact your grandparents if you want to do so. If your parents oppose this contact, then it becomes just like any other disciplinary matter between parents and teens.

STEP-PARENTS

Another issue that comes up relates to step-parents and their relationship to the children. As a general rule, step-parents do not have a legal relationship to the child unless they formally adopt. There are some states, however, that will allow a step-parent to have visitation with a step-child after a divorce from the child's parent.

KIDNAPPING

Finally, there are some parents who feel so strongly that the other parent should not be able to see the child that they will resort to kidnapping by taking the minor child and hiding him or her from the other parent. This is a crime, and should be reported to the police. (This is also true if you are kidnapped by a stranger.)

TEEN TIP

After your parents are divorced, they should communicate directly with each other about matters related to their children and not use you as messenger service. If your parents are using you to pass messages, ask them to talk to the other parent directly. It is not your responsibility to deal with those issues.

NOTE: *Custody and visitation orders end when you become a legal adult. Child support can continue beyond your eighteenth birthday if you are still in high school, but your parents are not legally obligated to pay for you to go to college.*

−18−
RUNNING AWAY

Many teens who are unhappy at home believe that running away is the answer to their problems. Of course, life on the run as a teen is very difficult, and many teens who make this choice end up homeless and living on the streets. As if these problems were not difficult enough, teens also face a trip through the juvenile system when they are caught. Most states have passed a version of the *Interstate Compact on Juveniles*, which states that a juvenile who is picked up in another state will be returned to his or her home state.

Just as with violations of criminal laws, being a runaway can cause you to end up on juvenile probation or even in placement. There have been many teens who started out on juvenile probation for running away and could not follow all the rules. The next step is some kind of placement, preferably in the teen's home town, but not at home. If you still cannot follow the rules there, you can end up placed in the state juvenile correction facility.

TEEN TIP

If you have run away and need help, you can call the local authorities or the National Center for Missing and Exploited Children at 1-800-843-5678.

One case that reviewed some of the laws on runaways is ***In the Matter of Charles Curran***, a 1985 New York case. In this case, the parent's child ran away from home and was placed in a runaway program under the Runaway and Homeless Youth Act of 1978. This act is a New York law that allows the runaway youth to voluntarily stay in the program for thirty days without the parent's consent. The

(continued)

parent in this case challenged the law, claiming that it unconstitutionally interfered with the parent's rights to the child. The judge
disagreed, and said the law was proper because the state has a duty
to protect runaway children. The teen was allowed to stay in the
runaway program in spite of his parent's objections.

Just because you leave home and live on your own for a while does not
mean that you will be legally considered an adult. Many states have laws
that have a way for a teen who would otherwise be too young to be considered an adult to be treated as an adult for legal purposes, but those laws
usually require a court order for a teen to qualify as an adult. This is called
emancipation and is addressed more completely in Chapter 14.

BEING THROWN OUT

Sometimes, the teen does not leave home voluntarily, but is thrown out by
the parents. This does not make you an adult for legal purposes, either, so
there may be issues on which you will still have to deal with your parents.
If you are in this situation, you should check the laws of your state to see
what the requirements for emancipation are.

If you are thrown out by your parents, are still under age eighteen, and
do not have a place to go, you should consider calling your local child welfare department. They may be able to provide some resources to help you
and also to deal with your parents. At a minimum, tell an adult you trust
or your school counselor about the problem. It is important for you to get
all the help you can and not try to handle a problem like this on your own.

In most states, until you are considered legally an adult, your parents
have an obligation to support you. They cannot get out of this duty just by
refusing to let you live at home. You may be able to force them to honor
this support obligation.

–19–
FINANCIAL RESPONSIBILITY

NEEDS OF THE CHILD

Parents are under a legal duty to provide the basic needs for their children. The basics include food, shelter, clothing, education, and medical care. This does not mean that your parents have to buy you the most expensive or most fashionable clothes, and you will note that cars are not found on the list of basics. The obligation really just extends to what is necessary, and not what might be desirable. Because the duty to support you ends when you become an adult, your parents will generally not be legally obligated to pay for you to attend college.

All of these obligations continue only as long as the child remains legally dependent on the parent. Once you reach the *age of majority* as determined by the laws of your state (usually 18), your parents' legal duty has ended and you are now responsible for yourself. Your parents' duty will also end if you go to court and become legally *emancipated* or if your status makes you a legal adult. (Emancipation is a procedure in which a judge signs an order making you an adult even if you are younger than the age of majority in your state.) For instance, in most states, getting married emancipates you so that you are treated as an adult. Joining the military also has the same result.

The parental obligation continues even if you do not live at home. Parents have to pay child support if their children are committed to a state juvenile correction facility or other placement outside the home. Your parents cannot get out of the duty to support you just by throwing you out of the house, either.

Getting a Job

Although your parents are obligated to support you, there is nothing that keeps them from making you get a job. As your parents, they have a constitutional right to control your upbringing; if they think it is good for you to work, they can make you go. If you have a job, however, you do not necessarily have a legal right to keep the money that you earn. Your parents have that right unless your state has a law, as many do, that allows minors to keep the money they earn. Even if you get to keep the money, your parents still have the legal right to discipline you and to direct your moral and religious training. That means they can tell you how to spend your money and impose discipline on you if you disobey their instructions. If you parents do not want you to work, they can legally forbid you from getting a job.

Chores and Allowance

Another right that goes along with being a parent is the right to the services and earnings of your children. The fact that they are entitled to your services means that they can also make you mow the lawn, clean your room, and wash the car. They are not legally obligated to pay you for these things or other things that you do around the house. There is no law that entitles you to receive any specific amount of money from your parents. They can determine how to provide you with the things you need. They decide how much, if any, money to give you to spend on yourself. The only limitation is that they cannot do anything that would constitute child abuse.

ACTS OF TEENS

Regardless of how old a person is, he or she is responsible for his or her own actions. Even if you are under eighteen and your actions cause damages to another person, you can be ordered by a judge to pay for those damages. This would mean that the judge would enter a *judgment* against you. Of course, you may not have any money or assets to pay a judgment. An unpaid judgment will have a negative impact on your credit rating, and the judgment can be renewed until it is paid. In some states, a monthly amount of money can be withheld from your paycheck and sent to the person to whom you owe the money. This is called *wage garnishment.*

Your *credit rating* reflects your payment history for all your bills. The current trend is to use something called *credit scoring*, which is where a potential creditor assigns a number to your credit history. This number is affected by the amount of overall debt you have and your history of paying on time or missing payments. The number is then used to decide whether you get credit on future items or not. A poor credit rating can keep you from being able to buy a car, renting an apartment, getting a job, or getting insurance.

Parental Responsibility

In some instances, parents can also be financially responsible for damages caused by their minor children. Some states have specific statutes that make parents responsible for property damages caused by their children; the extent of the liability and the upper limit of liability vary from state to state. These laws generally cover willful and intentional acts by minors that result in either property damage or personal injury.

Some states limit the recovery under these laws to governmental entities while other states allow anyone who has been damaged to proceed under the statute. Most states have some version of this law, which originally became popular as a way of controlling gang activity. An example of the use of these laws can be found in the following case.

In 1992, **In Re William George T**, a juvenile had been in the hospital. While he was there, he destroyed property belonging to the hospital. He was processed through the juvenile system and admitted to the offense. The court ordered his father to make *restitution* to (pay) the hospital for the full amount of the damage caused by the juvenile.

Parents can also be held financially responsible if they provide the method by which the child causes harm, for instance, for providing a gun or by being careless about storing guns they own.

Some states also allow parents to be sued for failing to control their children. In order for this to apply, the parent must have some reason to know that the child was likely to do whatever it was he did to cause the damage. If the parent has taken reasonable steps to control the child and prevent the harm caused, they will not be found liable.

Parents can also be financially responsible for the damages if the parent told the child to commit the act that caused the harm or consented to the act. If the parent participates in the act, they will be liable for the damages on that basis.

Curfew

Some courts have allowed parents to be fined for curfew violations by their children. Other states and courts have allowed parents to be held criminally responsible for the acts of their children if the parent instructed the child to do the act or the parent consented.

Assault

In one 1999 case from Alaska, the state tried to hold the parents responsible for an assault committed by their seventeen year old child.

In ***Dinsmore-Puff v. Alvord***, the child shot and killed someone after they had gotten into an argument. The court said that the parents could not be held liable in that case because the parents had been trying to control the violent behavior of their son since he was three years old. They had also sought treatment for him.

In this case, the juvenile was already on probation and had been complying with the conditions of his probation. He had assaulted someone else several months before the assault that resulted in a death, but his parents were not aware of that incident.

These judges let the parents off the hook by ruling that they could not have foreseen that their son would steal a gun and kill someone. It also made a difference that the parents had taken many steps to get their son's tendency to engage in violent behavior under control.

Another court in Nebraska refused to hold the parents liable for an assault committed by their child.

In ***Durkan v. Vaughn***, the juvenile did not have a history of violence and had not committed any other assaults. The court said that the parents had no way of knowing that their child was likely to assault someone.

The case that causes the financial liability may be part of some other proceeding, just like the William George T. case, was part of the proceeding against the juvenile. It can also be done as a separate proceeding, which will mean that the family will incur additional attorney's fees.

As you can see, there can be substantial financial consequences to the whole family when a teenager causes damage to someone or their property.

JUVENILE CRIMES

When a teen is accused of violating a criminal law, there are several areas of cost for the family. If the teen is found to have committed a crime and placed either on adult or juvenile probation, there will be monthly probation fees to be paid. This amount varies from case to case and state to state; in some instances in juvenile court, the judge will take the financial circumstances of the family into consideration when setting the fee. In adult court, the fee will likely be set by the county and financial considerations are not much of a factor. In adult court, there will also be a fine to be paid.

> ### PARENT TIP
>
> If your family financial situation is such that the judge thinks you can afford an attorney, you will have to pay several hundred dollars, and maybe more, in legal fees. This is an expense that usually falls on the parents.

Restitution is also a possibility in both instances. If the teen is over eighteen, then the parents have no legal obligation to pay these costs. In juvenile court, both the parents and the child are responsible unless the judge specifically makes the juvenile responsible.

If a juvenile is sent to a placement outside the home, the state pays the costs associated with the placement. Since parents have a legal duty to support their children, the juvenile court has the authority to order the parents to make child support payments to the state while the juvenile is in the placement.

Truancy (skipping school) also creates financial obligations for the family of the truant teen. Parents can be fined; usually, the fine is set at some dollar amount for each day the child is absent from school without a valid, approved excuse. Since habitually truant teens can end up being processed in the juvenile justice system, the costs discussed above will also apply.

Another significant costs to these proceedings is the cost for legal representation. If you qualify for a court appointed attorney, the judge can order you to reimburse a portion of the fees as part of the disposition of the case.

There will generally be more than one court appearance required. In juvenile court, the parents are required to be present in court for every hearing. This means that the parents will have to miss work in addition to the other costs involved.

–20–
INSURANCE

There are two kinds of insurance that are important for teens and their parents: health insurance and car insurance.

HEALTH INSURANCE

You can be covered on your parents' health insurance policy at least until you are eighteen. Sometimes, the cost of your coverage will be paid by your parent's employer; otherwise, the parent pays an extra premium to have you covered by the policy. Many policies will allow you to still be covered beyond age eighteen if you are unmarried and in school. Most states will not allow you to buy your own health insurance until you are eighteen, but you may be covered on your own if you are covered by insurance provided by your employer.

There are different kinds of health insurance policies. One kind is the *Health Maintenance Organization, or HMO*. Under this type of policy, you pay a specific amount of money as a premium, and the insurance company pays all of your medical costs but you have to be treated only at the HMO provider.

TEEN TIP

If your parents do not have insurance available to them through an employer and cannot afford to buy insurance, many states have created special insurance available at low cost for parents to get coverage for their children.

You can check with your state's insurance department to see if this insurance is available in your state. You can find the number for the state insurance department in the blue pages of your phone book.

A second policy is a *Preferred Provider policy*, called a *PPO*. In that type of policy, your insurance company contracts with specific providers like doctors, pharmacies, and hospitals. As long as you go to one of these providers, the insurance company will pay most of your medical costs and you will only have to pay a small co-payment.

The traditional PPO policy requires you to first pay out of your pocket an agreed upon amount, called a *deductible*. The lower this amount, the higher the cost you will pay for the insurance. Once you have met this deductible, then your insurance company will reimburse you for eighty percent of your medical bills and you will pay the other twenty percent.

CAR INSURANCE– LIABILITY STATES

Many states have laws that require drivers to be covered by a specific amount of *liability insurance*. You buy insurance by paying what is called a *premium*. The premium is the amount of money the insurance company charges you for providing the insurance. There are several kinds of insurance policies and coverage.

Liability insurance is the coverage that pays for damages you cause in a wreck to someone else. That type of policy does not pay to fix your car, just that of the other driver if the accident was your fault. If you want to have insurance available to fix your own car, you must purchase collision coverage for an additional cost. There are some additional coverages available for additional costs that you also might want to consider; we will discuss these coverages below.

Deductible

You will also have to meet a *deductible*, meaning that you will have to pay a preset amount of money out of your own pocket before your insurance begins to pay.

Another factor to keep in mind when asking an insurance company to fix your car is that the insurance company does not have to fix your car if the repair costs exceed the value of your car. If that happens, the insurance company considers the car to be a total loss and you will be paid only the value of the car. You and the insurance company can negotiate about what a fair value for your car is.

Injuries

You should also obtain coverage to cover *personal injuries* that you cause to others in a wreck. This is very important coverage to have, because the biggest expense in an accident is often not the cost of vehicle repairs, but the medical costs. These costs can add up very quickly and you will have to pay these costs yourself if the accident is your fault and you do not have this insurance.

TEEN TIP

If you have questions about what kind of coverage and what policy limits are best for you, you and your parents should meet with insurance agents to discuss the options and the cost for each option. Do not be afraid to shop around; there can be differences in the premiums charged for the same coverages.

Rental

Your insurance company does not have to give you a rental car to drive while your car is being repaired after a wreck unless you buy that coverage separately. You might also consider purchasing personal injury protection coverage, also called *medical payments coverage*, which will pay some specific amount of money to help you pay your expenses and medical bills if you are hurt in a wreck.

NOTE: *You may also want to buy insurance to cover having your car towed to the repair shop after an accident.*

Underinsured Motorist

If you are hit by a driver that does not have insurance or has an insurance policy with an upper limit that is insufficient to cover all of your damages, you will need to have purchased *uninsured/underinsured motorist coverage* to make up the difference.

Paying Claims

In states with liability insurance policies, your insurance company only pays for damages to the other driver's car or compensates the other driver and passengers for personal injuries if the accident is your fault. Under *liability policies*, the insurance company decides whether or not to pay a claim; as the policy holder, you do not have a say in this decision. If your insurance company decides not to pay, the other driver can file a lawsuit against you to recover the damages. If that happens, it is your insurance company's responsibility to hire an attorney to defend you in the lawsuit.

You may have to testify as a part of the lawsuit, but the insurance policy pays the costs and will pay for any judgement awarded against you by a judge or jury up to the limits of your policy.

Policy Limits

All insurance policies have what are called *policy limits*. What this means to you is that if your policy has a $20,000 limit and you cause damages of $100,000, you could have to pay the $80,000 difference. You can purchase additional insurance to increase these limits.

Parental Responsibility

As a minor, you can be held liable for the damages that you cause. Of course, you may not have any assets with which to pay a judgment. In that case, the injured party will look to your parents to pay the damages. Most states have laws that make parents financially liable for damages caused by their children when driving.

You should also remember that you and your parents can be liable for damages caused by someone to whom you have loaned your car, although these damages will generally be covered by your insurance. If you let your friend drive your car (or your parent's car), you are taking a big risk that you will pay a lot of money if that friend is in an accident.

NO-FAULT INSURANCE

There are some states, however, that use a different system of dealing with damages from car wrecks. This system is called *no-fault insurance*. Under those policies, your insurance company pays to fix your car and the other driver's car is fixed by their insurance company, no matter who caused the accident.

As a general rule, you have to be eighteen to enter into contracts. Since an insurance policy is a contract, many states will not let teenagers purchase their own insurance. Other states, however, have specific laws that authorize minors to contract for their own car insurance. However, the insurance company may not be willing to sell you insurance because teenage drivers are statistically more likely to get into accidents and are more likely to cause the insurance company to have to pay a claim.

Insurance premiums for young drivers are much more expensive than those for older drivers with good driving records. This is true whether you are able to get your own insurance or are covered by your parents' insurance. These premiums will remain high until you are in your twenties, and are affected by your driving record.

Regardless of your age, it is very important that you avoid getting traffic tickets or getting into accidents. When either one of those things happen to you, the insurance company considers you to be a greater risk and your premiums can be increased. Too many accidents or tickets can result in having your policy canceled altogether. You can also lose your driver's license.

TEEN TIP

If you cannot buy your own insurance, then you can be covered on your parents' insurance policy. The rules that apply are the same whether you or your parents are the policy holder.

–21–
DRIVING

If you are going to drive a vehicle on a public road, every state requires you to have a driver's license. You should have the license with you any time you are behind the wheel, because you will be required to show it to a police officer any time you are stopped.

DRIVER'S LICENSES

The new trend in driver's licenses for teenage drivers is the *graduated driver's license*. Almost all of the states have now passed some version of this program, which sets up a series of steps that lead to the unrestricted license. This is a significant change from the traditional method of getting an unrestricted license at sixteen, with the only requirements being passing driver's education class, the written exam, and the driving test.

The versions of this new law vary from state to state, but the underlying idea is the same. The point is to give new drivers some extra supervised driving experience; the hope is that this strategy will reduce the accident rate for younger drivers. Generally in the graduated system, the young driver starts out spending a period of time driving only with a licensed adult driver in the car. Most states require this adult driver to be at least twenty-one, so that older high school students will not qualify as the supervising driver.

The goal of this law is to have parents filling this role. Frequently, the laws restrict the passengers in cars driven by young drivers to family members. In some states, there is a second step that allows the teen to drive alone, but restricts the hours the teen can drive. Frequently, the teen has to be off the road by midnight and cannot drive before 5:00 a.m. Once these steps have been completed, then the teen is eligible for a regular driver's license.

States will require drivers under age eighteen to successfully complete an approved driver's education course. All drivers, regardless of age, must

PARENT TIP

Most state laws that deal with time restrictions have exceptions for work and school activities. You should check the laws of your state for more information.

pass a written test covering the traffic laws of the state and a driving test to get their first license. Subsequent licenses can be renewed without further testing, although you may have to take a vision test when you renew.

Suspended License

It is against the law to drive without a driver's license. If your license has been *suspended* for some reason by the state and you are caught driving, many states treat this as a crime for which you will be arrested and charged. You may end up having to hire an attorney and paying a significant fine. You may also have to serve a term of criminal probation if you are an adult.

One of the reasons your license can be suspended is if you are cited for underage drinking. Underage tobacco possession can have the same result as can illegal drug possession. And, if you do not yet have a license, you may have to wait for six months or so if you violate the drinking or tobacco laws. Many states also require school attendance as a condition to having a license before you are eighteen.

Since these laws vary greatly from state to state, you will need to check the laws of your state for all the particulars. There is information about the driver's license laws of each state in Appendix B and some addresses for websites that you can visit to learn more about the graduated license. Your state licensing department will have written materials available as does AAA Automobile Club. You can find the AAA for your state on the Internet at **www.aaa.com**.

TRAFFIC TICKETS

If you violate a traffic law of your state, the police can give you a traffic ticket. You will be required to either plead guilty and pay a fine or have a trial to determine whether or not you are guilty. If you are found guilty, the judge will order you to pay a fine.

As a general rule, you will not be sent to jail for violating a traffic law. However, if you either ignore the ticket or do not pay a fine once you have been ordered to, you can be arrested and put in jail.

Even though the police are involved when you are caught violating a traffic law, the case is treated differently from other law violations. Criminal cases for juveniles are handled in juvenile court, but when a juvenile gets a traffic ticket, it is handled by the same court that handles all the other traffic tickets.

DUI's

Be aware, though, that driving under the influence of drugs or alcohol (DUI) is different. Although you might think this is a traffic violation just like speeding, it is not handled in traffic court. It is treated like a criminal case. If you are a juvenile, your case will go to the juvenile court. If you are an adult, you will be arrested and you can be punished by spending time in jail.

Multiple convictions for DUI can result in the case being filed as a felony, which means that you could end up in prison. You will also have a permanent criminal record if you are convicted. There are many instances in the DUI process that can result in a temporary suspension of your driver's license.

Procedure

In many states, if you are under eighteen when you get a ticket, you will have to appear in court with a parent to take care of the ticket. This is true even if you are not contesting the ticket.

Since the maximum punishment for most traffic tickets is a monetary fine only, you are not entitled to have a court-appointed attorney to represent you.

You do have the right to hire an attorney to help you resolve your traffic ticket; in many cases, this is a good investment. There are things that an attorney will spot that might help you get the ticket dismissed. Also, your state may have options available that will

TEEN TIP

If you believe that you are not guilty of the offense, you have the right to have a jury trial.

let you take care of the ticket without a trial and without ending up with a conviction. This is an important goal to accomplish in traffic court.

If you are convicted on the ticket, the conviction goes on your driving record. Convictions on traffic tickets can cause your car insurance premiums to go up. Additionally, most states have rules about how many tickets you can get in a specific time period without losing your license. If you get too many, the state will automatically suspend your license.

AUTOMOBILE ACCIDENTS

Sometimes, no matter how careful you are as a driver, you may be involved in an accident. When that happens, there are things you need to do at the scene. First, determine whether anyone is injured or not. If there is any doubt, go ahead and call for an ambulance. You should also notify the police. In larger cities, the police will not respond to an accident if all of the vehicles can be driven and if there are no injuries, but you should call anyway. Later, your insurance company will ask you for a police report and you need to be able to say you called the police. Never leave the scene of an accident without stopping.

You may need to move your car if it is blocking traffic. On busy streets, you may be in more danger by leaving your car where it is, so you should get to a safe area. If you and the other driver are moving your cars, you should make note of where all the cars ended up in the wreck. You might also want to look at the other driver's license plate in case they try to leave the scene. If the police will not come to the scene, you and the other drivers should exchange information. Be sure you get the other driver's name, address, and phone number. You should ask to see their driver's license to verify this information.

Always be sure to look at their insurance card as well. They should have a card in their car; you should write down the name of the insurance company, the policy number, and the name of the policy holder. Also

---

TEEN TIP

When you are talking to the other drivers, do not admit to being at fault. If you admit to being at fault, this can be used against you later when the insurance companies or courts are deciding who has to pay for the damages. If the other driver admits to any fault, be sure to tell your insurance company.

look on the card for any phone numbers to use to make claims. You should also provide your information to the other driver. As soon as possible, you need to notify your insurance company about the accident.

If you are hurt, seek medical attention right away. Waiting to go to the doctor will weaken your position if you end up filing an insurance claim. Be sure to save all of your receipts for medical expenses. If you need ongoing treatment, be sure to go to all of your doctor's appointments. Gaps in treatment and failing to follow the doctor's instructions can make it more difficult for you to be successful in collecting on your claim.

TEEN TIP

If you are injured, you and your parents may want to hire an attorney to represent you in your claim against the insurance company.

Most lawyers handle cases like this on a *contingency fee basis*. This means that you do not have to pay the attorney unless he or she gets a settlement for you. You should expect to pay somewhere between one-third and forty percent of your *settlement* (winnings) to the lawyer. There is more information in a later chapter about hiring an attorney.

If the accident was your fault, the other driver may file a claim against you to recover their car repair expenses and medical expenses, unless you live in a no-fault insurance state. No-fault insurance means that each person's insurance company repairs the damage on their vehicle, and it does not matter who was at fault. If you are notified that a claim is being made, contact your insurance company right away. They will handle the claim for you.

If you fail to notify them, and you are later sued over the accident, your failure to notify your insurance company may mean that they can get out of paying the claim since most policies contain provisions requiring you to give them notice of the claim.

As a teenager, you can be held financially responsible for the damages you cause while driving, and so can your parents. It is important that you not do anything that would invalidate your insurance coverage.

Be sure you cooperate fully with both your insurance company and the police if they come to the scene. You should also be polite to the other people involved in the accident. Having a bad attitude or being rude or using obscenities will only make the situation worse. You will be much better off if you just exchange information and move on. If the police are there, do not leave until they tell you it is all right for you to go.

Sometimes, the police will give *citations* to one or more of the drivers involved in an accident. For information on what to do if you get a citation, review the section on traffic tickets found earlier in this chapter.

CURFEWS

Many cities have passed ordinances that restrict juveniles from being out during certain hours. These hours vary from place to place, but are generally the late night hours from midnight to early morning. Most curfews have exception for teens who are with their parents. There are also some other exceptions frequently found in curfew laws for things like school, work, church, social, or political activities.

Some states will have a state law that deals with curfews and some states do not. Just because your state does not have a specific statute about curfews does not mean that the city or town in which you live cannot have a curfew. In those states, the curfew just applies to the city or town that passed the ordinance. Neighboring cities may or may not have the same curfew regulations, so you should know the law of the area if you are going to be away from home without your parents late at night.

It should not come as a surprise that many cases about juvenile curfews have ended up in court. Courts have reached differing decisions about the validity of juvenile curfew, sometimes upholding the curfew and sometimes not. As areas learn from the mistakes of other cities and from the cases that have already been decided, it gets more and more difficult to successfully challenge the legality of a curfew law. Judge's decisions can also be affected by the fact the juvenile curfew laws have helped to lower the crime rate, particularly the crimes committed by juveniles, where they have been enacted.

In most instances, juveniles who are taken into custody by the police are not formally arrested for curfew violations. They are just taken in to the police station and held until their parents come to get them. The officer also has the option to escort the juvenile home. Of course, if the officer believes that the juvenile's reason for being out beyond the curfew is valid and falls under one of the exceptions, the juvenile will be allowed to remain out. The penalty for curfew violations is most often just a fine.

Not all states have a specific statute, but the ones that do are listed in Appendix B. Even though your state does not have a law listed, you may still be subject to a curfew passed by the city or town in which you live.

–22–
VANDALISM

Many communities have experienced problems with vandalism, often committed by minors. It has become such an issue that most states have passed laws to make parents liable for their children's vandalism.

Under traditional laws, one person is not automatically responsible for damages caused by another. When a person causes damages to another person or their property, they may have to pay for the damages. One way you can be held liable is to cause the damage intentionally. Another way is to be negligent. *Negligence* is generally defined as taking an action that a reasonable person knows or should know will cause harm. A person is always responsible for their own negligent and intentional acts, and has to pay for the damages caused.

There are ways that you can be responsible for the damages that someone else causes. For example, if you are his or her employer and he or she causes the damage while they are working for you, you might have to pay. If a plumber who works for the ABC Plumbing Company causes a car accident while he is driving the company truck on his way from one plumbing job to another, the plumbing company will have to pay to fix the car of the person the plumber hit. You might also be responsible if you allow a friend who does not have a driver's license and does not know how to drive to drive your car and they cause an accident.

PARENTAL RESPONSIBILITY

These same rules apply to parents and their children. If a *minor*, usually defined as a person under eighteen, goes into a store with a group of friends and they break something, their parents are not necessarily obligated to pay the store for the damages. The same thing was true for vandalism damages caused by children. The property owners did not have an easy way to make parents pay.

Many of the owners were government agencies like cities and school districts who had their property covered by graffiti or otherwise damaged by minors, usually teenagers.

So the *legislatures* (law makers) in most states passed laws to remedy this problem. They created specific laws that say that parents must pay for the damages caused by their children. Most of the states have some limit to the amount of money the parents can be made to pay. Some limits are as low as a thousand dollars, others are higher. The statutes vary from state to state in other ways as well.

Some states limit the financial responsibility to property damage while other states also cover personal injuries. In some places, only public entities like cities and schools can collect damages under the statute.

PARENT TIP

If you are the parent of a child who has been accused of damage to someone's property or of injuring someone, you should check the law of your state to see what the extent of *your* liability is. You should also check with an attorney to see if there is any insurance coverage available to help you pay the damages.

Other states extend the coverage to private property owners as well. If the damage was caused intentionally, it is very unlikely that any insurance policy will cover the claim, but it never hurts to check it out.

One case that looked at the parental liability issue is **Nationwide Insurance Company v. Love**, a 1984 Ohio case. In this case, a fourteen-year-old girl stole a car that belonged to someone who was at the girl's house visiting her mother. While she was out joy riding in the car, she had a wreck. Ohio has a law that says parents are liable when their child willfully damages property belonging to someone else. The owner of the car sued the girl's parents for the cost to fix her car.

In this case, the parents did not have to pay because the judges decided that, while the girl willfully stole the car, she did not willfully damage it because the car wreck was an accident. (As a reminder, the teen is still responsible for the damages to the car.

(continued)

Additionally, do not forget that, in some states, parents are liable by law for damages caused by their children when driving. In those states, the final outcome of this case would be different because of that additional law.)

TEEN RESPONSIBILITY

As a minor, you are responsible for your own acts and can be required to pay damages. In addition to the monetary penalties, you can also be charged with a crime if you are caught vandalizing.

Depending on your age and the laws of your state, you will either be processed through the juvenile justice system or through the adult system. As part of a criminal proceeding, you can be ordered to pay for the damages as part of your punishment. If the damages occurred as the result of gang activity, the penalties can be more severe.

TEEN TIP

If the property you damage is school property, the school can discipline you. There are laws that make damage to school property more serious than damage to other, privately owned property.

−23−

SEXUAL CRIMES AND PHYSICAL ABUSE

As has been noted in other places, being accused of a sexual crime has serious consequences that can last a lifetime. One area that gets teenagers into trouble is the case of the sexual encounter where one partner thought that it was consensual, only to find out that the other partner felt coerced. Another area has to do with the ages of the partners.

STATUTORY RAPE

Many teens assume that just because they are dating another student at their school, there cannot be a problem with *statutory rape*. Unfortunately, that is not always the case. If one of the partners is over eighteen and the other is not, the older partner risks being charged with a crime for having sex with an underage person who consents.

> **TEEN TIP**
>
> If you are under eighteen and your partner is younger than the minimum consent age in your state, you can still be charged with statutory rape.

Some states have exceptions that make allowances if the two people are close in age, but not always. And, if a teen who is legally an adult becomes involved with a partner who is very young, consent may not even be an issue.

Most states have laws that set a minimum age to be old enough to consent to sex. If you select a sexual partner who is below this age, you can be charged with rape (*statutory rape*).

If you are convicted in adult court, you now have a permanent criminal record that can make you appear to be a rapist. Whether you are convicted in adult court or in juvenile court, you may end up being subject to the sex offender registration laws. This means that you could be required to register with your local police department as a *sex offender*. You may have to do this for the rest of your life, re-registering every time you move. Your name and photograph may be publically released in the local newspaper and on the Internet, and you will be identified as a sex offender.

The bottom line is that you should be very cautious and take all of these factors into account before you enter into a sexual relationship with a fellow teenager. The consequences of your decision could be with you forever.

BEING UNDERAGE YOURSELF

If you are on the other side of the equation and are the underage person who is being asked for sex, you should notify the authorities. Particularly if you are engaged in a sexual relationship with an adult and you are under eighteen, you should report this matter to the police. If you voluntarily entered into this relationship and wish to continue it, you should know that you are putting your partner at risk for criminal prosecution if the relationship continues and is reported to the authorities.

If the adult who is exploiting you is a family member, you can also file the report with the child protective services agency in your area. As a minor, you do not have to put up with sexual exploitation and there are laws in place in every state to help you.

Every child protection agency has a hotline that you can use to make the report. You can also tell your family doctor, a teacher, or school counselor. Any time you report sexual abuse to one of these people, they are legally obligated to make a report to the authorities.

NOTE: *Date rape (forced sex occurring on a date) is treated the same as any other rape and is equally a crime.*

PHYSICAL ABUSE

The same thing applies if you are the victim of physical abuse. No one has the right to physically abuse you. This includes your parents and teachers. While they have the right to exercise reasonable discipline, they cannot do anything that constitutes abuse. Whether or not spanking is allowed depends mostly on the degree of spanking involved. One swat with an open hand on the backside may be OK, while repeated strikes on the legs with a belt is not. If you are suffering from abuse, you should tell an adult that you trust or report the matter to the police or child protective services agency.

In cases where children are being abused by their parents, regardless of whether the abuse is sexual or physical, the authorities have the authority to remove you from your parents' home and let you live somewhere else. They can help to get you counseling to deal with the

TEEN TIP

Do not accuse your parents of abusing you just because you are angry with them or want to live somewhere else.

psychological issues that arise when people are abused. They can also force your parents to get counseling so that they no longer are a danger to abuse you. Your parents can also be prosecuted criminally for child abuse. You should not let this fact keep you from filing a report. Your safety is the most important concern.

Child abuse charges are felonies in most states, and parents who abuse their children can be sent to prison. It can cost a parent thousands of dollars in legal fees to defend themselves against a charge such as this and can cause permanent damage to their reputation. A false allegation can destroy a family, and it may be impossible to later repair the damage.

By all means, if you are being abused by your parents, get help. The serious consequences to your parents in that situation are not your responsibility and you should not be concerned about what will happen to them. They are adults and are responsible for their actions. But, by the same token, do not use this avenue lightly. It should be reserved for real abuse and not just a quick response to the typical problems that teens have with their parents.

–24–
ALCOHOL, TOBACCO, DRUGS AND WEAPONS

The legal age for drinking and smoking is set by the legislatures of each state and not by federal law. However, the federal government does have ways to influence the decisions made by the various states. The most effective tool used by the federal government is the threat of withholding federal funds from the states unless certain laws are passed by the state legislature. This has occurred with both the drinking and smoking ages and, as a result, there is great uniformity among the states. The legal age to possess, use, or purchase tobacco products is eighteen and the drinking age is twenty-one.

Laws do vary somewhat between the states as to consequences to teenagers who violate the law, but there are similarities. Tobacco and alcohol possession charges are not usually treated as juvenile criminal offenses, but more like traffic tickets. You are likely to be cited to appear in court and, if found guilty, fined and ordered to perform some number of hours of community service. You may have to go to alcohol or tobacco awareness classes, and your parents may also have to go with you. In a lot of states, a conviction on one of these charges can cost you your driver's license for some period of time. Six months is fairly common.

DUIS
The situation is different, however, if your use of alcohol is combined with use of an automobile. If you are arrested and charged with driving under the influence of alcohol *(DUI)*, this is a much more serious matter. If you are still considered a minor under the criminal laws of your state, you will be processed through the juvenile courts system just like you are for any other violation of a criminal law. That means, depending on the facts and your history (do you have other criminal convictions or are you already on

juvenile probation for something else?), you could be sent to a juvenile detention facility or to jail.

If you are an adult, you will be dealing with the adult criminal system and can end up with a criminal conviction that will remain on your record for the rest of your life. In both the juvenile and adult systems, you can also lose your driver's license. Your car insurance costs will also increase dramatically.

In the adult system, if you have multiple convictions, you can end up in prison as a convicted felon. Felony convictions have life-long consequences—you can never vote or own a gun of any type. It can also make renting an apartment or getting a job more difficult. You may have a harder time being accepted into college and you can lose the ability to get a student loan if you have a felony on your record.

DRUGS

Drug cases are another matter entirely. Some drugs are always illegal. You can also get into trouble with prescription drugs that are not prescribed for you. Possession of illegal drugs is always treated as a crime. As with other crimes, your age and the laws of your state will determine whether or not you go through the juvenile system or through the adult system. A charge of selling drugs is even more serious. Drug cases can be either misdemeanors or felonies, depending on the exact charge and the type and amount of drugs.

You may have heard about *designer drugs*; you may have even heard things such as the drugs are legal and will not hurt you. Many of them are illegal and some of them can be deadly.

The overwhelming majority of schools have a *zero tolerance policy* where drugs are concerned.

TEEN TIP

If you have drugs and give them to someone else, you can be charged with a crime. In most instances, you can even be charged with the more serious offense of selling drugs.

You can count on being arrested if you are caught with drugs at school—even once. The school can discipline students for use of alcohol, drugs, or tobacco because these things will always be a violation of school policy. For questions about school discipline, please refer to Chapter 10.

GUNS AND WEAPONS

Schools are also *gun-free zones*. Bringing a gun to school will get you arrested and charged with a crime. Other types of weapons like knives are also prohibited at school. Depending on the particular weapon, it may also be a criminal violation.

Most states have laws governing gun possession in places other than school as well. There are laws that deal with registration of guns and permits to carry them, as well as laws that regulate minors' use of weapons. Often, you will find exceptions that allow minors to use guns while hunting when accompanied by a parent.

PARENT TIP

In many states, if a teen takes a gun belonging to a parent, even without the parent's permission, the parent may be subject to criminal charges for allowing a minor to have access to the gun.

SECTION III:

TEENS AND THEIR BODIES

–25–
EATING DISORDERS

Many teenagers suffer from an eating disorder. Although the majority of sufferers are female, males are also afflicted by these diseases.

TYPES OF DISORDERS

The phrase *eating disorder* actually encompasses three separate illnesses: *anorexia nervosa*, *bulimia nervosa*, and *binge eating disorder* (also called *compulsive eating disorder*).

The most familiar of the three is probably anorexia, but the other two are just as serious. All three can do lasting damage and, taken to the extreme, can be fatal. All three have common elements; the primary one is the unhealthy relationship the sufferer has with food. We sometimes think these problems are caused by the media and cultural emphasis on thinness and body image, but that is too simplistic an explanation. Each is a psychological disorder, with complex causes, and each can be difficult to cure.

TEEN TIP

Please be careful about searching for information on the Internet about eating disorders. Just because there is a website does not mean that the information is accurate or appropriate. There are actually websites in existence that promote anorexia, and relying on information from sites like this can literally be deadly. Be sure you are dealing with a reputable organization.

Anorexia

Anorexia is characterized by unnaturally low weight accompanied by an unrealistic body view. The sufferer thinks he or she is too fat, and tries to remedy the problem by dieting. This pattern continues even when body weight drops to dangerously low levels. Where other people see someone who is so thin that they could have just come from a concentration camp, the anorectic sees an overweight body that must be gotten into shape. Approximately 90 percent of anorectics are women. The disease most often begins during the teenage years.

No one knows what causes anorexia and there is no medical or psychological test that you can take to see if you are going to develop the disorder. It can start gradually, when a diet that was begun to lose a few pounds gives the dieter a feeling of control that he or she wants to keep. So he or she keeps on dieting long past the point of necessity, and the warning signs begin to appear. In most cases, even when the physical symptoms are present, the anorectic will not acknowledge that there is a problem.

This is one of the most dangerous components of the disease; victims' body weight can drop to dangerous levels and they still cannot see or accept that there is a problem. Even though there is a danger of dying, he or she may still be resistant to eating and gaining any weight.

Bulimia

Bulimia is a close relative of anorexia. The main goal is still the same—to lose weight—but the method of achieving the goal is different. The primary identifying characteristic of bulimia is the *binge and purge cycle*. This means that the classic bulimic will overeat and then feel so guilty about it that he or she feels there is no choice but to get rid of (throw up) the offending food.

Unlike the anorectic, the bulimic knows there is a problem and tries to hide it. While an anorectic's condition may become obvious to people because of the excessive weight loss, the bulimic can be harder to spot. Weight is more likely to be within the normal range and the bulimic will go to much greater lengths to keep the illness a secret. Bulimics are also more prone to suicide attempts than are people with other types of eating disorders.

The binge symptom can take different forms since some bulimics see a small amount of food as a binge. Others consume massive amounts of food over a short period of time. By massive, we mean an amount of food far in excess of the needed caloric requirements. A normal diet might consist of two to three thousand calories per day. A binging bulimic might eat thirty or fifty thousand calories worth of food.

Once he or she has had what he or she considers a binge, then the need to get rid of the food is overwhelming. Some bulimics will induce vomiting while others will use laxatives to ease the shame and guilt they feel about the binge. They see the binge as a loss of control over the food and the purge as a way of regaining the lost control.

Bulimia also starts gradually, with the occasional purge used as a way of controlling weight. But it eventually becomes a vicious cycle because the ability to control weight with purging makes the bulimic more susceptible to the desire to binge. Eventually, one becomes addicted to the cycle of binging and purging. As with other eating disorders, bulimia often begins in adolescence and can be triggered during times of high stress.

Compulsive Eating

The desire for control is a common characteristic that bulimics share with anorectics. The binge aspect is a trait that is shared with those who suffer from the third type of eating disorder, *compulsive eating*. Compulsive eating involves eating binges followed by guilt. In this respect, it is like bulimia, but the binge is not followed by a purge. Compulsive eaters are more likely to be overweight; however, being overweight does not necessarily make you a compulsive eater. The difference between someone who is overweight because they eat too much or eat the wrong kinds of food and a compulsive eater lies in the attitude towards food.

For the compulsive or binge eater, eating is an obsession and thoughts of food consume a large percentage of the compulsive eater's thoughts. Food is used as a coping mechanism and not just as a means to satisfy normal hunger. Of the three eating disorders, compulsive eating has the highest percentage of male sufferers. Compulsive eating can have its roots in childhood when attitudes about food are formed, but it also begins gradually.

Other conditions may accompany the eating disorder. Victims may exercise compulsively as a method of controlling weight and maintaining control. Depression may also accompany any of the three eating disorders.

Eating Non-food

A fourth problem that is related to food issues is the person who eats non-food items. Cases have been reported of people eating dirt, clay, kleenex, q-tips, and other such items. This is a sign of trouble. If you are engaging in this behavior, you should seek professional help and go for an evaluation.

> **TEEN TIP**
>
> If you think one of your friends has an eating disorder, it can be hard to know how to handle the situation. Talk to a trusted adult, such as a school counselor.

WHAT TO DO WHEN A FRIEND HAS AN EATING DISORDER

One of the first problems can be recognizing that your friend or family member has a problem. There is a very helpful book for friends and family members, *Surviving an Eating Disorder*, written by Michele Siegel, Judith Brisman, and Margot Weinshiel and published by Harper Perennial. If you cannot find this book in your local bookstore or library, you can order it from:

www.Amazon.com

Surviving an Eating Disorder contains checklists of behaviors that can help other people spot an eating disorder. You should not use these lists to diagnose an eating disorder since you are not a trained professional. The lists are only to be used as a tool to help you recognize when a friend or family member has a problem. Do not try to treat the problem yourself, but, instead, encourage the person to go for the professional help they need. You will note that these lists are similar to the symptoms of eating disorders we have previously discussed.

Surviving an Eating Disorder also contains many helpful suggestions about how to talk to the person you believe has the eating disorder and how to deal with the most likely reactions you will receive in that conver-

> **TEEN TIP**
>
> If death and suicide are likely, you should get the person to a hospital immediately. If the person will not go willingly, you may need to call for outside help.

sation. It is not uncommon for victims of eating disorders to deny that there is a problem, and you cannot force them out of their denial.

There are some instances that may be so severe that they are really emergencies. Some sufferers of eating disorders may attempt suicide, and anorectics can be near death as a result of the illness.

TREATMENT OF EATING DISORDERS

There are many components to treating an eating disorder. Generally, the primary therapy will be psychological, using things like individual, group, and family therapy. Support groups can be an important asset for both the person with the eating disorder and her family and close friends. There is a list of support groups in the appendix to this book.

Medical treatment may also be necessary. All eating disorders have the ability to cause serious physical problems that will require treatment. In many anorexia cases, feeding treatments may be needed. Nutritional and dietary guidance is also important in helping the patient develop healthy eating habits.

There have been many new developments in the medical arena, and there are now medications that can help with treatment. Part of any treatment plan should be a consultation with a psychiatrist so that the eating disorder patient can be evaluated for this purpose. It is important to select a team of professionals that specialize in the treatment of eating disorders so that you can benefit from the most current information.

Eating disorders present many challenges for both the person with the disorder and those around her. The most important step is to get professional help so that you do not try to travel this road alone. For more information, you can read the books we have referenced. Understanding Weight and Depression is part of a series of books published by Rosen Publishing Group, Inc. that have to do with eating issues and are directed at teens.

NOTE: *Please be sure to check Appendix A for other resources that can be of help to you as you confront this problem.*

–26–
SUICIDE

Sometimes, people with eating disorders and many other stresses are so depressed that they consider suicide. If someone you know begins talking about killing themselves, you should take that talk seriously, especially if it is accompanied by other things like giving their possessions away, undergoing a personality change, or suffering other signs of depression.

Talk to your school counselor, a teacher, parent, or other trusted adult. There is no problem or situation that is worth killing yourself over. Medication and therapy can help. If you cannot talk to your parents, call a suicide hotline. Help is available for you. There is a national hotline for suicide help; they can direct you to help in your local area. The number is 1-800-784-2433. See Appendix A for other resources that may be helpful.

–27–
BIRTH CONTROL

The issue of a minor's access to birth control has been controversial. There are many teenagers who want access to birth control without having to get their parents' permission. On the other side of the equation are the parents who do not want their children to have unlimited access to birth control. As with most other areas of the law, the outcome is based on a balancing of rights by the judicial system.

The parents have constitutional rights to direct the upbringing of their children and to the free exercise of religion. Many parents object to the use of birth control by their children on religious grounds, so this helps to make this a hot button issue. But children have constitutional rights also, including the right to privacy.

In most jurisdictions that have considered this issue, the courts have decided that minors have the right to access birth control devices, and have upheld condom availability programs. The Social Security Act, specifically the parts that provide for Medicaid and welfare, indicate that minors have the right to access to family planning services, including birth control, upon request.

There have been cases that have held that state statutes that required parental consent were invalid as an unconstitutional infringement on the minor's privacy rights. But, there have also been courts that have reached the opposite conclusion even though this would not seem to be possible given the federal regulations just mentioned.

CONDOM DISTRIBUTION PROGRAMS
There have been cases that have addressed the legality of condom distribution programs in public high schools.

In the case of **Curtis v. School Committee of Falmouth**, the junior and senior high schools in Falmouth had a condom availability program. Some parents sued, claiming that the program violated their right to family privacy; their right to control the rearing of their children; and, their right to freedom of religious exercise.

The school program allowed students at the junior high to receive free condoms from the school nurse. The nurse was required to counsel the students and to give them pamphlets on HIV and AIDS and other sexually transmitted diseases. The high school students could either get free condoms from the school nurse or buy them from vending machines located in the boys' and girls' restrooms. The students could ask for counseling from trained faculty members and printed information about AIDS and sexually transmitted diseases was available in the school nurse's office.

A memo from the Superintendent said that it would be stressed that abstinence was the only sure way to avoid a sexually transmitted disease. The program did not have a provision for parents to opt out and keep their children from getting the condoms. Nor was there a provision that required parents to be notified if their children requested condoms.

The court agreed that the parents have a constitutional right to be free from unnecessary government interference when it comes to decisions about their children. Areas that are specifically protected from intrusion by the government include the instruction in moral standards and religious beliefs.

However, the judge did not think that the parents had shown that the condom program unconstitutionally interfered with their rights. Part of the basis for this decision was that the students were not forced to participate in the program and the parents were free to instruct their children not to participate.

When the appeals court judges addressed the claim of interference with the parent's free exercise of religion, they pointed out that the school district does not have to design its programs to be in compliance with the tenets of any particular religion.

The parents tried to claim that the peer pressure their children would encounter constituted a burden on the exercise of their religious beliefs, but the judges did not agree with this claim. Once again, the judges pointed out that the students were not forced to take the condoms or otherwise participate in the program.

In the cases that reached this conclusion, the judges adopted the idea that condom distribution programs should be defined as a "health service" because they were a way to preserve health, by reducing the risk of getting AIDS or another sexually transmitted disease. "Health services" do not require parental consent in the state in which these courts are located. The courts that have reached the opposite conclusion on the legality of condom availability programs have classified the programs as "medical treatment" which does require parental consent.

Courts have reached these decisions regardless of whether the condom program was in a public school or at a family planning clinic. They have used the same reasoning and based their decisions on the same principles as the cases that deal with school programs.

If you want to use a birth control method that requires a prescription, you can either go to your family doctor or to a public clinic like Planned Parenthood. Of course, there are also birth control methods that are available over the counter. Condoms are one example. Parental consent is not required to purchase over the counter birth control.

–28–
ABORTION

Access to abortion is a very controversial issue, and the controversy is even greater when the person seeking the abortion is a teenager. The primary case in the abortion arena is **Roe v. Wade**. This was the first case to legalize abortion and set up parameters for its regulation. The earlier in the pregnancy it is, the less regulation allowed. This means that women who are very early in their pregnancy have easy access to abortions while women in the second and third trimesters have increasingly difficult challenges.

In later cases, the United States Supreme Court has said that states cannot keep minors from getting an abortion, but that they can impose a *parental notification requirement* (discussed in the next section). Each state determines its own laws in this area, taking into account the various rulings of the Supreme Court. (See Appendix B for the laws in your state.)

PARENTAL NOTIFICATION

States are not required to have parental notification laws and not all do. Some states say that the notification and consent laws apply to women under eighteen. Other states allow older teenagers who are not yet eighteen to consent to their own abortions without their parents. You will need to check the laws of your state for this in Appendix B. You can usually find this information by looking to see how the statute defines the word *minor*. If the law does not have a specific definition, then it is the overall *age of majority* for your state that controls.

In the states that do have such laws, there are two types. One is the law that requires *parental consent* and the other simply requires *notification*. In all cases, the Supreme Court requires that the state provide what is called a *judicial bypass procedure*. This allows pregnant teens who do not want to tell their parents about the pregnancy to go to court and get permission from a judge to have an abortion. If you are a teen who does not feel like you can go to your parents, you can get information on the judicial bypass procedure by either contacting an attorney or researching the laws of your state yourself.

Appendix B contains information about what the laws of each state were at the time of the writing of this book and the statute number so that you can check the current status since all laws change from time to time. You may also be able to get some information about the judicial bypass procedure from the district clerk's office in your home county. If you are going the judicial bypass route, you can also consult with an attorney about the process. Many attorneys will give you some information for either little or no charge.

TEEN TIP

If you are pregnant and unsure about what options are available to you, clinics like Planned Parenthood can offer you information and counseling services. See Appendix A for additional resources.

TEEN FATHERS

Often, prospective fathers want to have input in the decision to seek an abortion. Under the law in states as of the writing of this book, the decision belongs totally to the mother. The father can neither force the woman to have an abortion nor keep her from having one.

FORCING TEENS TO HAVE ABORTIONS

The other side to the parental consent issue arises when the parents want the teenager to have the abortion and the teen wants to have the baby. In that case, the minor's decision controls. Parents cannot force a teenager to have an abortion if she does not want to have one.

Parents cannot generally force their children to have a child when the teen does not want to give birth. Most states that require parental notification have a provision that allows the minor to go to a judge and get permission for an abortion without her parents' consent. This is called the *judicial bypass procedure* discussed in this chapter. Other states have provisions that allow an abortion provider to perform the abortion without parental notifications.

Federal laws govern the availability of abortions at federally funded clinics. The status of abortion availability can change based on the regulations requested by the President of the United States. As the president changes, the regulations can change. Right now, the federal government will not pay for most voluntary abortions that are not medically necessary.

–29–
MARRIAGE

Marriage laws vary from state to state and, in order for you to be legally married, you will need to comply with the laws of your state. There are, however, some general guidelines that will apply wherever you are.

All states allow marriages between adults of opposite sexes. Parties desiring to wed will have to obtain a marriage license from the state. Each state has different rule about things like *residency* requirements and waiting periods between the issuance of the license and wedding itself. You may also have to have a blood test in order to get a marriage license.

PARENTAL CONSENT

All states require people under age eighteen to have the consent of at least one parent before a marriage can occur. Many states have minimum ages and will not allow children under that age to marry under any circumstances. In some states, teenagers who are under a certain age (frequently sixteen) are required to get permission from a judge before they can get married. In those instances, you may have to undergo premarital counseling or stay in school as a condition of the judge granting you permission to marry. States with minimum marriage ages may also have exceptions if the prospective spouses are expecting a child together.

MARRIAGE AND "LEGAL" ADULTHOOD

In most instances, being married means that you are legally considered an adult, even if you are under the age of majority for your state. The exceptions to this are the legal ages for tobacco and alcohol. You must still be eighteen to legally use or purchase tobacco and twenty-one to drink.

TEEN TIP

If you get married without following the laws, your marriage may not be valid. This may not seem like that big a deal to you, but there can be serious legal consequences to you if your marriage is later declared invalid. Your rights in relation to property ownership and other contractual matters can be negatively affected as described in this chapter.

TEEN TIP

If you are under the legal age to marry in your home state and plan to go to another state to get around this problem, you need to check the laws of your home state to see if your marriage will be legal once you get home.

PROPERTY OWNERSHIP

Laws about property ownership between spouses are passed by the state legislature and can be different from one state to another. Although the terms and rules are different, all states have laws that create some form of jointly owned property for things that are bought during a marriage. Also, if one of the spouses gets into debt, the states have laws that can make both spouses liable for the debt.

LEGAL MARRIAGE

As a general rule, if you get married legally in one state, your marriage will be valid in all of the other states. However, not all states recognize marriages if the marriage would have been illegal if performed in that state. If your marriage is not legal because you were underage, it becomes valid once you are over eighteen if no court action to void the marriage has been taken.

Common Law Marriage

There are some states that have laws that recognize *common law marriage*. This means that the law will treat you and your partner as legally married even though you have never gotten a marriage license and been through a marriage ceremony. These laws will only apply to you once you are over eighteen. If you are over eighteen and living with someone of the opposite sex, you should familiarize yourself with the laws of your state to see if there is a chance that your living arrangements could create a common law marriage issue.

DIVORCE

If your marriage does not work out and you decide to get a divorce, the divorce laws of your state apply to you just like they apply in divorces between spouses who are over eighteen. The divorce judge will sign orders about custody of any children you have and one of you will probably be ordered to pay child support to the other. This is true even if you are both still teenagers when you divorce. You will be able to file for divorce on your own and will not need your parents to file for you.

Getting a divorce does not undo the fact that your marriage emancipated you. You will still be treated as an adult even though you are no longer married.

PARENTAL SUPPORT

Because marriage may emancipate you, your parents probably no longer have a legal obligation to support you once you are married. If your parents are divorced, the orders from their divorce that deal with your custody, visitation, and child support all terminate in that case. Marriage may also mean that you cannot be carried on your parents' health and car insurance. You will need to check with your insurance agent or company to see what the eligibility rules are. If you get into any debts and sign any contracts, you cannot get out of them based on your age. Emancipation means that you are an adult for all of these purposes and no longer eligible to be treated as a child.

Appendix B contains information about the legal ages for marriage in the various states. It also includes the statute number so that you can check the current status of the law in your state if you are planning to get married.

SAME-SEX MARRIAGES

There are no states at the present time that offer the option of marriage for same sex couples. Vermont does offer same sex couples an option to register as a couple and obtain the same legal rights and protections given to married persons, but this option is not called a marriage. There are some cities and companies that offer the same benefits to same sex couples as to other, heterosexual couples who are not married.

–30–
MEDICAL CARE

In most instances, medical professionals will not provide medical care without the consent of the patient. If you are in a car accident or have another medical emergency, you should receive the care that you need without the issue of consent coming up. But, in other situations, someone with the legal authority to do so will have to consent to the medical treatment.

The laws for medical consent do vary some from state to state, but the general rule is that you must be a legal adult to consent to medical care. Therefore, your parents will have to consent to all of your medical treatment. There are a few exceptions, which we will address, but in most instances parental consent will be the rule. If your parents are divorced, their divorce decree and the law of your state will determine the rights each of them has to consent to medical care for you.

CONSENTING TO YOUR OWN CARE

Most states allow minors to consent to their own medical care in cases where it is an emergency. What constitutes an emergency will be decided initially by the doctors. If it becomes disputed later on, and a lawsuit is filed, a judge could end up making the final determination. Receiving medical care creates a contractual situation where the doctor is obligated to provide appropriate medical care to the patient and the patient is obligated to pay for the care.

If, as a minor, you consent to your own medical care, you will be legally obligated to pay for it. Because emergency medical care will also generally be classified as a necessary, your parents will also probably be legally obligated to pay.

INSURANCE AND PAYMENT

The fact that you have insurance does not get you out of the legal obligation to pay unless you are part of an *HMO* and receiving care directly from
the HMO provider. (HMO's are a specific type of insurance with strict
rules on who can provide your care and how.) In other than the HMO situation, the contract is between you and the medical provider and not the
medical provider and your insurance company. Therefore, if your insurance
does not pay, you still have to.

The same rules apply if you are injured by someone else, for example
in a car accident. If you are in a car accident and go to the emergency room,
you will be legally obligated to pay that bill even if it was someone else's
fault. That's because, once again, the contract for the services is between
you and the hospital, not the hospital and the other person or their insurance company.

DRUG AND ALCOHOL TREATMENT

Many states have special laws that allow minors to consent to their own
treatment for alcohol and drug abuse without their parents. If you need
treatment for one of those issues, you will need to check the laws of your
state if you are unwilling or unable to get your parents to consent to the
treatment. The treatment facility will be able to give you information
about the rules that apply.

ABORTION

Abortion is a type of medical care, but it is not treated the same as medical care for other purposes. To determine whether you need your parents'
consent or not, you will need to check the abortion laws in your state and
not the regular medical care laws. For more information on abortions,
please refer to Chapter 28 in this book.

BIRTH CONTROL

Some types of birth control also involve medical care. Birth control pills are
the best example of this, because they are only available with a prescription. In some states, there are specific laws that allow minors to obtain
birth control on their own. In all states, minors can legally go to family
planning clinics like Planned Parenthood and get confidential counseling
and prescriptions. For more information about birth control, please see
Chapter 27.

PRENATAL CARE

Another type of medical care that minors sometimes need is prenatal care when they are pregnant. All states will allow minors to consent to their own medical care in that situation. Additionally, when the baby is born, the minor parent has the right to consent to medical care for the child. (In most states, the father who did not marry the mother has these rights as well, after *paternity* (who is the father) is established by blood tests.)

This can create an interesting situation; the minor parent can consent to major surgery for her child but, if she needs a wart removed herself, she must have her parent's consent.

TEEN TIP

If you need treatment for a sexually transmitted disease, there are low-cost clinics in many cities that can help you if you do not have a family doctor or prefer not to seek treatment from that professional. Check your phone book or the Internet.

SEXUALLY TRANSMITTED DISEASE

Minors who have a sexually transmitted disease are also authorized to consent to their own medical treatment for that disease. Many states also have laws that specifically authorize minors to consent without their parents for treatment for AIDS and HIV. In states that do not have that specific law, minors would still be able to consent without their parents under the sexually transmitted disease law.

YOU AS AN ADULT

If you have become a legal adult, you can consent to your own medical care. Your parents lose the authority to consent for you. That is why some adults have a *medical power of attorney* so that someone else can authorize medical treatment for them if they are unable.

–31–
CONFIDENTIALITY

In addition to the rules about confidentiality of school records discussed in Chapter 6, there are other kinds of information and records that are confidential. In most of those instances, the confidential information can be accessed by the teenager and the teenager's parents. In fact, the parents may be the only ones with the legal right to get to the information since the teen is not legally an adult.

MEDICAL RECORDS

Medical records are covered by rules about confidentiality. The general rule is that your medical records are confidential and access to them is limited only to those people to whom the patient gives authorization. However, if you are not legally an adult, your parents have an automatic right to those records. If your parents are divorced, then each parent has an independent legal right to these records.

When you file a claim on a health insurance policy or seek treatment with your HMO, you (or your parents) consent to the release of your records to the insurance company.

> **TEEN TIP**
>
> Information that you tell a psychologist or psychiatrist can be treated the same way as with a physician. Your parents have a legal right to access these records unless, in the judgment of the therapist, it will harm the juvenile patient to release the records.

Another exception to the medical records confidentiality rule has to do with child abuse. If you tell your doctor that you are being abused or if your doctor has some other reason to believe that you are a victim of child abuse, then the doctor is legally obligated to report the suspected abuse to the authorities. In addition to the report that the doctor makes, the child welfare authorities can have unrestricted access to all of your records.

Mental health records can be withheld from the patient if the treating professional believes it would be harmful for the patient to see his or her records.

TEENS WITH ATTORNEYS

There are some instances in which a juvenile is represented by an attorney. The ethical rules for attorneys require that information given them by a client be kept confidential unless the client authorizes its release. There are a few exceptions to this rule, such as the requirement to report child abuse and the authorization to break confidentiality if a client says he or she is going to commit a crime. What this means for you is that, if you are the attorney's client, your parents are not automatically entitled to information, even if your parents are the ones paying for the lawyer. The protection goes to the client, who is the person being represented, and not to the person paying the bill.

NOTE: *You will find some additional information on confidentiality in the chapters on working, relating to your personnel file and other records that employers will maintain.*

SECTION IV:

TEENS AND WORK

–32–

LIMITATIONS ON
YOUNG WORKERS

JOB LIMITS

Both federal and state laws limit the ages and jobs at which teens can begin working. Those same laws also set limits for the amount of time young workers can spend on the job. The primary law that sets the rules for workers under age eighteen is the federal *Fair Labor Standards Act*, which is sometimes referred to as the *Wage and Hour Law*. In this book, we will refer to the law as *FLSA*.

Lots of employers are covered by the this law and have to comply with its provisions. Employers may also have to comply with state laws that relate to the employment of children. If the state law provisions are more lenient than the federal ones, then the employer is held to the higher standards of the federal law. However, if the state law provides more protection to the minor worker, then the employer must be in compliance with the state standard.

The federal law provides a minimum required level of protection, but states are free to pass laws that provide extra protection for minor workers. State law cannot be used to help employers avoid at least following the federal regulations. If an employer is not covered by FLSA, it can still be covered by the state law.

One area that is covered by both state and federal law is the type of job younger workers can hold. These laws can apply to workers up to age eighteen, and generally cover jobs that would be considered hazardous. Most state child labor laws have a list of specific occupations that are defined as hazardous, and the laws will set out the minimum age for workers in those jobs.

FLSA also contains a list of hazardous occupations. Children under sixteen cannot have the following jobs:

- manufacturing, mining, or processing occupations, including jobs where any of the work is performed in areas of the facility where goods are manufactured, mined, or otherwise processed;
- jobs involving the operation or tending of hoisting equipment or power-driven machines (here, they are talking about large machinery and not office equipment);
- jobs that require the operation of motor vehicles or that require working as a helper on motor vehicles; or,
- pubic messenger service, transportation occupations, construction work, and communications and public utility work.

The law also contains a list of jobs that workers under eighteen cannot have. This list includes:

- working in plants that manufacture explosives and components of explosives;
- motor vehicle driver and helper jobs;
- mining, logging, and sawmill operations;
- jobs that require operation of power-driven woodworking, metal-working or hoisting equipment;
- jobs that involve exposure to radioactive substances;
- slaughterhouse and rendering plant jobs;
- jobs that involve operation of bakery equipment, paper products machines, circular saws, bandsaws, and guillotine shears;
- brick and tile manufacturing jobs;
- demolition or wrecking jobs;
- roofing jobs; and,
- excavation jobs.

Your state must prohibit underage workers from all of these jobs because the federal law controls this issue. However, your state can *add* jobs to the list of dangerous occupations and you will also be prevented from having those jobs, at least in that state.

There are some limited exceptions under FLSA for workers who are apprentices or who are working as part of a school-sponsored work program.

LIMITS ON WORK HOURS

The other significant issue covered by child labor laws deals with the hours that workers under age eighteen can work. Each state has passed its own version of these laws. Once again, the federal law provides a level of protection that employers must meet, but state laws can be more restrictive on the employer and provide additional protection for workers under eighteen. The most restrictive version is the one that employers must follow.

> ## TEEN TIP
>
> If an employer is violating any of the child labor laws, report that employer to the Department of Labor.

Under the federal law, workers between fourteen and sixteen can only work for three hours on a school day and only up to eighteen hours in a school week. Non-school days are limited to eight hours and non school weeks to forty hours. They may only work between the hours of 7 a.m. to 7 p.m. during the school year. During the summer, the hours extend to 9 p.m. Minors are prohibited in most cases from working during school hours unless they are part of a school program. State laws have similar rules and regulations. The hours your state permits can be found in Appendix B.

There are special rules that apply to some occupations. Some states have laws that allow teens with paper routes to deliver their papers outside of the stated hours. Most states also have special rules for children performing in movies or theatrical productions and to teens working in agricultural jobs and in family owned businesses.

When you apply for a job, you will need to be prepared to provide proof of your age. Generally, a certified copy of your birth certificate will suffice. If you do not have a copy, you can request it from the county in which you were born.

If you need more information about the child labor laws in your state, Appendix B in this book will give you the statute number for your state so that you can look up the laws for yourself if you want to. The appendix also sets out the rules for your state relating to hours that you can work. You can also find more information about child labor laws on the U.S. Department of Labor web site, www.dol.gov.

Most cities have a local Department of Labor office. You can find the office closest to you by looking in the government pages of your phone book, under United States government, or by checking the Labor Department's website.

–33–
RIGHTS AND OBLIGATIONS OF WORKERS

Other than the special rules that apply to child laborers discussed in this chapter, the rules that apply to adult workers also apply to workers under age eighteen. Let's review some of the rights employees have. These rights are established primarily under federal law, but your state may also have laws that give residents more protection than that afforded by the federal law.

MINIMUM WAGE

In many jobs, your employer will be required to pay you the *minimum wage*. This is a dollar amount of compensation per hour that you must be paid. The minimum is set by federal law and Congress may change it. (At the time of this book's publication, the minimum wage is $5.15 per hour.) Your state may also have a minimum wage. In that case, your employer must pay you the higher of the two amounts.

Commission

You must remember that not all jobs are covered by the minimum wage law. Many professional and administrative jobs do not have to follow this law. Other jobs that pay *commissions* may be covered by the law in some instances. If you are working in a job that just pays you commissions, your employer does not have to pay you the minimum hourly wage in addition to your commissions. But if your commissions applied to the number of hours that you worked mean that you made less than the minimum wage, your employer has to make up the difference.

Be aware, though, that most employers who pay on a commission basis will set certain sales levels that you are required to meet. If you consistently fall below those levels and the employer is always making up the difference between your commissions and the minimum wage, you could be in jeopardy of being fired from your job.

Tips

Another occupation that is treated differently under the minimum wage law is that of the employee who works for tips. If an employee regularly earns a certain amount of money per month in tips, then the employer can pay the employee a much lower minimum wage. The amount the employee can earn in tips without triggering the lower minimum wage level is determined by state and federal law and may change. The most common job category to which this rule applies is that of waiter or waitress.

NOTE: *Determining whether a specific job is covered by the minimum wage law can be fairly complex, and is certainly beyond the scope of this book. If you have questions about whether a job is covered by the minimum wage law, you can contact the U.S. Department of Labor. Ask for the Wage and Hour Division. (Check the Internet at* **www.DOL.gov.**)

OVERTIME

As a teenage worker, you are technically eligible for overtime pay, but as a practical matter, these rules will not apply to most of you. That is because overtime pay rules generally become effective when the employee has worked more than forty hours in one week. Since child labor laws prohibit worker under eighteen from working more than forty hours, you should not become eligible.

If you are over eighteen, however, you may qualify. If you do, federal law says that you are entitled to be paid one and one-half your regular rate of pay (commonly referred to as time and a half) for every hour over forty that you work in a given week.

DEDUCTIONS FROM YOUR CHECK

Any time you are an employee, your employer will have to deduct certain taxes from your check. Federal law requires withholding for *federal income taxes, social security tax,* and *Medicare tax.* These are taxes that every worker has to pay. They will be automatically held out of your check each time you are paid. You will be asked to fill out a form telling your employer the number of dependents you have; this affects the amount of taxes that are withheld. The more dependents you have, the smaller the amount of taxes withheld.

However, at the end of the year, you are responsible for paying all of the taxes due on the amount of money you made. If you did not have enough taxes held out of your check, you will have to come up with the difference out of your own pocket. If you do not pay on time, the Internal Revenue Service will add penalties and interest to any amount you owe. If you live in a state that also has a state income tax, an amount will be held out to cover that tax as well.

For each year that you work, you may have to file a *tax return*. If you are just babysitting or mowing lawns, you probably will not make enough money to have to file. But to be on the safe side, you should tell your parents how much you made from working so that no one gets in trouble for not paying taxes. If you work for an outside employer who takes taxes out of your check, you will need to file. If you did not make enough money to owe any taxes, or you owe less than what was taken from your check, the government will refund the money.

EXTRA BENEFITS

If you have a full time job and your employer provides health insurance as a benefit, there may be an amount withheld from your check to pay for this. If you are still eligible for coverage on your parents' insurance, you may be able to opt out of participation in your employer's insurance. An employer is not obligated to offer health insurance as a benefit, and, if they do, they may pay all or part of the premiums or the employee may be required to pay the entire amount. Your employer will give you this information when you are hired.

Many employers also offer retirement plans to their employees. Even as a minor, you are eligible for the plan if you otherwise qualify. There are many different kinds of plans and a thorough discussion is too detailed and complex for this book. When you are hired, your employer will explain how your company's retirement plan works. If you have any questions about the plan, the personnel director will be able to answer them. For our purposes, you just need to know that you may be eligible to participate. Many

> **TEEN TIP**
>
> If you are a teen and have been with your employer for over a year and worked enough hours to qualify, you may be eligible for unpaid time off from work if you have a child.

employers restrict participation to full time employees. Since many minors only work part time, the retirement plan may not be available to you.

The Family and Medical Leave Act will allow you a twelve week unpaid leave with a guarantee that you will be allowed to return to the same job you had before or one similar to it. Your own state may also have laws in this area. There is another federal law, the *Pregnancy Discrimination Act*, which prohibits employers from discriminating against workers just because they are pregnant.

RIGHTS TO PRIVACY IN THE WORKPLACE

As an employee, you have certain privacy rights on the job. Your employer will collect a certain amount of information about you; most of this will end up in your personnel file. Employers are supposed to keep this information confidential, but very often do not. State and federal laws govern who can get access to your file and under what circumstances.

> **TEEN TIP**
>
> If you believe that an employer has given out confidential information about you, you should contact either your state labor department or an attorney to see what options are available to you.

Your employer may have access to information that will come as a surprise to you. For instance, your employer may have access to a great deal of medical information about you, especially if the employer is self-insured (meaning that the employer does not contract with an insurance company to pay your medical expenses; the employer pays them directly).

There are some employers who will want to require you to be tested for a genetic predisposition to certain diseases; if you find yourself in this situation, you should contact an attorney or your state labor department since there may be laws that prohibit the employer from requiring such a test.

> **TEEN TIP**
>
> If you believe that an employer has violated these acts, you can file a complaint with the Equal Employment Opportunity Commission.

Drug and Alcohol testing

There are a number of laws that deal with drug and alcohol testing of employees. As a general rule, the employer can legally require these tests of both prospective employees and, in certain instances, of employees already on the job.

Psychological Testing

Another testing issue is that of a psychological test for prospective employees. Many states have laws regulating their use, but it can be legal for you to have to take such a test.

> **TEEN TIP**
>
> If your employer requires a medical examination as a condition for hiring you, you should talk to an attorney or the labor department since there are numerous laws that regulate this procedure.

Lie Detector Testing

For the most part, it is now illegal for an employer to require you to take a lie detector test. There are a few exceptions, of course, mostly for jobs in the security industry and jobs that require you to handle drugs.

Credit Reports

When you apply for a job, your prospective employer can look at your credit report. That is why it is important to pay your bills on time and avoid as much as possible having negative credit information on your report. Employers use this report as a tool to help them evaluate whether you will be a responsible employee for them or not.

DRESS AND CONDUCT CODES

Your employer has the right to set up dress codes for the employees as well as conduct codes. For example, many companies prohibit their employees in supervisory positions from dating employees they supervise and many companies require their employees to wear uniforms.

DISABILITIES

Employees with disabilities are covered by the *Americans with Disabilities Act (ADA)*. While a thorough analysis of this law is too complex for this book, the law generally prohibits employers from discriminating against employees with disabilities. The employer must reasonably accommodate the disabled employee or prospective employee. For more information on this act, you can contact the Civil Rights Section of the United States Department of Justice.

LOSING YOUR JOB

In most instances, your employer can fire you for any reason or for no reason at all. This is called the *employment-at-will doctrine*. There are some jobs, such as jobs where you have an employment contract that sets out the reasons for which you can be fired, to which this doctrine does not apply. But for most jobs, it does.

If you are fired without cause, you may be entitled to receive *unemployment compensation*. Your state will have an unemployment benefits office that administers these claims and you should contact them for more information. They can be located by looking in the government pages of your phone book. If you were fired *for cause*, for example because you stole from your employer, you are not entitled to receive unemployment benefits. You are also ineligible if you quit voluntarily. The laws of each state are different, but you will usually receive a weekly benefit for a certain number of weeks. The particulars are determined by the law of your state.

JOB TIPS

As an employee, it is important that you follow all of your employer's rules. You should always be on time to work; have a good attitude while you are there; get along as well as possible with your co-workers and, especially, your supervisor; and not miss work unnecessarily. Call in sick only when you are really sick. A good employee will receive raises and promotions and a bad employee will eventually end up looking for another job.

–34–
DISCRIMINATION IN THE WORKPLACE

Federal law prohibits employers from discriminating against anyone on the basis of race, national origin, religion, or gender. The *Americans with Disabilities Act* (ADA) protects citizens with disabilities from discrimination. There are also laws that prohibit age discrimination, but these laws apply to older workers, not young ones.

These laws do not mean the job applicants are entitled to be hired for jobs even when they are not qualified for the job just because they are members of a class that cannot be discriminated against according to the law (*called a protected class*). Examples of protected classes are women (for gender discrimination) and African-Americans (for race discrimination).

AFFIRMATIVE ACTION
You may have heard references in the media to *affirmative action*. These are programs that are designed to help groups of people who have historically been discriminated against to achieve equality. Affirmative action programs do things like set *minority* goals for projects that receive federal funding. The purpose is to encourage project administrators to solicit minority bidders for contracts and to ensure that these classes of people have an equal chance to get the contract.

It is illegal for employers to award contracts and job positions and promotions to members of protected classes just because they are members of those classes. If someone unqualified for the position is hired or promoted based strictly on his status as a minority, that is also considered discrimination; it is called *reverse discrimination*. These rules apply to all workers, including workers under the age of eighteen.

GENDER DISCRIMINATION

An area of gender discrimination has to do with the issue of pay for women and men, also called *equal pay for equal work*. Federal law makes it illegal for women to be paid less than men in the same job.

Your state may have a state civil rights office that accepts complaints for discrimination. You will need as much documentation as you can get for your claim. You can file these complaints without hiring an attorney, but you should consider at least consulting one.

> ## TEEN TIP
>
> If you believe that you have been the victim of discrimination, you should file a complaint with the *Equal Employment Opportunity Commission* (EEOC).

Many attorneys will meet with you for an initial consultation for little or no cost, and this can be money and time well invested. A lawyer can help you determine whether what happened to you is legally actionable discrimination or not and they can help you to know what facts to include in your complaint and what to leave out.

If the EEOC does not act on your complaint, you can still file a civil lawsuit against your employer. (The EEOC will issue a "right to sue" letter.) Federal law requires you to file discrimination complaints with the EEOC before you go to court, but once you get the right to sue letter, you can then file your lawsuit. While you have a legal right to represent yourself, handling a civil rights/ discrimination lawsuit on your own will be very difficult.

SEXUAL HARASSMENT IN THE WORKPLACE

A subcategory of discrimination is sexual harassment. *Sexual harassment* consists of unwanted sexual advances or other offensive conduct that is sexual in nature, especially if the conduct is by someone in authority over the recipient. Just as with sexual harassment at school, there are two types of harassment at work.

One type is the *hostile environment* and the other is the *quid pro quo*. Hostile environment cases involve situations in which the harasser makes the work environment intolerable for the victim. In the other type of case, the victim is required to perform a sexual act in order to get a job benefit, like a raise or assignment or promotion. Both situations are illegal.

The first requirement for sexual harassment is that the offensive conduct be sexual in nature. Examples of sexual conduct, in addition to the outright proposition, are things like sexually explicit or pornographic pictures in open view in the workspace. Sexually explicit jokes and comments can also create a hostile environment.

Supervisor Harassment

Unwanted sexual advances by an employee's supervisor are the classic signs of sexual harassment. Although it is less clear cut and will require more proof of the overall work atmosphere, it is possible to have illegal sexual harassment of one co-worker by another. In those types of cases, it is important for the employer to be put on notice of what is happening.

The law says that, in cases of harassment by supervisors or other authority figures, the employer is presumed to know that the harassment is occurring; in co-worker harassment cases, this presumption does not apply. If the employer does not know what is happening, you cannot win your case against them because they are not responsible for what they do not know.

It is also illegal for employers to allow their employees to be harassed by the employer's customers or other salespeople. And while the most common cases involve men as the perpetrators of harassment and women as their victims, it is just as illegal for a woman to sexually harass a man.

Same-Sex Harassment

Another issue that has been litigated involves same-sex harassment. The Unites States Supreme Court has ruled that there can be a viable sexual harassment case when both employees are of the same gender. The same rules about hostile environment and quid pro quo apply in these cases as well.

Minors

The sexual harassment laws apply to minors just like they do to adults. That means that a minor can be guilty of sexual harassment and, if victimized, can recover damages.

You will need to be prepared to provide documentation of the harassment. In order to do this, you will need to keep a written log of the harassment; there is no magic formula for this log, but it should include the date and time of the harassment and a description of exactly what was said and done. You should also always notify your immediate supervisor. If that is the person who is harassing you, then you should notify the administrator at the next level.

TEEN TIP

If you are the victim of sexual harassment, you should file a claim with the *Equal Employment Opportunity Commission* (EEOC).

When you first notify your employer, and nothing is done to address your complaints, you might consider giving future notifications in writing as well as verbally. You should also consider consulting an attorney before you file with the EEOC to get advice about your case and what you will need to do to win.

SECTION V:

TEENS AND PROPERTY

–35–

TEENS AND PROPERTY OWNERSHIP

The right to own property and to manage it is determined by the age of majority in your state. If you have reached the age of majority, you have the right to own and manage property. If you are married, you also have this right in most states. In some states, an emancipation proceeding gives you this right; in other states, it does not. You will need to check the laws of your state to determine exactly where you stand.

But what happens if you have an ownership right to property and you are still considered a minor? As a minor, you may own the property, but lack the right to manage it. One way this situation occurs is when a minor's parent dies and the minor inherits property from the parent. This is not a problem if the property was left in trust, but that is not always the case. If there is no trust, there can be a problem.

The minor becomes the owner of the property when the parent dies, but the minor effectively cannot sell the property, because the minor lacks the legal capacity to enter into a contract that will be permanently binding on the minor. For more information about this issue, please refer to Chapter 36 on contracts.

GUARDIANS

In most cases, someone will have to go to court and set up a guardianship for the minor. This is a very expensive process, and it is best to avoid it if possible.

Guardianships require ongoing legal expenses and trips to court to show the court that

TEEN TIP

If the property you own is money in a bank account, there are special rules that may apply, and you will need to read Chapter 36 on contracts.

the property is being managed appropriately. A *guardian* is the person who is appointed by a judge to manage the property of the minor, and the guardian has a legal duty to act in the minor's best interest. The guardian will have to file regular reports with the court showing just exactly how the minor's property has been managed. The guardian owes a legal duty to the minor to manage the property carefully and conservatively.

One way to avoid the expense and extra trouble of a guardianship is to set up a *trust* to manage the property until the minor reaches legal adulthood. Another way is to transfer the property, as long as it is not real estate, into a special account under the *Uniform Transfers to Minors Act*. The property is managed by a *custodian* until the minor becomes an adult. This is much cheaper than a guardianship, and can be effective in many situations as a way to avoid the expense of *probate* court (the court that decides where someone's property goes when he or she dies).

The above information applies to major categories of property, like real estate, stocks, and bonds. Most personal belongings, like baseball card collections, sports equipment, and other smaller items can be bought and sold by the minor without any problem. Courts do not get into these smaller details of property ownership.

If a minor becomes the owner of property that would require a guardianship, the fact that a minor still has a living parent will not avoid the problems associated with minor's ownership of property. If the property is inherited by or given to just the minor, the parents have no ownership interest in the property and no inherent right to manage it. Of course, the parent can serve as the guardian or as the custodian of a Uniform Transfers to Minors account.

INHERITING FROM PARENTS

Minors can inherit property from their parents in one of two ways. If the parent has a will, the minor can be given property under the terms of the will. If the parent dies without a valid will, then state law determines who inherits the property.

Parents are not legally obligated to leave anything to their children, however; they can completely disinherit one of their children and leave property to the other children if they wish. They can also disinherit all of their children. Furthermore, the parents are not obligated to divide their property equally among their children.

All state laws give some or all of a deceased parent's property to the children if the parent dies without a will. This is true even if the children are adopted; they are treated the same as a biological child would be. The exact percentage belonging to the child depends on whether the deceased parent has a surviving spouse or not; a surviving spouse is entitled to a percentage of the property.

If the parents have more than one child, the siblings share the property equally. If your parents were never legally married to each other, you may have to go to court to prove *paternity* (establishing that a man is the father through a blood test) before you can inherit from your father.

DEATH OF MINORS

If a minor dies owning property, state law determines who inherits the property. Minors cannot have legally binding wills, so there is no way around the state law division. If the minor has children, the children would inherit the property. If the minor does not have children, then the parents will inherit.

NOTE: *Once the minor becomes an adult, all of these problems go away because the minor has acquired the right to manage his or her own property.*

–36–
SIGNING CONTRACTS

As a general rule, individuals under eighteen do not have the legal capacity to sign contracts. This is because most states set eighteen as the age of majority. If, however, you are legally considered an adult by your state, then you can sign a legally binding contract.

There is nothing that makes it illegal for a minor to sign a contract. It is just that most businesses that require written contracts will not deal with you or allow you to sign because the law says that contracts signed by minors are voidable at the minor's insistence.

Getting out of the contract is called *disaffirming* the contract. That means that you could force the other party to the contract to perform all of their obligations under the contract but they would not have that same protection because you could get out of the contract if you changed your mind about the deal.

As with most areas of law, there are exceptions to that general rule. For instance, if the contract was for *necessaries* for you, you would still have to honor the contract. Necessaries, as you might expect from the word, means contracts to provide you with things that you need to live. Food, clothing, shelter, and medical care are examples of necessaries.

As a practical matter, though, people will be reluctant to sign a contract with you while you are under age even for necessaries. If you do sign such a contract, your parents can be required to fulfill your contractual obligations if you do not. That means if you sign a contract for an apartment because you need a place to live and you are under eighteen, your parents could have to pay your rent if you fail to pay. Of course, failing to pay your bills can cause you to end up with a bad *credit rating*. If your parents *cosign* with you and you do not pay, your parents could also end up with negative information on their *credit report*.

BANKING

Another exception to the general rule relates to banking. Every state has passed some version of a uniform law that allows minors to open bank accounts. Without this special law, you could not open an account because that would require the bank to enter into a contract with you to establish the terms of your account. This law gets around that problem by specifically authorizing banks and credit unions to open deposit accounts for minors.

Under that law, the minor has full rights to the account, and the parents do not have any rights to it unless the minor agrees to put the parent on the account. The minor is the only one who can make withdrawals from that account. This allows minors to have checking accounts as well as other deposit accounts such as savings accounts. The minor is bound to the account terms with the bank and cannot get out of that contract based on his or her age.

INSURANCE

Some states also have laws that specifically authorize minors to sign legally binding contracts for insurance. This means that, in those states, you can purchase your own car insurance without your parents' assistance. However, insurance rates for minors are much higher than those for adults over age twenty-five, and you will probably find it much better to be covered on your parents' policy.

EDUCATION

There are also laws that permit minors to sign binding contracts for educational purposes. This allows those who are still not legal adults but who are enrolled in college or trade schools to legally contract with the school and to borrow money so that then can legally obtain school loans.

CANCELLING CONTRACTS

If you buy a bicycle from your neighbor down the street when you are sixteen and sign a contract with him to make monthly payments for the bike, you cannot cancel the contract based on your age and then keep the bike without paying for it. If you decide to cancel, you will have to return the bike.

It is only the minor who has the right to cancel the contract. If your neighbor changes his mind and wants his bike back, you do not have to return the bike as long as you have fully complied with the contract by making your payments on time. Once you reach eighteen, however, you can no longer cancel the contract even though you were still a minor when you signed it.

GETTING IT IN WRITING

If you are entering into an agreement with someone, it is always safer to make the agreement a written one. A contract is basically just a document that sets out the rights and obligations of each party. Sometimes verbal agreements can be enforced in court and sometimes they cannot, so you should get a written contract.

TEEN TIP

If you are a minor and enter into a contract that you later cancel based on your age, you will have to return anything you received under the contract.

In our bicycle example, your written agreement would need to say that your neighbor, Joe Blow, was selling his red mountain bike to you for a hundred dollars and that you would pay Joe a down payment of fifteen dollars and pay the balance off at the rate of ten dollars per month until the balance was paid. You would also need to say what day of the month your payments would be due and when the first payment was due. This is because a contract must contain all of the basic terms of the agreement.

CO-SIGNERS

If an adult *co-signs* on a contract with a minor, that means that the adult has also agreed to be responsible for complying with the contract just like the minor. If the minor does not do what he is supposed to according to the contract, then the adult would have to do whatever the minor had failed to do.

Let's go back to our bicycle example and assume that Joe did not trust you to make the payments so he asked your mother to cosign the contract. If she agrees and signs, then she will have to pay Joe for the bicycle if you quit making you payments. While you may be able to cancel the contract because you were under age, your mother cannot cancel on that basis. She is obligated to pay even if you do not.

BREACH OF CONTRACT

If one of the parties to the contract does not do what he or she is supposed to according to the contract, then he or she has *breached* the contract. The person who didn't breach can sue the person who breached the contract. A judge can either make the person pay money for breaching the contract or enter a court order making the person do whatever it was he or she did not do.

As a minor, if you breach a contract, you can be sued. You can also sue if someone does not honor a contract with you. Please see Chapter 37 on suing and being sued for more information about how this is done.

TEEN TIP

If you are considering signing a contract, you should check the laws of your state to determine exactly what the rules are.

AUTHORIZATION TO SIGN CONTRACTS

Your state may have laws that authorize minors to sign other types of contracts. There may also be different rules about what kinds of contracts you can cancel based on your age and what kinds you cannot.

SECTION VI:

TEENS AND THE COURTS

–37–
SUING AND BEING SUED

There are generally two kinds of cases: civil and criminal. A *criminal case* is filed when someone is accused of violating a *penal law*. These laws are simply the sets of laws that have been passed by the state legislature that determine whether or not a specific act is a crime. The law has to say that the act is a crime for it to be classified as one. For example, robbing someone's house is a crime because there is a law that says it is.

Agreeing to paint someone's house and then not doing a good job may result in the homeowner suing you and getting a court order that says you have to pay for the damage you caused, but it is not a crime. This is an example of the other type of case, the *civil case*. Any case that is not criminal is classified as a civil case.

Within the civil category are many different kinds of lawsuits. There can be *civil rights* suits like many of the cases discussed in the school section. There can be *employment* related lawsuits, for example when you file a claim against your employer for not paying you what you were owed. *Breach of contract* is another kind of suit; these suits are filed when there is a dispute between the parties to a contract.

Other suits are called *tort* suits. These suits include cases about car accidents. Other examples are suits that are filed when someone falls in a store and gets hurt or a suit against a doctor for poor medical treatment, called a *medical malpractice* suit. A tort is basically a wrong committed that causes harm. It can also be a crime, but it is not necessarily one.

For instance, if you hit someone, you can be charged criminally with assault. The person you hit can also file a civil tort suit against you to make you pay money to reimburse him for the damages you caused. In that example, you could be ordered to pay his medical bills and repay him or her for any wages he or she lost while recovering from the injuries you caused. You could also have to pay him money for the pain he or she suffered.

For example, let's say that you were driving your car down the street near your house. You were busy talking to your friends and changing the radio station and did not notice that there was a stop sign at the next intersection. You drove into the intersection without looking and without stopping, and hit another car. The police could give you a ticket for running the stop sign. Although you will not be sent to jail for running the stop sign, it is a violation of the traffic laws and is a type of criminal case.

TEEN TIP

As a teenager, if you do something that caused another person harm, you can be sued in a civil suit. Your parents do not also have to be sued unless there is some state law that makes them equally liable with you.

Let's also assume that the driver of the other car was hurt in the wreck. She ended up with a sore neck and a broken leg and was too hurt to go to work for several days. She would file a claim against your insurance policy in most instances and the insurance company would pay her medical bills and other damages. If she could not work out a deal with the insurance company, she would file suit against you. Your insurance company would hire a lawyer and handle that case for you and pay if the judge or jury said that the accident was your fault and you owed the other driver money.

But what if, instead of a car accident, you got caught spray painting an insult on the side of your former best friend's house after the two of you had a fight. Your friend's father caught you in the act. The father could sue you for the costs to get the paint off his house. Because most states have laws that make parents liable for intentional property damage caused by their children, the friend's father could also sue your parents in court for the damages. This is not the type of thing that would be covered by insurance, so the money would have to be paid by you and your parents out of your own pockets.

Most states have laws that say that minors cannot file lawsuits themselves. If you are the one who wants to file a suit, your lawsuit will have to be filed by one of your parents, or your legal guardian if you do not live with your parents. The person who files this suit for you is sometimes called a *next friend*.

If you win your lawsuit and the other person has to pay you money, the judge may not give the money directly to you if you are still a minor when the case is concluded.

This issue is handled differently from state to state and case to case, but the judge may set up some kind of trust that has someone else mange the money for you until you are eighteen. Sometimes, your parent will be the one who gets to manage the money, but in other instances it may be the court system that manages the money. Once you become an adult, the money is turned over to you.

Sometimes, children want to sue their parents. In some instances, they can. For example, if you are hurt in a car accident and your parent was the driver, you can file a claim against your parent for your injuries. Of course, insurance will generally cover that claim. You can also sue your parent if they have abused you or if they have failed to fulfill their obligation to support you with the basic necessities.

HOW A LAWSUIT WORKS

A civil suit is begun by filing a document called a *complaint* or *original petition*. This paper tell the judge who you are suing and why. The person who files the suit is called the *plaintiff*. The person who is getting sued is the *defendant*. The "why" of your lawsuit is called the *cause of action*. Breach of contract is a cause of action; so is negligence in operating your car.

A suit is filed by taking the complaint or petition to the clerk's office and paying a filing fee. Once the suit is filed, the defendant has to be *served with* (be handed) the suit. Methods of service differ from state to state, but this basically means that someone who is authorized by the courts to serve papers hands the defendant a copy of the petition or complaint that was filed.

The defendant then files a document in court called an *answer*. The answer just denies the claims in the complaint and says that one should not have to pay the plaintiff. If the defendant does not file this response, the plaintiff can go to court and get the judge to enter a judgment against him or her without saying in advance. If you ever find out that you are being sued, you and your parents should contact an attorney right away and set up a meeting. There is additional information about hiring and working with an attorney in Chapter 38.

If the plaintiff and defendant can reach an agreement, then the case is settled. If not, then you will have a trial. Either the judge or a jury will decide who wins the case. The judge enters a judgment against the person who lost. The judgment may be to make the loser pay money to the winner or to take some specific action or both. The losing party then has a certain number of days (this number is determined by state law) to appeal to the next highest court.

The first court to hear the case is called the *trial court*. It may be labeled something like county court, district court, or superior court. It can either be a state court or a federal court. Federal courts hear cases that involve either violations of federal laws or disputes between residents of different states. State courts can also hear civil cases that involve federal law in addition to the cases they hear that involve state law.

APPEALING

After the case is heard by the trial court, it can just end there if neither side *appeals*. Most cases end at this point because it costs a lot of money to appeal. If you do appeal, your next stop is the *court of appeals*. State court cases are appealed to a state appeals court. Federal cases go to the Circuit Court of Appeals that hears cases from your state. The country is divided into regions called circuits, and all states belong to a specific region.

If you still aren't happy with the result in appeals court, then state cases can be appealed first to the *state supreme court* and then to the *United States Supreme Court*. Federal cases go straight from the Circuit Court of Appeals to the U.S. Supreme Court. The U.S. Supreme Court does not have to hear your case just because you ask it to.

The justices vote on which cases to accept, and they usually take only cases of national importance (like the case of how to count the votes in the presidential election between Vice President Gore and President Bush) or cases where the various states and circuit courts have different opinions on the same area of law. The U.S. Supreme Court has the final word on the law, and what they say in one case applies to every other case in every other state.

–38–
ROLE OF THE LAWYER

As with anything, there are advantages and disadvantages to having an attorney represent you in your lawsuit or give you advice about your rights and legal duties. As a minor, you may find yourself working with an attorney. Even though your parents may be the ones who sign the contract with the attorney and pay the bill, if the attorney is representing you, you will be the client in most instances.

With the exception of the confidentiality issues discussed in Chapter 31, the lawyer will work with both you and your parents. The following information should be helpful to both you and your parents if you are thinking of hiring a lawyer.

ADVANTAGES OF HAVING A LAWYER

The advantages are fairly obvious. An attorney knows the law, the rules of evidence, and the rules of procedure; these are all things you will be responsible for knowing just as if you were a lawyer if you represent yourself. The lawyer also has experience in trying cases, and will know what evidence will be most helpful to you in trial and what evidence will hurt your chances of victory.

Complications that only an attorney would notice can arise in many cases. If you mishandle your case, it may not be possible for an attorney to fix it later. Even if they can, it will usually be much more expensive than if you had just hired them in the first place.

Another advantage the attorney has is objectivity. You are a party to the case, and, as such, you have a big emotional investment in the outcome. Lawsuits can be very stressful, but your attorney will be able to help you maintain perspective and help you make decisions regarding your case with a clearer head and with more emotional distance. Also, you may be taken more seriously in court if you have an attorney. Having an attorney also reduces the chance that you will have fatal drafting errors in your *pleadings* and *final orders*. You may be able to keep your case moving faster, since most attorneys have a heavy caseload and sometimes work on your case will come behind work on other cases, but the attorney has more experience in working within the system. And, finally, you will not have to be responsible for all of the administrative details that go along with a lawsuit if you hire an attorney.

ADVANTAGES TO REPRESENTING YOURSELF

This freedom from details comes at a price. Cost is the main advantage to representing yourself. Depending on the type of case, most lawyers will either handle the case on a contingency (percentage of winnings) fee or charge you an hourly rate, and require some sort of retainer (money up front) to be paid before they will begin work on your case. The hourly rate will vary, depending on your geographical location, the years of experience the lawyer has, the type of case it is, and the complexity of the case.

Personal injury cases, like car accident cases, are usually handled on a contingency fee. This means that you do not pay the attorney any money until your case settles. The attorney will take a percentage of the money you get; the percentage will be set by the contract you sign with the lawyer and will depend on where in the process your case ends. Contingency fees generally range from one-third to one-half. In an hourly fee case, you should always receive an itemized bill from your lawyer so that you know how your money is being spent.

You need to be prepared to pay for all things done by the lawyer that relate to your case. This includes talking to you on the phone, talking to the other attorney, and writing letters.

SELECTING AN ATTORNEY

If you decide that the advantages of having a lawyer to represent you outweigh the disadvantages, you will face the problem of selecting an attorney. It is important that you hire an attorney that is knowledgeable and experienced in the type of law your case concerns. Law can be a very specialized field, and attorneys do not handle all kinds of cases. You should be sure the attorney you select has experience in the area of law you are dealing with.

You also need to feel comfortable working with that lawyer. It does not matter how good a lawyer is if you are not comfortable with them. You should feel like all of your questions are being answered and answered correctly. There are some answers no lawyer can give you, particularly as to the final outcome. No attorney can guarantee you what the outcome of a contested case will be, and you should be wary of anyone who says they will give you a 100% guarantee.

If you do not already know a good *domestic relations lawyer*, there are several sources for referrals. One of the best ways to find a lawyer is through someone you know. Ask around to get names from acquaintances of lawyers they have worked with and liked. In larger cities, the local bar association will maintain a referral list. You might also check with your employer as many offer a prepaid legal plan or a plan for discounted legal services as an employment benefit.

TEEN TIP

If you are a low income individual, you may be eligible for services from a legal clinic.

Most large cities offer some form of low-cost legal clinic. You can always check the phone book and the Internet as well. Many law firms maintain websites that provide information about their firm. There is a website that has information and referral links, **www.findlaw.com**. There is also a legal directory called Martindale-Hubbell that contains information about law firms and lawyers. Not all attorneys are listed, and the absence of a listing does not mean an attorney is not good.

Feel free to schedule consultations with more than one lawyer. Many will give you a free initial consultation; others may require a small fee. You should be able to find out in advance what the charge will be. When you meet with the lawyer, do not be hesitant about asking the attorney about his or her educational background and experience.

You should also come away from your initial consultation with a good idea of how the lawyer plans to handle your case and what you can expect during the course of the *litigation* (case in court). You should have confidence in this person. And, remember, if at any time you become dissatisfied, you can fire that lawyer and hire another.

BUILDING A RELATIONSHIP WITH YOUR ATTORNEY

Once you have made the decision to hire an attorney, there are several things you can do to make the experience better.

Ask Questions

One of the keys to a good relationship with your lawyer is to understand what is going on with your case and the law that applies to it. If you do not understand something, keep asking questions until you do. The law can be complicated and you should not be embarrassed if you do not understand something the first time. Your lawyer should be willing to take whatever time is necessary to answer your questions.

On the other hand, once you do understand, do not keep covering the same ground over and over. Also, do not waste the lawyer's time complaining about the unfairness of the legal system. This is frustrating for the lawyer and costly for you. You are paying for the lawyer's time, and complaining about things that are not within the attorney's control accomplishes nothing.

Tell Your Lawyer Everything

It is also important that you tell your lawyer everything that might apply to your case. It is much better to let your lawyer decide what is important; things that may not seem important to you may in fact be very critical. If you withhold information because it is damaging or makes you look bad, your lawyer will not be able to prepare properly for your case and minimize the damage this information will cause when it comes out in trial. Remember, anything you tell your lawyer is *confidential*.

Be Realistic

Another key to being satisfied with the way your case is handled is to be realistic. In many more instances than you may realize going in, the system is not going to work the way you think it should. The law may seem unfair to you and you may not understand why the procedures are the way they are.

However, these are things over which your lawyer has no control and, being angry with your attorney does not help either one of you. It may, however, damage the working relationship between the two of you. When you find yourself in that situation, do not vent your frustration; instead, accept the situations and do your best to work with your attorney within the system to get the best outcome you can.

Be Patient

You will also need to be patient. Our legal system will often move at a frustratingly slow pace. In many places, the courts are very busy and it may take a long time before your case can be heard. There is nothing either you or your lawyer can do about this, and you will simply have to accommodate your schedule to that of the court.

You also need to have some patience with your lawyer. You are not the only client your lawyer has, and it is unrealistic to expect your attorney to always be available to you. Lawyers often spend a significant amount of time in court. When in court, they devote their full attention to that client and that case, and they will have to get back to you at another time. When your time comes to go to court, you will expect this same treatment. So you will need to understand when your lawyer takes several hours, or maybe even a day or more, to return your call.

Talk to the Assistant, Too

When these things happen, talking to the secretary or assistant can be a big help. There are many questions that this person can answer for you. This enables you to get the information you need more quickly and less expensively. Many lawyers now use a voice mail system for messages. If this is the case, do not just leave your name and phone number. Tell the lawyer why you are calling and what information you need. That way, if the attorney calls you back and gets your voice mail or answering machine, they may be able to leave you the information you need without a long game of telephone tag.

Be Concise

It is important that you not become a pest. When you need information from your lawyer or need to pass information to him or her, be organized when you call. Get your questions answered, find out what happens next, when you should expect to hear something, and then finish your call. Do not make frequent, unnecessary calls, as this just runs up your bill and irritates the lawyer. You should also always be on time–both for appointments and for court settings.

Pay Your Bill

Pay your bill on time. Clients who pay on time almost always get prompt attention. While you should review your bill carefully and be sure you understand the fee arrangements, you should not have to discuss each item with the attorney.

Ask before Acting

Finally, before taking any action related at all to your case on your own, ask your lawyer first. Decisions and actions while the case is pending are important and can dramatically impact the final outcome.

–39–
JUVENILES AND THE CRIMINAL JUSTICE SYSTEM

Hopefully, you will never find yourself charged with violating a criminal law. But, if you do, this chapter will provide some information about what you can expect. How your case will be handled depends greatly on whether you are considered an adult or a juvenile. Adults and juveniles are treated differently and processed through different systems.

The first question to answer is which system applies to you. This is a matter that is determined by the laws of your state, your age, and the law that you are accused of violating.

AGE OF MAJORITY
Each state sets the age at which you must go through the adult criminal system. In most states, this will either be seventeen or eighteen. In Appendix B, you will find a reference to the *age of majority*; this is not necessarily the age limit that applies to the criminal system. The age of majority deals with civil matters, and your state legislature can set a different age for the criminal system. A *civil matter* is any legal matter that is not criminal, and includes things like contracts, marriage, employment, family law, and car wrecks.

Once you reach the age specified by the laws of your state, you will automatically be charged and tried in the adult criminal system. But even if you are less than that age, you may still be subject to prosecution as an adult. Most states have laws that say that people who would otherwise be treated as juveniles can have their cases transferred to adult criminal court under certain circumstances. We will address these situations later and will first direct our attention to the juvenile justice system.

Although your state may have a different limit, many states use eighteen as the line that differentiates juveniles from adults. In all states, you cannot be treated as a juvenile if you were over eighteen when the crime was committed. If you are treated as a juvenile under the laws of your state and you are put in a juvenile placement, however, you can be held until you are twenty- one.

DELINQUENCY

In the juvenile system, you are not convicted of a crime; instead, you are found to be a delinquent child. This is called an *"adjudication."* The reason for this is the differing purposes of the adult criminal system and the juvenile justice system. The adult criminal system is designed to punish wrongdoing while the juvenile system's purpose is to rehabilitate.

Although there are differences between the states, there is also a great deal of common ground in how states treat juvenile offenders. This is because there are several federal laws that apply and several sets of laws that the states have passed that are all modeled on the same format. Although some of the terminology and procedures will vary, most of the information that follows will be the same in every state.

Although a proceeding in juvenile court is not called a criminal charge, it usually is the result of the violation of some law by a juvenile. Habitual truancy can cause a teenager to end up in juvenile court. So can more serious crimes like robbery and murder. One word of warning, however: if you are over fourteen in most states (although this can be younger in some states), being charged with a serious crime like murder can get your case transferred to adult court.

PLEAS AND DISPOSITION

Because juvenile court is considered a civil court and not a criminal court, you are not *indicted* (charged) by a *grand jury* (a group of people that decides whether there is enough evidence against you). The reason for this is that, in juvenile court, you do not get an adult criminal record so different rules apply. This means that you do not have to say anything that admits to a crime. Instead, the state files what is generally called either a *petition* or *complaint* against you. When you enter your plea, it is not the "guilty" or "not guilty" that you are familiar with. Instead, you will plead "true" or "not true." If the judge finds that you committed whatever act with which you are charged, then the allegation will be found to be true and the court will decide that you are a *delinquent child*.

Instead of the judge imposing a sentence on you as would happen in adult court, the judge will make a *disposition order*. The judge has several options for disposition. The judge will consider factors like your age, the seriousness of whatever it was that you did, and your previous history.

Probation

One option is to place you on juvenile probation. In that situation, you still get to live at home, but you have to comply with a list of rules, called *conditions of probation*. Typical of these rules are:

- ◆ some sort of curfew, which will be much earlier than a regular juvenile curfew ordinance;
- ◆ a requirement that you obey the rules at home and follow your parents' instructions;
- ◆ a requirement that you maintain decent grades at school and an excellent attendance record there;
- ◆ a schedule to regularly report to a juvenile probation officer and pay a monthly probation fee; and,
- ◆ a dollar amount to be paid to the victim of your actions to reimburse them for any damages you caused.

You may also have to do *community service*, which is basically volunteer type work, at a location or agency selected by the judge or probation department. The judge can also tell you that you cannot hang around with certain people (these will generally be the friends with whom you have been getting in trouble) and you can be ordered to undergo drug testing. If you violate any of these rules, the judge can modify your disposition and send you into a placement away from home.

Before you are put on probation, the court will have the probation department prepare a report about you to help determine whether or not you are a candidate for probation. This is usually called a *pre-disposition report*, and will cover issues including your home situation, your family situation, and your performance at school. The judge will rely on the recommendation made by the probation department in making a final decision on your disposition.

If the judge does not put you on probation, then you will be committed to some sort of placement. There may be some placements in your city or near your home area, or you may be sent to a state juvenile correction facility.

Teen Court

In some places, another alternative may be available to you. It is teen court, and is a program that uses teenagers to serve in the role of prosecutor, defense attorney, and judge. Other teens will also serve as the jury. Before you are eligible for teen court, you will have to admit to the offense. Teen court is not set up to determine whether you are guilty of violating the law or not; it just lets your peers determine your punishment.

Felony Sentencing

In some states, the legislatures have passed rules that impact juveniles charged with serious felonies. Even if you are not transferred to adult criminal court, you can receive a lengthy sentence from the juvenile court, such as a sentence of forty years in prison. Until you are eighteen, you serve the time in the juvenile correction facility. On your eighteenth birthday, you are transferred to adult prison to serve the remainder of your sentence.

PROCEDURE

When you are first accused of a crime and arrested, you will be taken to a juvenile detention facility. It may be a totally separate facility; in smaller towns, it will be a separate part of the jail. Juveniles are supposed to be kept separate from the adult jail population. As soon as possible, you will be taken before the juvenile detention judge for a detention hearing. At that first hearing, the judge will decide whether to release you into the custody of your parents or to hold you in detention. You can be held for up to ten days at a time.

If the judge says you have to stay in *detention*, you will have another hearing in ten days. That process repeats itself as long as you remain in detention. As soon as you are taken into custody, the authorities will notify your parents that you are in custody; however, because juvenile proceedings are not legally considered criminal, you are not entitled to post *bail* and get out of detention. You have to stay until the judge decides you can leave.

The judge will make the decision on how long you have to stay in detention based on the overall circumstances, your family situation, your previous history, the nature of the acts that got you placed into detention, and your behavior while you have been held in detention. The judge will also take into consideration how likely they think it is that you will get into trouble again if they let you out.

CONSTITUTIONAL PROTECTIONS

Although juvenile court is not technically a criminal proceeding and you do not get an adult criminal record, juveniles do still get some of the same constitutional protections that adults have in criminal court. The state still has to prove the allegations against you *beyond a reasonable doubt* (a lot more likely than not that you did the crime).

Double jeopardy also applies, which means that you cannot be tried twice for the same offense. You have the right to confront the witnesses that the state has against you and to cross-examine those witnesses.

You also still have your Fifth Amendment right to not *incriminate* yourself. This means that you do not have to say anything that admits to a crime. And, any time the proceedings could result in your placement in a juvenile correction facility, you have the right to have an attorney represent you. If you and your family cannot afford an attorney, the state will appoint one for you. You should always take advantage of this right and never try to represent yourself in a juvenile proceeding.

You also have the right to be officially informed about these rights by the police officers when you are arrested. These are called the *Miranda* warnings. They are named after the case in which the United States Supreme Court first ruled that anyone who was under arrest had to be told about the rights they have.

One constitutional right you do not have is the right to a jury trial. The decisions in your case will be made by a judge unless your state has a specific law that authorizes jury trials for juveniles.

CONFESSING

A particular area of interest in juvenile proceedings is obtaining and using a confession by the juvenile accused of a crime. You do not have to talk to law enforcement officials, but if you do and confess to a violation of a criminal law, this admission can be used against you in court. Of course, the confession must be voluntary, and the police are forbidden from *coercing* (persuading in a manipulative manner) a confession.

In deciding whether a confession was voluntary, the judge will consider factors such as your age, your maturity and intelligence level, and your ability to understand the consequences of confessing. Let's look at the leading case in this area.

In Re Gault, a 1966 United States Supreme Court case, Gerald Gault and a friend were taken into custody as the result of a verbal complaint made by a neighbor about an obscene phone call. This was not Gerald's first trip to the police station; he was already on probation for six months for theft.

Gerald's parents were not told that Gerald had been taken to the police station, and they spent the evening looking for him. Finally, they tracked him down and went to the detention center to pick him up. The officer on duty told them Gerald could not come home, but that a hearing would be held the next day.

The state filed a basic petition, which did not really contain any specific allegations against Gerald. It just said that he should be adjudicated as a delinquent. The petition was never given to Gerald's parents.

The hearing, such as it was, took place in the judge's office. The neighbor who made the complaint was not there to testify against Gerald, there were no other witnesses sworn in to testify, and there was no court reporter to make the official transcript of the proceedings. The judge questioned Gerald about the phone call, and he admitted to participating in the call but denied making the most offensive of the statements. At the end of the hearing, the judge said Gerald had to stay in detention. No time limit was set, but Gerald ended up getting sent home three days later.

Another hearing was scheduled, and the parents were notified only by a note from the police officer. Once again, the neighbor was not there to testify, and there was some dispute as to exactly what Gerald admitted to doing and what he denied. At the end of this hearing, Gerald was committed to the State Industrial School until he was twenty-one. Interestingly enough, if Gerald had been an adult, the maximum punishment he could have received was a fine of between five and fifty dollars and two months in jail. Instead, he ended up being ordered confined in the juvenile facility for six years.

He and his parents appealed, claiming that the whole process had been unfair to Gerald. The Supreme Court agreed, ruling for the first time that juveniles were entitled to fair notice of the charges, a right to confront the witnesses against him (the neighbor who received the call in this case), and the right to have an attorney. The Court also said that Gerald should have been told of his Fifth

(continued)

Amendment right not to say anything incriminating that could be used against him. Additionally, the Court said that, with juveniles, officials must take special care to insure that any confessions made by a juvenile are really voluntary and not coerced in any way.

USE OF JUVENILE RECORDS

Now, let's assume that you have a juvenile criminal record and maybe have spent time in a juvenile correction facility. Can that record be used against you later? For what purposes? The answer is yes, there are instances in which your juvenile record can be used again. If you get into trouble again as a juvenile, the courts will have access to your records and your history will have an impact on the dispositions made in any future case.

Your juvenile record can also be considered in some instances in adult criminal court. It will be used for assessing punishment in that case and can cause you to get a greater penalty in adult court than you would have, had you not had a juvenile record. It is not used as a direct method to increase the penalty as regular adult convictions can be used, but it is used in the preparation of the *pre-sentence investigation and report* when you have been convicted of a felony.

A pre-sentence report is a report prepared by the probation department. It covers your family, employment, school, and criminal history situations and makes a recommendation to the judge about whether or not you should be given probation or put in jail (or a placement if you are in juvenile court). (In adult court, convictions can result in the law mandating a more severe minimum punishment that if it were your first offense.)

The judges use that report to determine whether you should be placed on probation as punishment for the felony or

> **TEEN TIP**
>
> Even if you are a juvenile who never gets into trouble again, if the original case involved a sex offense, you could be required to register as a sex offender for the rest of your life.

sentenced to serve time in prison. The reason the law allows juvenile records to be used in this way is to identify those individuals with a history of criminal activity who have clearly not been rehabilitated by the juvenile system.

But, for many teenagers, it only takes one trip through the system for them to change their ways. For those individuals, there is a desire by many states to give them a fresh start and not hold their juvenile problems against them forever. For that reason, many states have passed laws that allow a juvenile's records to be destroyed if the juvenile meets the requirements of the statute. Usually, the statute requires some period of time to pass without any further charges of criminal activity after the juvenile becomes an adult. Most states say that, once that period of time passes, the state will automatically destroy the records. Other states, rather than destroying the records, will have the *records sealed*. When the records are sealed, they can only be reopened if the juvenile consents and a court order approving the reopening is obtained.

While the record is in existence, it is a confidential record and can only be accessed by court and law enforcement personnel. Additionally, juveniles do not have to answer yes when asked if they have been convicted of a crime at jobs, on school applications, on apartment applications, or anything.

ADULT PROCEEDINGS FOR JUVENILES

Most states have provisions for children under eighteen to be tried as an adult when they commit certain acts. Each state sets the age at which this can happen; fourteen is a common age but it is younger in some states. The state law will set out a list of crimes that can trigger transfer to adult court. Generally, these crimes are the more serious felonies like murder, rape, and robbery.

If you are old enough under the laws of your state to be treated as an adult and you are charged with one of the crimes on the list in your state, your case will start out in the juvenile court. The transfer to adult court is not automatic, but is a decision that is made by the juvenile judge after conducting a hearing in juvenile court. Once your case is transferred, you are treated just like you would be if you were already legally an adult. If you are sent to prison, it will be to adult prison and not to a juvenile facility, even if you are still under eighteen.

The one exception is that, in death penalty states, juveniles that have been transferred to adult court may not be eligible for the death penalty. In a case that could result in death for an adult charged with the same crime, the juvenile's maximum sentence will be life in prison.

THE ADULT CRIMINAL SYSTEM

Once you are old enough under the laws of your state to be charged as an adult, you no longer deal with the juvenile justice system. Instead, you go through the adult criminal system.

When you are charged with a crime as an adult, you are arrested and placed in jail. You are entitled to have a reasonable bail set. This amount will be set based on the charges against you. When that happens, you will either have to post the entire amount of the bail in cash to get out of jail or you will have to hire a *bonding company* to post the bond for you. You, or someone who is willing to post the bond for you, will have to pay the bonding company a percentage of the bond amount (often ten or fifteen percent). If you do not post the bond, you do not get out of jail. You will have to stay in jail until your case is concluded.

There are two classes of crimes: *misdemeanors* and *felonies*. *Misdemeanors* are the less serious crimes and *felonies* the more serious ones. If you are charged with a misdemeanor, your case does not go before a grand jury and you are not indicted. Instead, the state files what is usually called an *information*. This is a piece of paper that sets out the elements of the crime with which you are accused.

In most states, if you are accused of a felony, the state must present these allegations to a grand jury. This jury does not decide whether or not you are guilty; their role is to decide whether or not there is enough evidence to justify charges being filed against you. If they think there is enough evidence, then you are indicted. If there is not enough evidence, then you are not indicted and your case is over. If you are indicted, then you will either have to plead guilty or have a trial.

If you plead guilty, you will be convicted of the charge to which you pled guilty. If you plead not guilty, you will have a trial. You can be found guilty and convicted or found not guilty. Once you have been convicted, you will receive a sentence, or punishment, of some sort. The options for that punishment are either for you to be put on probation or sentenced to jail. You can also be fined. The maximum length of the jail term and the fine are set by state law and depend on the charge. The more serious the offense, the longer the jail time and the higher the fine.

You may also have to perform a certain number of hours of community service; in some states, community service is a mandatory part of any probationary sentence. You will have conditions of probation that you must follow, such as reporting to a probation officer, paying a monthly probation fee, and undergoing random drug testing. If you fail to abide by the conditions, your probation can be revoked and you can be sent to jail.

Conviction in Adult Court

Once you are convicted of a crime in adult court, that conviction permanently remains a part of your record. Those records will not be sealed or destroyed. A criminal record can keep you from joining the military, getting into college, renting an apartment, or getting the job you want. Remember, if you are convicted of a sexual crime, you could have to register as a sex offender for the rest of your life.

Plea Bargain

Many cases are resolved by a *plea bargain*. That just means that you and your attorney and the attorney for the state reach an agreement as to what your punishment will be instead of letting a judge or jury decide what the punishment will be.

Constitutional Rights

When you are charged with a crime in the adult system, you do have constitutional protections. You have a right to have a jury trial, to confront and cross-examine the witnesses the state has against you, and the right not to incriminate yourself. You also have the right to have an attorney, and you should always have an attorney to represent you in a criminal case. It is never wise to try to represent yourself when you may be faced with spending time in jail. If the judge finds that you qualify, you can get a court-appointed attorney.

–40–
DEPENDENCY AND NEGLECT CASES

Each state has an agency that is responsible for investigating child abuse and neglect cases. If it can be done without any danger to the child, the agency will try to keep the family together. This is done by offering services to the family; which services are offered depends on the facts of each case and the needs of the family. Frequently, the parents will be required to undergo counseling and a psychological evaluation; the children may have to participate in these services as well. The parents may also have to go to parenting classes to learn how to be better parents.

If the children would be in danger by staying at home with their parents, then the state agency will remove the children and place them in foster care. If the parents cooperate with the state agency and correct the problems that led to having their children taken away, then the children may be allowed to be return home to live. If not, then the parents' rights to the children can be terminated and the children placed for adoption. Sometimes, the children may go to live with another relative instead of being adopted by strangers.

The two conditions that warrant the removal of children from their parents' care are abuse and neglect. *Abuse* is an obvious category–any sort of child abuse will qualify, whether it is physical abuse or sexual abuse. *Neglect* can be in the form of a parent's failure to meet the child's basic needs. It can also occur when the parent leaves children unsupervised or abandons them. The state can also intervene in cases where the parents are not getting their children the medical care they need.

ABUSE
When a report of abuse is received, the agency will prioritize the report. Children that are in immediate danger can be taken from their parents

right away and kept in foster care while the investigation is done. The children have no right to decide to stay if they want. If the risk level to the child is lower, then the authorities will investigate first and then decide whether the child needs to be taken from the parents or not.

Under the laws of most states, anyone who suspects that a child is being abused is legally obligated to report that fact to the police or child welfare agency. Many abuse cases are reported by school counselors and by health care providers, but this law applies to everyone.

If you know of someone who is being abused, you should notify the police. In most places, there will be a child protective services hotline that you can also call to make this report. The identity of the person making the report is kept confidential.

TEEN TIP

If you are a teen who is being abused by a family member, you should either tell your doctor, school counselor, other trusted adult, or call the authorities yourself. See Appendix A for additional resources

As long as you are under eighteen, you are eligible for services against abuse and the authorities will investigate. You may end up in foster care if there is not another relative with whom you can live, but it is better to be out of an abusive family. If you are the victim, you should not need your own attorney. The state should take all of the legal steps necessary to protect you.

A couple of cases that have looked at abuse by parents will be helpful to show how courts treat these types of case. Neither of the following cases is published in the regular reporter system, which means that other judges do not have to go by the decisions these judges made. It does show, however, at least how the judge in each case viewed the facts. If you want to read these decisions for yourself, the reference information is in the Table of Cases, page ___, so that you can look the case up on Lexis-Nexis™, a computer legal research service.

In the first case, *In the Interest of Storee J.*, a fifteen-year-old girl accused her father of sexually abusing her. Storee, for most of her life, lived with her mother and maternal grandparents. At fifteen, she decided she wanted to live with her father. The evidence

(continued)

showed that, within two weeks of her moving in with the father, he had taken her to the doctor and had her given a birth control shot. By the end of the first month, the father had begun sexually abusing her. Storee reported the abuse to the school, and the child protective services department investigated. Eventually, the state filed a suit to terminate the father's rights. Because of the abuse, the judge agreed with the state that the father's parental rights to Storee should be terminated.

In the second case, ***In Re Interest of Krystal K., April Z., Cody Z., and Kaleb Z***, a mother's parental rights were terminated because she failed to protect her children from abuse. The biological father of some of her children had been in prison for drug use, armed robbery, and second degree murder. By the time the appeals court reached its decision, Gary was back in jail for attempted manslaughter and sexual assault of two of the mother's children from a previous marriage. In addition to the sexual abuse, the mother testified that Gary was extremely violent toward her and that the children had witnessed a lot of the violent episodes between Gary and the mother. Because the mother did not believe her daughters when they told the child welfare caseworkers that about the abuse and downplayed the level of Gary's violence, and admitted to abusing drugs and alcohol, the court terminated the mother's parental rights even though she was not the one who actually committed the abuse.

TEEN PARENTS

When a baby is born, hospitals routinely do testing. If the mother has used drugs during the pregnancy, the drugs may show up in the baby's blood work. When that happens, the hospitals automatically notify the child welfare department. Most of the time, the state will take custody of the baby from the hospital. Therefore, if you are pregnant, it is very important that you not use drugs not prescribed by your doctor. Alcohol can also damage an unborn baby and should not be used during pregnancy.

If a baby does not grow and develop at a normal rate, doctors may end up reporting the family to child welfare. These are called *failure to thrive cases*, and they will be investigated. The baby's failure to develop on schedule can be the result of improper care by the parent.

It is only natural to be angry if your child is taken away from you, but taking your frustration out on the caseworker only makes your situation more difficult. As soon as possible, you should contact an attorney to help you navigate your way through this system.

Teen parents who do not have good support systems sometimes find themselves involved with the child welfare system. If you find yourself in this situation, you should, at a minimum, schedule one appointment with an attorney.

TEEN TIP

As a parent, if you have contact with the child welfare department, it is very important that you cooperate fully with them. Remember that they can use any information you give them—against you.

–41–

TEENS AS CRIME VICTIMS

If you are the victim of a crime, the first thing you should do is call the police. When a crime is reported, the police will send one or two officers to take your report. They will ask you questions so that they can get the basic facts of the alleged crime. You may have to talk to the police again if the case is assigned to detectives to complete the investigation.

If you do not know the person who committed the crime against you, but you saw them, you may be asked to participate in a *lineup*. Sometimes the lineup is done as you see it on television; you actually look at a group of people that includes the suspect to see if you recognize the person who committed the crime.

More frequently, however, you will be asked to view a photo lineup. The police are supposed to pick the other participants in the lineup carefully so that they resemble the suspect as closely as possible. If you pick someone out of a lineup and he or she is later charged with the crime, you may have to identify them again in court if the case goes to trial.

When a suspect is arrested and charged with the crime, you may have to testify in court. Many cases are resolved by a plea bargain, in which the suspect admits to being guilty. In those cases, you will not be required to go to court. However, if there is no plea bargain and the case is tried, you will probably have to testify.

The *prosecutor* (the lawyer for the state against the criminal) will contact you and tell you if and when you have to appear in court. They should also tell you what to expect and what kind of questions you can expect to be asked. Once the prosecutor has questioned you, then the attorney for the person charged with the crime gets to ask you questions. This is called *cross examination*. The prosecutor should be able to tell you what to expect as part of this process as well.

As a crime victim, you may also be asked to approve a *plea agreement* before it is presented to the judge. (see Chapter 39.) This is not a right that you have; the prosecutors have complete discretion in offering a plea bargain and in deciding what the terms of the offer are. However, as a matter of policy and public relations, many prosecutors will consult with the crime victim before making an offer to the defendant to resolve the case. If you want to have a say in any plea bargain, you should ask what the policy is as soon as you know which prosecutor is handling the case.

As a crime victim, you certainly have the right to hire an attorney to help you with this process. However, you do not really need an attorney of your own. The prosecutor will help you through the process and answer any questions you have.

You should let the authorities know what your *damages* are and be prepared to provide them documentation of the financial loss. Most judges will make *restitution* a part of a probationary sentence, which will make it easier for you to get your money. However, if the case results in a prison sentence for the defendant, you will have a hard time collecting any money.

> **TEEN TIP**
>
> If you have lost money as a result of the crime, you can probably get *restitution* (paid back) from the defendant.

–42–
LEGAL RESEARCH

If you are interested in researching the law yourself, here are a few pointers to make the job easier. If you live in a larger city or a city with a law library, you should be able to find all of the laws of your state there as well as other information about how the laws work. If you are going to be representing yourself in court, you can also find books that will contain samples of the forms you will need to file papers in court. Your public library may also have copies of the laws of your state. A third source for legal research is the Internet. One site that contains listings for the laws of all of the states as well as copies of written opinions in cases that have been decided is:

www.findlaw.com

If you are handling your own case, the librarian at both the law library and the public library can only direct you to the books where the laws and forms are located. They cannot tell you which forms to use in your situation or give you any other sort of legal advice. You will find that some states have forms that are very easy for non-lawyers to use while some states are a little more difficult to work with.

STATUTES AND CODES
The laws are found in sets of books. The book will have a title that usually includes either the word *statute* or *code*. Appendix B to this book will tell what the books that contain the laws for your state are called. Many of these have the words *revised* and *annotated* in the title. Annotated simply means that the book also contains a listing of some cases that have been decided under a particular section of the law. *Revised* means that the laws have been updated to reflect changes to the law that have been made by your state legislature.

Every time your state legislature meets, it is possible that some changes to the laws will be made. Therefore, you should always check for any supplements. Sometimes, the publisher may just issue a completely new volume; other times, they will just do a *supplement*. The supplement may be found in the front or back of the main volume. Sometimes, it will be contained in a separate, soft-cover book that is kept near the main volume.

CASES

Decisions by courts can also change the law; just because a statute still appears "on the books" does not guarantee that it is still valid law. Before relying on a law listed in the statute books, you will need to look at the annotations to be sure it has not been found unconstitutional or interpreted in such a way that your case is not as strong as you first thought.

If you want to read any of the cases cited in this book or you are researching how the courts in your state apply the law, you will need to read the written opinions. These are found in a set of books called the *reporter*.

The country is divided into several regions, and all of the reported decisions of the courts in your state will be found in the book for your region. Not all court decisions are published. Most of the cases you will find come from either the appeals court level or the state supreme court.

In state court, the decisions of the trial courts are not usually published; in federal court cases, they sometimes are. The federal trial court decisions are published in the *Federal Supplement* set of books. Federal appeals court cases are found in the *Federal Reporter*. The United States Supreme Court decisions are published in three different sets of books. One is called the *Supreme Court Reporter*, the second is the *Lawyer's Edition*, and the third is the *United States Reporter*.

TEEN TIP

If you will be representing yourself in court, you will also need to familiarize yourself with the *procedural* rules that will apply. You will find books containing the rules in the same place that you find the books with the other laws. This book will be titled something like the Rules of Civil Procedure.

Decisions from state courts come in various reporters.

♦ Atlantic Reporter:

Connecticut, Delaware, District of Columbia, Maine, Maryland, New Hampshire, New Jersey, Pennsylvania, Rhode Island, and Vermont

♦ Northeastern Reporter:

Illinois, Indiana, Massachusetts, Ohio, and New York

♦ Northwestern Reporter:

Iowa, Michigan, Minnesota, Nebraska, North Dakota, South Dakota, and Wisconsin

♦ Pacific Reporter:

Alaska, Arizona, California, Colorado, Hawaii, Idaho, Kansas, Montana, Nevada, New Mexico, Oklahoma, Oregon, Utah, Washington, and Wyoming

♦ Southeastern Reporter:

Georgia, North Carolina, South Carolina, Virginia, and West Virginia

♦ Southern Reporter:

Alabama, Florida, Louisiana, and Mississippi

♦ Southwestern Reporter:

Arkansas, Kentucky, Missouri, Tennessee, and Texas

A case will be cited as *Jones v. Jones*, 750 N.E. 2nd 555 (Illinois 1999). To find this case, you would look in volume number 750 (the first number) of the Northeastern Reporter 2nd series and turn to page 555 (the second number). The other items in the citation mean that the Illinois Supreme Court ("Illinois") decided the case in "1999".

Another set of books that can help you locate cases is the *digest*. Each state has a digest. It is grouped by subject matter and it will tell you the citation of cases that relate to each subject. The digest also has an index to help you find the correct subject matter listing.

> **TEEN TIP**
>
> If you have questions, the law librarian will be able to help you get started on your research.

A good source of general information is a legal encyclopedia. There are two national ones: *American Jurisprudence* and *Corpus Juris Secundem*. Additionally, many states have their own encyclopedias. This material will also be grouped by subject matter and will contain a list of a few cases as well as specific information about what the law is. If you are looking for an overview of the law in a particular area, the encyclopedia is an excellent place to start, especially if your state has its own.

GLOSSARY

A

age of majority. Legally defined as no longer a child and has full legal rights. Also called an *adult*.

C

censored. Items removed from publication.

charter school. A school that is not a regular public school, but is funded by the government.

contempt of court. Violation of a court order. Can be punished by jail time.

contract. An agreement between two parties that imposes rights and duties on them.

corporal punishment. Type of punishment that involves physical contact.

credit rating. The record of how much money you owe and how well you pay your bills.

curriculum. The program of study at school.

D

deductible. The amount of money you must pay on an insurance claim before your insurance will begin to make payments on the claim.

due process. The requirements that must be met to protect your rights.

emancipation. The process by which a court makes one a legal adult even though the legal age has not been reached.

F

felony. The most serious classification of crime carrying longer jail time.

first amendment. The addition to the constitution that protects free speech, freedom of religion, and freedom of association.

free association. The right to spend time with people of your own choosing.

fundamental right. A right guaranteed by the U.S. Constitution.

I

immunity. Rule that says that governments cannot be sued unless they pass a law that allows the particular type of lawsuit.

insurance premium. The amount of money you pay to buy the insurance policy and coverage.

J

judgment. A court order that if not followed, can cost a person money or jail time.

jurisdiction. The geographical area governed by a court.

L

liability. Doctrine that makes one person or entity owe money to another.

liability insurance. A contract that requires the insurance company to pay expenses for you.

litigation. A lawsuit where parties present evidence and resolve issues.

M

minor. A child, or one not legally an adult.

misdemeanor. The less serious classification of crimes carrying lower sentences.

N

negligence. Carelessness.

non-custodial parent. The parent that you do not live with.

P

probate. The process of going to court to deal with property titles and debts when someone dies.

probable cause. Facts that would lead a reasonable person to believe a crime has been or is about to be committed.

R

reasonable suspicion. Some facts that could indicate that a crime may have been committed.

S

segregated. Divided by some common characteristic. Often refers to division along racial lines.

statutory rape. Sexual contact between a person and another person who is too young to be legally able to consent to the sexual contact.

subpoena. A document that requires a person to come to court or to provide records.

T

tort. A wrong that is not a crime but when money is paid to the victim.

truancy. Absence from school without an excuse.

trust. A legal creation that provides for management of money by one person for the benefit of another.

TABLE OF CASES

CHAPTER 8: DISCRIMINATION IN ATHLETICS

CHAPTER 10: SCHOOL DISCIPLINE

APPENDIX A:
LIST OF RESOURCES

This appendix contains many helpful resources for the topics covered in this book. This resources will help you deal with any issues you are currently faced with. However, you can also use these resources to assist you in research for class projects and papers. You may find some resources listed under more than topic. This is because many of the topics overlap and you can benefit from the same resource for more than one situation.

If there are any resources that you know of that are not listed in this appendix, please share them with us. Contact us at:
info@SphinxLegal.com.

SECTION 1:
TEENS AND SCHOOL

BOOKS AND
MAGAZINE ARTICLES

Anger Management Workbook for Kids and Teens
Anita Bohensky

The Complete Home Learning Source Book
Rebecca Rupp

"The Crackdown on Teen Rights."
The New York Times upfront, 1999, volume 132, no. 1, pp.10
Detention, suspension, or worse: For high schoolers, free speech suddenly gets costly.

Cybersafety: Surfing Safely Online
Joan Vos MacDonald

Education, Religion, and the Common Good:
Advancing a Distinctly American Conversation About Religion's Role in Our Shared Life
Martin E. Marty, Jonathan Moore

Helping Teens Stop Violence: A Practical Guide for Educators, Counselors, and Parents
Allan Creighton, Paul Kivel

Internet and Online Privacy: A Legal and Business Guide
Andrew Frackman, Claudia Ray, Rebecca Martin

I Will Remember You: What To Do When Someone You Love Dies: A Guidebook Through Grief for Teens
Laura Dower, Elena Lister

Justice Talking: Censoring the Web: Leading Advocates Debate Today's Most Controversial Issues
Kathryn Kolbert, Zak Mettger

Legal Rights, Local Wrongs: When Community Control Collides With Educational Equity
Kevin Grant Welner, Jeannie Oakes, Martin Lipton

Negotiating the Special Education Maze: A Guide for Parents and Teachers
Winifred Anderson

Odd Girl Out: The Hidden Culture of Aggression in Girls
Rachel Simmons
Queen Bees and Wannabes: Helping Your Daughter Survive Cliques, Gossip, Boyfriends, and Other Realities of Adolescence.
Rosalind Wiseman

Ralph Nader presents Practicing Democracy: A Guide to Student Action
Katherine Isaac, Ralph Nader

Republic.com
Cass R. Sunstein

Reviving Ophelia: Saving the Selves of Adolescent Girls
Mary Pipher

The Rights of Students: The Basic ACLU Guide to Student's Rights.
Janet R. Price, Alan H. Levine, Eve Cary
Saying Goodbye When You Don't Want To: Teens Dealing With Loss
Martha Bolton

School Prayer and Discrimination: The Civil Rights of Religious Minorities and Dissenters
Frank S. Ravitch

School Prayer: The Court, the
Congress, and the First
Amendment
Robert S. Alley

Search and Seizure in Public
Schools
Lawrence F. Rossow,
Jacqueline A. Stefkovich

Sexual Harassment and Teens
Susan Strauss, Pamela Espeland

Sexual Harassment: What Teens
Should Know
Carol Rust Nash
Student Rights: A Reference
Handbook
Patricia H. Hinchey

Taking Religion to School:
Christian Theology and Secular
Education
Stephen H. Webb

Teen Dropouts
Elizabeth Weiss Vollstadt

Teen Privacy Rights: A Hot Issue
Deanne Durrett

Understanding the Human
Volcano: What Teens Can Do
About Violence
Earl Hipp, L. K. Hanson

We the Students: Supreme Court
Decisions for and About Students
Jamin B. Raskin

You, Your Child, and 'Special
Education': A Guide to Making
the System Work
Barbara Coyne Cutler

WEBSITES AND ORGANIZATIONS

ACLU Freedom Network
www.aclu.com
*American Civil Liberties Union website
includes info about such topics as: school
prayer, disability rights, free speech, lesbian and gay rights, students' rights,
drugs, etc.*

Center for Adult Learning
Educational Credentials
www.gedtest.org
*Information for prospective GED test
takers*

Continuing education
http://eoc.icontech.com
*Provides students interested in continu-
ing their education with free services,
such as GED preparation, study-related
workshops and admission information.*

Education Law Association
www.educationlaw.org
*The official website for the Education
Law Association*

Freedom Forum
www.freedomforum.org
*A non-partisan foundation based in
Arlington, VA dedicated to "free speech,
free press and free spirit for all people."*

GED preparation
www.gedonline.org
*Helps prepare students for taking the
GED.*

Homeschool World
www.home-school.com
*Official website of Practical
Homeschooling Magazine.*

Legal and law related journals
www.usc.edu/dept/law-lib/legal/jour-
nals.html
A resource for legal or law journals

Narcotic Canine Legal Update and Opinions

www.k9fleck.org/narlegal.htm
Includes a suggested flow chart of proper procedure when conducting school searches, a summary of school searches, and US Supreme Court decisions regarding school searches.

National Disabled Students Union

www.disabledstudents.org
A national organization for any student with a disability looking for community.

Special Olympics

www.specialolympics.org
Official website of Special Olympics, an international organization dedicated to empowering individuals with mental retardation.

State Compulsory School Attendance Laws

www.infoplease.com/ipa/A0112617.html
Lists school attendance requirements by state.

State constitutions and codes:

www.law.cornell.edu
A list of individual state constitutions and codes used statewide.

The State of Charter Schools 2000 Fourth Year Report

www.ed.gov/pubs/charter4thyear/
Study sponsored by the US Dept. of Education, part of a four-year research program to document and research the charter school movement.

Student legal stories

www.splc.org/newsflash.asp
Provides different legal stories about students and their schools.

Students' rights

http://members.tripod.com/sky-hawk13/index2.html
Discusses students' rights at school.

University of Iowa Gender Equity in Sports Project

www.bailiwick.lib.uiowa.edu/ge/
Includes overview of Title IX, related complaints and lawsuits, related actions, and resources.

US Constitution and Youth

www.topica.com/read/home.html
Discusses how the constitution and other US laws apply to the youth of America.

US Department of Education

www.ed.gov
For publications about students and hate crimes and sexual harassment.

Whole Family-About Teens Now

www.wholefamily.com/aboutteensnow/
Information and articles on a variety of topics such as family relationships, sexuality, school, substance abuse, etc.

SECTION II: TEENS AND HOME

BOOKS AND MAGAZINE ARTICLES

The 7 Habits of Highly Effective Teens: The Ultimate Teenage Success Guide
Sean Covey

Addiction: The 'High' That Brings You Down
Miriam Smith McLaughlin, Sandy Peyser Hazouri, Sandra Peyser Hazouri

Alcohol 101: An Overview for Teens
Margaret O. Hyde, John F. Setaro

American Bar Association Guide to Family Law: The Complete and Easy Guide to the Laws of Marriage, Parenthood, Seperation, and Divorce
Time Books, 1996.

An Educated Guide to Speeding Tickets: How to Beat and Avoid Them
Richard Wallace

Battered Women and Feminist Lawmaking
Elizabeth M. Schneider

Child Custody Made Simple: Understanding the Law of Child Custody and Child Support
Webster Watnik

Children of Alcoholism: A Survivor's Manual
Judith S. Seixas, Geraldine Youcha

Different Like Me: A Book for Teens Who Worry About Their Parent's Use of Alcohol/Drugs
Evelyn Leite, Pamela Espeland
Domestic Violence: Facts and Fallacies
Richard L. Davis

Domestic Violence: The Criminal Justice Response
Eva Schlesinger Buzawa, Carl G. Buzawa, James A. Inciardi

Drug Abuse Relapse: Helping Teens Get Clean Again
Barbara A. Moe

Drug Abuse and Teens: A Hot Issue
Shelagh Ryan Masline

Every Parent's Guide to the Law
Deborah Foreman

Everything You Need to Know About Teen Motherhood
Jane Hammerslough

Facing Teen Pregnancy: Your Choices, Dreams and Decisions
Shirley M. Arthur

Families and the Law
Lisa J. McIntyre, Marvin B. Sussman

Family Law: The Essentials
William P. Statsky
Family Violence: Legal, Medical, and Social Perspectives
Harvey Wallace

How to Fight Your Traffic Ticket and Win!: 206 Tips and Techniques
Mel Leiding

How to Say No and Keep Your Friends
Sharon Scott

Keeping Your Life Together When Your Parents Pull Apart: A Teen's Guide to Surviving Divorce
Angela Elwell Hunt
Kid's Allowances-How Much, How Often & How Come, A Guide for Parents
David McCurrach

License to Drive
Alliance for Safe Driving

The Peer Partners Handbook: Helping Your Friends Live Free from Violence, Drug Use, Teen Pregnancy & Suicide: A Guide for Students in Leadership
Jerry Kreitzer, David Levine

Runaway Kids and Teenage Prostitution
Ronald B. Flowers

A Safe Place: A Guidebook for
Living Beyond Sexual Abuse:
Hope and Healing for Teens
Jan Morrison

Safe Young Drivers 2000: A Guide
for Parents and Teens
Phil Berardelli

Stepliving for Teens
Joel D. Block, Susan S. Bartell, Jennifer
Frantz

Teen Alcoholism
Hayley R. Mitchell

Teen Challenges and Choices:
Assessing and Addressing
Adolescent Health Issues"
Journal of Technology in Human
Services, 2002, volume 19, no. 1,
pp. 57-62
Describes the health related issues facing
teenagers.

Teens and Divorce
Gail B. Stewert

Teens and Drunk Driving
Nathan Aaseng

Teen Parenting
Gail B. Stewert, Jacqueline McLean

Teen Smoking:
Understanding the Risks
Daniel McMillan

Visitation Handbook: The
Complete Guide to Parenting
Apart
Brette McWhorter Sember

Your Pregnancy and Newborn
Journey: A Guide for Pregnant
Teens
Jeanne Warren Lindsay, Jean Brunelli,
David Crawford

CRISIS HOTLINES

ChildHelp USA: National Child
Abuse Hotline
800-4-A-Child
www.childhelp.org
Hotline for teens in abusive situations.

National Center for Missing and
Exploited Children
800-843-5678
Call to report a missing child or to seek
assistance.

National Domestic Violence
Hotline
800-799-7233
800-787-3224 (TDD)
Provides assistance to victims of domestic
violence or friends and family of victims.

National Runaway Switchboard
800-621-4000
24-hour crisis hotline
www.nrscrisisline.org
Provides resources for teens and parents.

Planned Parenthood
800-541-7800
www.plannedparenthood.org
Provides family planning advice and
information.
Rape, Abuse, and Incest National
Network (RAINN)
800-656-4673
800-656-HOPE (for emergencies)
Provides counseling for victims of sexual
assault.

Teen Help: Support for Families
with Teen Challenges
800-840-5704
Provides assistance to gaurdians of
struggling adolescents.

W.E.A.V.E.: Women Escaping a Violent Environment

1-916-920-2952
www.weaveinc.org
This crisis line directs abused women toward safety.

WEBSITES AND ORGANIZATIONS

Alcoholics Anonymous

www.alcoholocs-anonymous.org
Official website for Alcoholics Anonymous, a twelve step program designed to help those who have problems controlling their alcohol intake.

Center for Law and Social Policy

www.clasp.org
Organization which concentrates on family policy and access to legal assistance for low-income families. This site includes a fact sheet for emancipated teen parents.

Children of Separation and Divorce Center, Inc.

2000 Century Plaza
Suite 121
Columbia, MD 21044
410-740-9553
www.divorceabc.com
Provides services and resources for children, adults and families coping with divorce.

Divorce Source: A Legal Resource for Divorce

http://www.divorcesource.com
Divorce law website that features a "Rights of Children" section.

Do it Now Foundation

www.doitnow.com
Provides realistic information on drugs, alcohol, and sexuality to young adults and teens.

National Center for Victims of Crime

http://www.ncvc.org
Provides a network of services, from health professionals to attorneys, for those who have been victimized.

National Institute of Drug Abuse

www.nida.nih.gov
Discusses the many aspects of drug abuse.

Office of Child Support Enforcement

http://www.acf.dhhs.gov/programs/cse
Website links to child support laws of each state.

Teen Health Help

http://depts.washington.edu/ecttp/index.html
Discusses teen sexuality, alcohol, tobacco, food, suicide, body image, and drugs.

Whole Family-About Teens Now

www.wholefamily.com/aboutteen-snow/
Information and articles on a variety of topics such as family relationships, sexuality, school, substance abuse, etc.

SECTION III: TEENS AND THEIR BODIES

BOOKS

The 7 Habits of Highly Effective Teens: The Ultimate Teenage Success Guide

Sean Covey

Addiction: The 'High' That Brings You Down

Miriam Smith McLaughlin, Sandy Peyser Hazouri, Sandra Peyser Hazouri

AIDS: Why Should I Care?
Robert Starr

American Bar Association Guide to Family Law: The Complete and Easy Guide to the Laws of Marriage, Parenthood, Seperation, and Divorce
Time Books, 1996.

Anger Management Workbook for Kids and Teens
Anita Bohensky

Birth Control and Protection: Choices for Teens
Judith Peacock

A Bright Red Scream: Self Mutilation and the Language of Pain
Marilee Strong

Changing Bodies, Changing Lives
Ruth Bell

Children of the Horizons: How Gay and Lesbian Teens Are Leading a New Way Out of the Closet
Andrew Boxer, Gilbert H. Herdt

Children of Rage: Preventing Youth Violence After Columbine
Carole Corner McKelvey, Conrad J. Boeding

Commercial Sexual Exploitation of Children: Youth Involved in Prostitution, Pornography & Sex Trafficking
Laura A. Barnitz

Coping With the Dangers of Tattooing, Body Piercing, and Branding
Beth Wilkinson

Coping With Teen Suicide
James M. Murphy

Drug Abuse Relapse: Helping Teens Get Clean Again
Barbara A. Moe

Drug Abuse and Teens: A Hot Issue
Shelagh Ryan Masline

The Eating Disorder Sourcebook
Carolyn Costin

Everything You Need to Know About Teen Motherhood
Jane Hammerslough

Facing Teen Pregnancy: Your Choices, Dreams and Decisions
Shirley M. Arthur

Girl Power: Self-Defense for Teens
Burt Konzak

Helping Teens Stop Violence: A Practical Guide for Educators, Counselors, and Parents
Allan Creighton, Paul Kivel

How to Say No and Keep Your Friends
Sharon Scott
Is It a Choice? The Most Frequently Asked Questions About Gay and Lesbian People.
Eric Marcus

The Journey Out: A Guide For
and About Lesbian, Gay, and
Bisexual Teens
Rachel Pollack, Cheryl Schwartz

Lost Boys: Why Our Sons Turn
Violent and How We Can Save
Them
James Garbarino

"The New Gay Youth Revolution"
Sabrina McIntosh
The Advocate, April 10, 2001

Odd Girl Out: The Hidden
Culture of Aggression in Girls
Rachel Simmons

The Peer Partners Handbook:
Helping Your Friends Live Free
from Violence, Drug Use, Teen
Pregnancy & Suicide: A Guide for
Students in Leadership
Jerry Kreitzer, David Levine

Queen Bees and Wannabes:
Helping Your Daughter Survive
Cliques, Gossip, Boyfriends, and
Other Realities of Adolescence.
Rosalind Wiseman

Recovering From Depression: A
Workbook for Teens
Mary Ellen Copeland, Stuart Copans

Reviving Ophelia: Saving the
Selves of Adolescent Girls
Mary Pipher

Runaway Kids and Teenage
Prostitution
Ronald B. Flowers

Sexual Health Information for
Teens: Health Tips about Sexual
Development, Human
Reproduction, and Sexually
Transmitted Diseases
Deborah A. Stanley

Straight Parents, Gay Children:
Inspiring Families to Live Honestly
and With Greater Understanding
Robert A. Bernstein

Tattooing and Body Piercing
(Perspectives on Physical Health)
Bonnie B. Graves

Tattooing and Body Piercing:
Understanding the Risks
Kathleen Winkler

Teen Eating Disorders
Elizabeth Weiss Vollstadt

Teen Parenting
Gail B. Stewert, Jacqueline McLean

Teen Smoking: Understanding the
Risks
Daniel McMillan

Teen Suicide At Issue
Tamara L. Roleff

Teen Suicide: Perspectives on
Mental Health
Judith Peacock

Things Get Hectic: Teens Write
About the Violence That
Surrounds Them
Youth Communication,
Philip Kay (editor), Al Desetta (edi-
tor), Andrea Estepa (editor)

Understanding the Human
Volcano: What Teens Can Do
About Violence
Earl Hipp, L. K. Hanson

When Nothing Matters Anymore:
A Survival Guide for Depressed
Teens
Bev Cobain

Your Pregnancy and Newborn Journey: A Guide for Pregnant Teens
Jeanne Warren Lindsay, Jean Brunelli, David Crawford

CRISIS PHONE NUMBERS

The Eating Disorder Connection
900-737-4044
A hotline for those suffering from eating disorders.

KidsPeace: The National Center for Kids Overcoming Crisis:
800-8KID123
www.kidspeace.org
Kidspeace is a nonprofit organization designed to help children and teens overcome crisis through treatment and education.

National Domestic Violence Hotline:
800-799-7233
800-787-3224 (TDD)
www.ndvh.org
The National Domestic Violence Hotline is a crisis service for those who are experiencing domestic abuse or those who would like to report an incident of violence.

National Food Addiction Hotline
800-USA-0088
Help for those inflicted with food addiction.

National Suicide Hotline
800-784-2433
http://suicidehotlines.com
Suicide Hotline offers crisis counselors willing to listen and who can provide further assistance.

ORGANIZATION MAILING ADDRESSES, PHONE NUMBERS, AND WEBSITES

American Academy for Child and Adolescent Psychiatry,
3615 Wisconsin Ave.
NW, Washington, D.C. 20016
800-333-7636
www.aacap.org
The American Academy for Child and Adolescent Psychiatry is an organization geared toward public awareness of mental, behavioral, and developmental disorders in children and adults.

American Anorexia/Bulimia Association,
165 West 46th St., Suite 1108,
New York, NY 10036
212-575-6200
http://www.serpell.com
Provides information on eating disorders.

The American Civil Liberties Union
www.aclu.org.
The American Civil Liberties Union works in many different areas related to civil rights.

American Foundation for Suicide Prevention
http://www.afsp.org
Information on suicide prevention.

Anorexia Nervosa and Related Eating Disorders, Inc.,
P.O. Box 5102,
Eugene, OR 97405
541-344-1144
www.anred.com
Non-profit organization that provides info about common and less-well-known food and weight disorders. Site materials include self-help tips and info about recovery and prevention.

Center for Law and Social Policy
www.clasp.org
Organization which concentrates on family policy and access to legal assistance for low-income families. This site includes a fact sheet for emancipated teen parents.

Children Now
www.talkwithkids.org
Discusses issues on sex, alcohol, drugs, violence, and HIV with teens.

Divorce Source: A Legal Resource for Divorce
http://www.divorcesource.com
Divorce law website that features a "Rights of Children" section.

Do it Now Foundation
www.doitnow.org
Provides realistic information on drugs, alcohol and sexuality to young adults and teens.

Eating Disorders Awareness and Prevention,
603 Stewart St. #803,
Seattle, WA 98101
206-382-3587
www.nationaleatingdisorders.org
Extensive information provided about programs to help battle eating disorders, as well as information about the disorders themselves.

Go Ask Alice
www.goaskalice.columbia.edu
Sexual health site which answers questions about reproduction, contraception, STDs, etc.

Mental Health
www.mentalhealthabout.com
Links to many different sites of interest to teens and their parents.

National Alliance for the Mentally Ill
http://www.nami.org
Discusses warning signs of suicide and how others can help.

National Association of Anorexia Nervosa and Related Disorders,
P.O. Box 7,
Highland Park, IL 60035
847-831-3438
www.anad.org
Gives general information about eating disorders and offers additional resources and services for education and prevention.

National Eating Disorders Organization,
6655 South Yale Ave.,
Tulsa, OK 74136
918-481-4044
www.laureate.com
Hard to find eating disorders are part of this website. Clinical references are included for definitions of eating disorders and treatment programs.

National Institute of Drug Abuse
www.nida.nih.gov
Discusses the many aspects of drug abuse.

Planned Parenthood
800-541-7800
Provides planning advice and information.
www.plannedparenthood.org
Links to www.teenwire.com, Planned Parenthood's youth oriented, health website.

SuicideHotlines.com
www.suicidehotlines.com
State-by-state listing of toll-free suicide hotlines.

Teen Health Help
http://depts.washington.edu/ecttp/index.html
Discusses teen sexuality, alcohol, tobacco, food, and suicide, body image and other drugs.

Teen Out Reach
www.teenoutreach.com
Provides teens with educational support on pregnancy, childbirth and postpartum issues.

Teenparents.org
www.teenparents.org
Fact sheets for teen parents.

Truth
www.thetruth.com
Website that provides information about nicotine addiction and the practices of cigarette companies.

Whole Family-About Teens Now
www.wholefamily.com/aboutteen-snow/
Information and articles on a variety of topics such as family relationships, sexuality, school, substance abuse, etc.

Youth Health
www.health.org
Has an entire section devoted to young people with links to a variety of sites.

SECTION IV:
TEENS AND WORK

BOOKS

The Employee Rights Handbook: The Essential Guide for People on the Job
Steven Mitchell Sacks

Neighbor Law: Fences, Trees, Boundaries, and Noise
Cora Jordan

The Rights of Employees and Union Members: The Basic ACLU Guide to the Rights of Employees and Union Members
Wayne N. Outten, Robert J. Rabin, Lisa R. Lipman

Sexual Harassment and Teens
Susan Strauss, Pamela Espeland

Sexual Harassment: What Teens Should Know
Carol Rust Nash

Step Forward: Sexual Harassment in the Workplace
Susan L. Webb

The Things Your Boss Won't Tell You
Leo James Terrell

HOTLINES

Sexual Harassment Hotline Resource List:
800-522-0925
Will provide answers to job-related sexual harassment questions.

WEBSITES AND ORGANIZATIONS

Department of Labor:
www.dol.gov
Everything you ever wanted to know about work-related issues.

Disability Rights Section and Civil Rights Division
U.S. Department of Justice
P.O. Box 66738
Washington, D.C. 20035
800-514-0307
800-574-0383 (TDD)
www.usdoj.gov
Government regulations and information about the rights of those with disabilities.

The Minimum Wage
www.dol.gov/esa/minwage/main.htm
US Dept. of Labor site that includes information about the history of minimum wage and current minimum wage rates for each state.

Rock the Vote
http://www.rockthevote.org
Information on current political affairs,
how they effect America's youth, and
how teens can get involved.

SECTION V:
TEENS AND PROPERTY

BOOKS

Street Wise: A Guide for Teen Investors
Janet Bamford

Teen Guide to Personal Financial Management
Marjoliijn Bijlefeld, Sharon K. Zoumbaris

Money: Save It, Manage It, Spend It
Mary Bowman-Kruhm

97 Ways to Protect What's Left of Your Privacy and Property Rights
Mark Nestmann

SECTION VI:
TEENS AND
THE COURTS

BOOKS

American Bar Association Guide to Family Law: The Complete and Easy Guide to the Laws of Marriage, Parenthood, Seperation, and Divorce
Time Books, 1996.

Battered Women and Feminist Lawmaking
Elizabeth M. Schneider

The Death Penalty for Teens: A Pro/Con Issue
Nancy Day

Domestic Violence: Facts and Fallacies
Richard L. Davis

Domestic Violence: The Criminal Justice Response
Eva Schlesinger Buzawa, Carl G. Buzawa, James A. Inciardi

Everybody's Guide to Small Claims Court
Ralph E. Warner

Every Parent's Guide to the Law
Deborah Foreman

Everything You Need to Know About Teen Motherhood
Jane Hammerslough

Facing Teen Pregnancy: Your Choices, Dreams and Decisions
Shirley M. Arthur

Families and the Law
Lisa J. McIntyre, Marvin B. Sussman

Family Law: The Essentials
William P. Statsky

Family Violence: Legal, Medical, and Social Perspectives
Harvey Wallace

How and When to Be Your Own Lawyer: A Step-by-Step Guide to Effectively Using Our Legal System
Robert Schachner, Marvin Quittner

I Will Remember You: What To Do When Someone You Love Dies: A Guidebook Through Grief for Teens
Laura Dower, Elena Lister

Legal Research: How to Find and Understand the Law
Stephen Elias, Susan Levinkind, Lisa Sedano

Legal Research Made Easy
Suzan Herskowitz
On Trial: Lessons From a Lifetime in the Courtroom
Henry G. Miller

Punitive Damages: How Juries Decide
Cass R. Sunstein, Reid Hastie, John W. Payne, David A. Schkade

Readings in Juvenile Justice Administration
Barry C. Field

Represent Yourself in Court: How to Prepare and Try a Winning Case
Paul Bergman, Sara J. Berman-Barrett

A Safe Place: A Guidebook for Living Beyond Sexual Abuse: Hope and Healing for Teens
Jan Morrison

Saying Goodbye When You Don't Want To: Teens Dealing With Loss
Martha Bolton

Teen Parenting
Gail B. Stewart, Jacqueline McLean

Your Lawyer on a Short Leash: A Survivor's Guide
Avi Azrieli

Your Pregnancy and Newborn Journey: A Guide for Pregnant Teens
Jeanne Warren Lindsay, Jean Brunelli, David Crawford

HOTLINES

ChildHelp USA: National Child Abuse Hotline
1-800-4-A-Child
www.childhelp.org
Hotline for teens in abusive situations.

W.E.A.V.E.: Women Escaping a Violent Environment
www.weaveinc.org
916-920-2952 (crisis line)
The crisis line directs abused women toward safety.

WEBSITES AND ORGANIZATIONS

The American Civil Liberties Union
www.aclu.org.
The American Civil Liberties Union works in many different areas related to civil rights.

Juvenile Justice
www.ncjrs.org
A reference website for National Criminal Justice.

Juvenile Justice: An Overview
www.law.cornell.edu/topics/juvenile.html
Cornell University's legal site concerning juvenile rights.

National Center for Juvenile Justice
www.ncjj.org
According to the website, "a resource for independent and original research on topics related directly and indirectly to the field of juvenile justice."

National Center for Victims of Crime
www.ncvc.org
The homepage for the National Center for Victms of Crime, recognized as the nation's leading advocate for crime victims.

Office of Juvenile Justice and Delinquency Prevention
www.ojjdp.ncjrs.org
Federal office of juvenile rights discusses the law and gives contact information.

US Constitution and Youth
www.topica.com/read/home.html
Discusses how the constitution and other US laws apply to the youth of America.

APPENDIX B:
STATE-BY-STATE LAWS

What follows is a list of some of the state laws that have been discussed in the book. We have included several categories for each state. Following is an explanation:

The Law	This tells you what the laws of your state are called and gives you some pointers on finding the statutes we have listed.
Abortion	Law that applies to teens is listed if the state has one. If there is one, we have included the statute number in parentheses.
Age of Majority	This is the age of adulthood for your state. If the statute is available, it is listed at the end in parentheses.
Driver's Licenses	Laws of your state and the statute numbers for those laws are given in parentheses.
Marriage	This tells you how old you must be to get married in your state. Then it gives the statute number in parentheses.
Compulsory School Attendance Ages	We have included the ages during which your state requires you to be in school. The statute is listed in parantheses.
Criminal Law	This gives you the age you can be tried as an adult for crimes. The statute is listed in parentheses

Child Labor Law

This section tells you where to find the rules about teen workers for your state and the general work hours that apply to teens. The statute information is in parentheses.

Curfew

This final section tells you whether your state has a curfew law.

NOTE: *Your town or city may have a curfew law even if your state does not.*

ALABAMA

The Law: Code of Alabama. Ignore volume numbers and use title numbers.

Abortion: Parental consent required. *(beginning with Sec. 26-21-1)*

Age of Majority: 19 if single; 18 if married

Driver's Licenses: Age 16. If under 16, must be enrolled in driver's education and have a licensed driver in the car with you. If under 19, license conditioned on being high school graduate, enrolled in high school, or GED program or job training program. *(Sec. 32-6-7)*

Marriage: Minimum age 14. If under 18, parents must consent. *(Secs. 8n 30-1-4 and 30-1-5)*

Compulsory School Attendance Ages: 7-16 years old

Criminal Law: At age 14, can be transferred to adult court for certain serious crimes. At age 16, certain serious crimes cause you to be automatically treated as an adult. *(Sec. 12-15-34)*

Child Labor Law: At 14 and 15, can work no more than 6 days per week and 8 hours per day, after 7 a.m. and before 7 p.m. (9 p.m. in the summer).
At 16, when school is in session, limited to 8 hours per day on a nonschool day or 3 hours per school day. Maximum of 18 total hours during the school week. Work hours 7 a.m. to 7 p.m. (9 p.m. in summer).*(beginning with Sec. 25-8-33)*

Curfew: No specific statute.

ALASKA

The Law:	Alaska Statutes "A.S.". Ignore volume numbers and look for title numbers.
Abortion:	Parents must consent if unmarried; unemancipated minor under 17. Alternate court order method authorized. *(beginning with Sec. 18.16.20)*
Age of Majority:	18 years old
Driver's Licenses:	At 14, get instruction permit, which allows driving only when accompanied. At 16, get provisional license once you have had instruction permit for one year. Regular driver's license after you have had provisional license for 1 year. *(beginning with Sec. 28.15.011)*
Marriage:	Ages 16-18, requires written consent of parent. Minimum age 14. Under16 requires court permission. Between 14 and 18, court can grant permission even without parent's consent. *(Sec. 25.05.171)*
Compulsory School Attendance Ages:	Ages 7-16. School board can approve earlier withdrawal. *(Sec. 14, 30.010)*
Criminal Law:	At 16, can be treated as an adult if charged with a serious felony. Also treated as an adult at any age for traffic violations, tobacco possession if under 19, alcohol curfew, fish and game, and driver's licenses violations. *(Sec. 47.12.030)*

(continued)

Child Labor Law:

Between ages 14 and 16, total of nine hours school attendance and work in one day, and only between the hours of 5 a.m. and 9 p.m. Maximum of 23 hours per week. From 16 to 18, 6 days per week maximum.
(beginning with Sec. 23.10.325)

Curfew:

City can order curfew for those under 18 and not emancipated or married. Violators can be fined up to $250.
(Sec. 29.35.085)

ARIZONA

The Law:	Arizona Revised Statutes Annotated "A.R.S." Ignore volume numbers; look for section numbers.
Abortion:	Parental consent or court approval required. *(Sec. 36-2152)*
Age of Majority:	18 years old
Driver's Licenses:	Generally 18, but can get restricted license at 15 to take driver's education class. Instructional permit at 15 years and 7 months, which requires supervised driving at all times. Get class G license at age 16. *(beginning with Sec. 28-1851)*
Marriage:	If under 18, parents must consent. If under 16, must also have court approval and required counseling. As a condition of the *marriage*, court can mandate staying in school. *(Sec. 25-102)*
Compulsory School Attendance Ages:	6-16 years old
Criminal Law:	10 and over go to juvenile court and any felony can be transferred to criminal court. At ages 15, 16, and 17, certain crimes are *automatically* transferred to adult court. At 14, can be tried as an adult for certain felonies. *(Secs. 8-302, 13-501)*
Child Labor Law:	Under 16, maximum of 40 hours per week, 8 hours per day when not in school, 18 per week and 3 per day during school term. Must be 10 to have a paper route. *(beginning with Sec. 23-230)*
Curfew:	No specific statute.

ARKANSAS

The Law:	Arkansas Code of 1987 Annotated "A.C.A." Look for title or chapter numbers.
Abortion:	No abortions on unemancipated minors until 48 hours after notice given to parents or with court approval. *(Sec. 20-16-801)*
Age of Majority;	18 years old
Driver's Licenses:	At 14, can apply for an instructional permit. Allows driving if accompanied by a licensed driver over 21 in the front seat. At 16, get an intermediate license if you have had an instructional permit and a clean driving record. *(beginning with Sec. 27-16-101)*
Marriage:	Males must be 17, females 16. Under 18, must have parental consent. Exception to the minimum ages if the prospective spouses are expecting a child; prove pregnancy, and have parental consent.
Compulsory School Attendance Ages:	Until 17 years old
Criminal Law:	Automatically treated as a juvenile if under 15. Also, if under 18 and are charged with a misdemeanor. At 14, serious felonies can be transferred to adult court. Also, at 14, if you are charged with any felony and have three previous "convictions." *(Sec. 9-22-318)*

(continued)

Child Labor Law: Must be at least 14 to work, unless it is a family business. Under 16, 8 hours per day, 6 days per week maximum and 48 hours per week maximum. Must be after 6 a.m. and before 7 p.m. (On the night before a nonschool day, can work until 9 p.m.) Between 16 and 18, can work 54 hours per week and ten hours per day between the hours of 6 a.m. and 11 p.m. *(beginning with Sec. 11-6-101)*

Curfew: No specific statute.

CALIFORNIA

The Law:	Deerings California Codes Annotated or West's Annotated California Codes.
Abortion:	Parents must either be notified or have court approval. *(Sec. 6925, Family Code 6925)*
Age of Majority:	18 years old
Driver's Licenses:	Generally 18. If taking driver's education, can get permit at 15 years and 6 months. At 17 and 6 months, get instruction permit, which requires licensed driver 25 or over. A junior permit is valid for getting to school, between ages 14 and 18. *(Sec. 15509, Vehicle Code 15509)*
Marriage:	If under 18, need parent's written consent and court order granting permission to marry. Pre-marital counseling required for those under 18. *(Sec. 302, Family Code 302)*
Compulsory School Attendance Ages:	6-18 years old
Criminal Law:	At 16, can be transferred to adult court for serious felonies. Otherwise, age is 18. *(beginning with Sec. 827. 1, Welfare and Institutions Code 827.1)*
Child Labor Law:	For ages 15 and under, maximum 8 hours per day, 40 hours per week, between 7 a.m. and 7 p.m. (9 p.m. in summer). For ages 14 and 15 during school term, maximum of 3 hours per school day and 18 hours per week. *(beginning with Sec. 1390, Labor Code 1390)*
Curfew:	No specific statute.

COLORADO

The Law:	West's Colorado Revised Statutes Annotated. "C.R.S.A."
Abortion:	Parental notice required and 48 hour waiting period *(beginning with Sec. 12-37.5-101)*
Age of Majority:	18 years old *(Sec. 13-22-101)*
Driver's Licenses:	At 15 and six months, can get temporary instruction permit, which allows driving with licensed driver over 21 in car. Must take driver's education class. At 16, get licensed as a minor driver. Under 17, cannot drive between midnight and 5 a.m. unless supervised. *(Sec. 42-2-108)*
Marriage:	18 to consent to marriage. At 16, can marry with parent's consent. If under 16, must also have permission from judge. (Sec. 14-2-106)
Compulsory School Attendance Ages:	Ages 7 to 16 *(Sec. 22-33-104)*
Criminal Law:	Can be transferred to adult court at 14 if charged with a serious felony or if habitual juvenile offender. Can be transferred at 16 if charged with any felony and previously been "convicted." *(Sec. 19-2-517)*
Child Labor Law:	No employment under 14, with some exceptions. Limited to six hours on school days, unless the next day is not a school day. Work hours between 5 a.m. and 9:30 p.m., except for babysitters. When out of school, 40 hours per week maximum and 8 hours a day. *(beginning with Sec. 8-12-101)*
Curfew:	No specific statute.

CONNECTICUT

The Law:	Connecticut General Statutes Annotated. "C.G.S.A." Ignore chapter numbers and look for title numbers.
Abortion:	Minor defined as under 16 for this law. Minors must have counseling, part of which discusses involvement of minor's family. Minor decides if best not to involve parents. *(Sec. 19a-601)*
Age of Majority:	18 years old *(Sec. 1-1d)*
Driver's Licenses:	At 16 or 17, can get a learner's permit with parental consent, which allows driving when accompanied by driver over 20 who has been licensed at least 4 years. At 16, can get regular license if complete driver's education class. *(Sec. 14-36)*
Marriage:	If under 18, must have parent's consent. If under 16, must also have permission from a judge. *(Sec. 46b-30)*
Compulsory School Attendance Ages:	Ages 5-18. Can leave school at 16 with parent's consent. *(Sec. 10a-76a)*
Criminal Law:	At 14 with a serious *felony*, transfer to adult court is *automatic*. For less serious felonies, judge has discretion to transfer. At age 16, treated as adult for *all* criminal charges. *(Sec. 46b-127)*
Child Labor Law:	If under 18, during non school periods, 8 hours per day, 6 days per week, 48 hours per week. During school term, 6 hours per day on a school day and 32 hours per week. *(beginning Sec. 31-12 et seq)*
Curfew:	No specific statute.

DELAWARE

The Law:	Delaware Code Annotated. "D.C.A." Ignore volume numbers. Look for title numbers.
Abortion:	Minor defined as under 16 for this law. Parents get 24 hours actual notice or court permission. *(beginning with Sec. 24,1780)*
Age of Majority:	18 years old *(Sec. 1-701)*
Driver's Licenses:	At 15 and 6 months, can get learner's permit. After 12 months, can get Class D license if complete driver's education class. Allows driving when supervised by licensed driver over 25. After six months of supervision, then six months supervised only between 9 p.m. and 6 a.m. At 16 and 10 months, get unrestricted license, but requires adult sponsor. *(beginning with Sec. 21,2710)*
Marriage:	Statute says no male under 18 or female under 16 can marry. Females under 18 need parental consent. Exception to age limits if expecting a child. *(Sec. 13,123)*
Compulsory School Attendance Ages:	5-16 years old *(beginning with Sec.14,2729)*.
Criminal Law:	Under 16, treated as a juvenile, but juvenile court can sentence offenders to sentences that last beyond age 16; time served in juvenile facility until age 16, then transferred to adult prison. At 16, automatically treated as adult.

(continued)

Child Labor Law:

If under 16, on school day 4 hours per day, 18 hours per week, 6 days per week. When school not in session, 8 hours per day, 40 hours per week. Can work between 7 a.m. and 7 p.m. only (9 p.m. during summer). No more than 12 hours combined school and work per day.
No employment under 14.
(beginning with Sec. 19,501)

Curfew:

No specific statute.

DISTRICT OF COLUMBIA

The Law:	District of Columbia Code. "D.C.C."
Abortion:	No statute regarding minors.
Age of Majority:	18 years old *(Sec. 46-101)*
Driver's Licenses:	Get learner's permit at 16, which allows driving only between 6 a.m. and 9 p.m. Get operator's permit at 17, but must have had provisional permit for at least 6 months and no violations for at least 12 months and 10 hours of supervised night driving. If under 18, no more than 2 passengers and no driving between 11 p.m. and 6 a.m.(Midnight on Saturday and Sunday and during the summer.) *(Sec. 50-1401.01)*
Marriage:	Under 18, need parent's consent. Minimum age is 16. *(Sec. 46-403-46-411)*
Compulsory School Attendance Ages:	5-18 years old. At 17, can get flexible hours to accommodate work. *(beginning with Sec. 38-201)*
Criminal Law:	Generally 18. Transferred at adult court at 15 for felony or if 16 and already committed to a placement. Can be transferred at any age for firearm charge. *(Sec. 16-2307)*
Child Labor Law:	Under 18, limited to 6 days per week, 48 hours per week, 8 hours per day. If under 16, only between 7 a.m. and 7 p.m. At 16 and 17, between 6 a.m. and 10 p.m. *(Sec. 32-201)*
Curfew:	If under 17, prohibited from 11 p.m. Sunday through Thursday until 6 a.m. on the following day, midnight to 6 a.m. on weekends. *(Sec. 2-1541)*

FLORIDA

The Law:	Florida Statutes. "F.S." A new set is published every odd numbered year, with hard cover supplements every even-numbered year. Ignore volume numbers and look for chapter numbers. There is also a set called West's Florida Statutes Annotated.
Abortion:	48 hours notice to parents unless permission from judge. *(Sec. 390.01115)*
Age of Majority:	18 years old *(Sec. 743.066)*
Driver's Licenses:	At 15, get learner's permit if completed driver's ed. At 16, can get regular license if you have had learner's permit for at least 12 months and no moving violations and 50 hours of supervised driving experience. *(beginning with Sec. 322.05)*
Marriage:	Between 16 and 18 need parental consent. If under 16, only if pregnant or already have child together and judge grants permission. *(Sec. 741.0405)*
Compulsory School Attendance Ages:	Until age 16. *(beginning with Sec. 232.001)*
Criminal Law:	If 14, will be transferred to adult court for serious felonies. Can also be transferred at 14 if you have three previous felonies and the present charge is also a felony. *(Sec. 985.226)*

(continued)

Child Labor Law: No work under age 14. Ages 14 and 15, work only between 7 a.m. and 7 p.m. Limited to 15 hours per week and 3 hours per day on any day before a school day. When school not in session, can work until 9 p.m. and work 8 hours per day and 40 hours per week.
At 16 and 17, limited to 6 consecutive days per week. During school, maximum of 30 hours per week and 8 hours per day, between 6:30 a.m. and 11 p.m. only. *(beginning with Sec. 450.001)*

Curfew: Curfews allowed for those under sixteen. (Sec. 817.20)

GEORGIA

The Law:	Official Code of Georgia Annotated. "C.G.A." Ignore volume numbers and look for title and chapter numbers. This is not the same set as the Georgia Code, which uses a completely different numbering system. If all you can find is the Georgia Code, look for a cross reference table to the Official Code of Georgia.
Abortion:	Must have written acknowledgment of notice by parent or doctor must give 24 hour notice to parent or permission from judge. *(Sec. 15-11-110)*
Age of Majority:	18 years old *(Sec. 39-1-1)*
Driver's Licenses:	At 15, get instruction permit. Can get license at 16 if in school upon completion of drug and alcohol awareness course, driver's education, and 40 hours of supervised driving. *(beginning with Sec. 40-5-22)*
Marriage:	Must be at least 16. If under 18, need parental consent. Age limit can be waived if pregnant or already have a child together. *(beginning with Sec. 19-3-2)*
Compulsory School Attendance Ages:	6-16. *(beginning with Sec. 20-2-690)*
Criminal Law:	Automatically treated as adult at 17. At 13, can be transferred to adult court for serious felony. Even if not transferred, juvenile court can give long sentences; serve time in juvenile facility until age 17, then transferred to adult prison. *(Secs. 16-3-1, 15-11-28)*
Child Labor Law:	If under 16, between 6 a.m. and 9 p.m. only. *(beginning with Sec. 39-2-1)*
Curfew:	No specific statute.

HAWAII

The Law:	Hawaii Revised Statutes. "H.R.S." Ignore volume numbers and look for title numbers.
Abortion:	No parental consent or notice required.
Age of Majority:	18 years old *(Sec. 577-1)*
Driver's Licenses:	At 15 and 6 months, can get instruction permit. Can get license at 16. *(beginning with Sec. 286-110)*
Marriage:	Under 18, need parental consent. 16 minimum age, except can marry at 15 with judge's permission. *(Sec. 571-1)*
Compulsory School Attendance Ages:	6-18 years old. At 15, can leave school if employed, and school superintendent consents, and judge grants permission after family court investigation. *(Secs. 302A-1132)*
Criminal Law:	Treated as adult at 18. Are not transferred to adult court, but can receive lengthy sentence in juvenile court. Serve time in juvenile facility until 18, then transferred to adult prison. *(Sec. 571-11)*
Child Labor Law:	At 14, limited to 5 continuous hours, 6 consecutive days, 40 hours per week, 8 hours per day, only between 7 a.m. and 7 p.m. during school term, 6 a.m. to 9 p.m. in summer. School and work combined cannot exceed 10 hours per day. *(Sec. 390-2)*
Curfew:	Counties can enact curfews for persons under 16, can apply from 10 p.m. to 4 a.m. *(beginning with Sec. 577-18)*

IDAHO

The Law:	Idaho Code. "I.C." Ignore volume number.
Abortion:	Must have written consent or court permission. *(Sec. 18-614)*
Age of Majority:	18 years old *(Sec. 32-101)*
Driver's Licenses:	If under 17, must take driver's education. At 15, drive in daylight only. At 16, get full license. *(beginning with Sec. 49-303)*
Marriage:	At 16 with parental consent. Under 16, must also have judge's permission. *(beginning with Sec. 32-202)*
Compulsory School Attendance Ages:	7-16 years old *(beginning with Sec. 33201)*
Criminal Law:	Can be transferred to adult court at age 14. Automatically treated as adult at age 18. *(Secs. 18-216, 19-402, 18-113B)*
Child Labor Law:	Can work during school vacation at 12. If under 14, can only work between 6 a.m. and 9 p.m. If under 16, only work 54 hours per week, 9 hours per day, between 6 a..m. and 9 p.m. *(Sec. 44-1301)*
Curfew:	Counties authorized to enact curfews. *(Secs. 20-549, 32-1301)*

ILLINOIS

The Law:
West's Smith Hurd Illinois Compiled Statutes Annotated. "I.L.C.S." This is different from the Smith-Hurd Annotated Statutes; a different set of books with a different numbering system.

Abortion:
Parents must get 48 hours actual notice unless child abuse present or judge gives permission. *(Sec. 750 ILCS 70/1)*

Age of Majority:
18 years old
(Sec. 755 ILCS 5/11-1)

Driver's Licenses:
At 15, get instruction permit with driver's education enrollment. Without driver's education, can get instructional permit at age 17 and 9 months. Must have instructional permit for at least 3 months and have 25 hours of supervised driving to get regular license.
(Sec. 625 ILCS 5/6-107)

Marriage:
If under 18, need parent's consent. 16 is minimum age. *(Sec. 750 ILC 5/208)*

Compulsory School Attendance Ages:
Ages 7-16. *(Sec. 105 ILCS 5/26-1)*

Criminal Law:
Treated as adult at 17. *Automatic* transfer to adult court at 15 for serious crimes. *(beginning with Sec. 705 ILCS 405/5-105)*

(continued)

Child Labor Law:

At 14, 3 hours per school day, 24 hours per week maximum, only between 7 a.m. and 10 p.m.

If under 16, 3 hours per school day, 24 hours per week, 6 days per week, 8 total hours per day school and work combined.

At 16, 6 days per week, 8 hours per day, between 7 a.m. and 7 p.m. (9 p.m. in the summer).

(beginning with Sec. 820 ILCS 205/1)

Curfew:

If under 17, prohibited from public places without an adult at the following times: 12:01 a.m. to 6 a.m. Saturday and Sunday, and between 11 p.m. and 6 a.m. on the following day Sunday through Thursday. *(Sec. 720 ILCS 555/0.01)*

INDIANA

The Law:	West's Annotated Indiana Code. "A.I.C." Look for title numbers.
Abortion:	Must have parental consent or judge's permission. *(Sec. 16-34-2-4)*
Age of Majority:	18 years old *(Sec. 31-9-2-13)*
Driver's Licenses:	Can get learner's permit at 15. At 16 plus 30 days, get full license if complete driver's education class and have had learner's permit for at least 60 days. At 16 and 6 months, and learner's permit for 60 days without driver's education. *(Sec. 9-24-3-2)*
Marriage:	At 17 with parental consent. If at least 15 and pregnant or already have child together, can get judge's permission to marry. *(Sec. 31-11-1-4)*
Compulsory School Attendance Ages:	Can leave school at 16 after exit interview with school administrator. *(beginning with Sec. 20-8.1-3-1)*
Criminal Law:	Can be transferred to adult court at 14 for serious crimes. For murder charges, can be transferred at age 10 to adult court. *(Sec. 31-30-3-1)*

(continued)

Child Labor Law:

At 14, can work at some jobs. Between 14 and 16, can only work between 7 a.m. and 7 p.m. (9 p.m. in the summer). Limited to 3 hours per day, 18 hours per week during school term, 8 hours per day and 40 hours per week when school not in session. At 16, can work 8 hours per day, 30 hours per week, 6 days a week, between 6 a.m. and 10 p.m. on school nights, midnight on non-school nights. *(Sec. 20-8.1-4-20)*

Curfew:

At ages 15, 16, and 17, cannot be in public place without adult between 1 a.m. and 5 a.m. on Saturday and Sunday, after 11 p.m. on Sunday through Thursday or before 5 a.m. Monday through Friday.
If under 15, cannot be out between 11 p.m. and 5 a.m.
(beginning with Sec. 31-37-3-1)

IOWA

The Law:	Iowa Code Annotated. "I.C.A." Ignore volume numbers and look for section numbers.
Abortion:	Must give parents 48 hours notice or have judge's permission. *(Sec. 135L.3)*
Age of Majority:	18 years old *(Sec. 599.1)*
Driver's Licenses:	Can get instruction permit at 14. At 16, can get intermediate license if you have had instruction permit at least 6 months, 20 hours of supervised driving experience, and had driver's education class. Intermediate license is revoked if you are not in school. Full license at 18. *(Sec. 321.180B)*
Marriage:	Not allowed if under 16. If 16 or 17, must have parental consent and permission from judge. *(Sec. 595.2)*
Compulsory School Attendance Ages:	Must attend until 16 years old. *(Sec. 299.6)*
Criminal Law:	Treated as an adult at 14. *(Secs. 356.3 and 702.5)*
Child Labor Law:	If under 16, only between 7 a.m. and 7 p.m. (9 p.m. in summer), 8 hours per day, 40 hours per week when school not in session, 4 hours per day and 28 hours per week when it is. *(beginning with Sec. 92.1)*
Curfew:	No statute listed.

KANSAS

The Law:	Kansas Statutes Annotated. "K.S.A." You may find these either as Vernon's Kansas Statutes Annotated or Kansas Statutes Annotated Official. The index system can be difficult to use.
Abortion:	Minors must have counseling and parental consent or judge's permission. *(Secs. 65-6704 and 6705)*
Age of Majority:	18 years old or 16 if married. *(Sec. 38-101)*
Driver's Licenses:	At 14, get instructional permit, which allows only supervised driving. At 15, get restricted license if have taken driver's education, had instruction permit for 6 months, and have had 25 hours of supervised driving. Must be either accompanied by licensed driver or going to and from school or work. Full license at 16. *(Secs. 8-236, 8-296, and 8-1586)*
Marriage:	If under 18, need consent of both parents or a judge's permission. *(Sec. 23-106)*
Compulsory School Attendance Ages:	Until age 18, except that at 16, can withdraw with parental consent and judge's permission. *(Sec. 72-1111)*
Criminal Law:	Can be transferred to adult court at 14 for serious felonies. Otherwise, treated as adult at 18. *(Sec. 38-1636)*
Child Labor Law:	No working under age 14; but there are some exceptions. Under 16, only work between 7 a.m. and 10 p.m. on school days, limited to 8 hours per day and 40 hours per week. *(beginning with Sec. 38-601)*
Curfew:	No specific statute.

KENTUCKY

The Law:	Kentucky Revised Statutes. "K.R.S." Ignore volume numbers and look for chapter numbers.
Abortion:	Minors must have parental consent or judge's permission. *(Sec. 311.732)*
Age of Majority:	18 years old *(Sec. 2.015)*
Driver's Licenses:	To get license if under age 21, must have had instructional permit for at least 120 days. If under 18, must take driver's education class and stay in school. Get full license at 16. *(Sec. 186.450)*
Marriage:	If under 18, need parental consent. If under 16, must also have judge's permission. *(Sec. 402.210)*
Compulsory School Attendance Ages:	Can withdraw at 16 with notice to parents and after a conference with the principal. *(Sec. 159.010)*
Criminal Law:	Treated as a juvenile until age 18. At 16, can be transferred to adult court for some crimes. *(Sec. 510.020)*
Child Labor Law:	Generally cannot work under age 14. Between 14 and 16, cannot work during school hours. *(Sec. 339.205)*
Curfew:	No specific statute.

LOUISIANA

The Law:	Louisiana Statutes Annotated-Revised Statutes. "LSA-R.S.", Children's Code "Ch.C.", and Civil Code "C.C."
Abortion:	Under 18, must have parental consent or judge's permission. *(beginning Sec. 40:1299.33)*
Age of Majority:	18 years old *(Sec. 29, Civil Code 29)*
Driver's Licenses:	At 15, can get instructional permit if in driver's ed. At 16, if you have had instructional permit for at least 90 days, can get intermediate license. Intermediate license allows driving only between 5 a.m. and 11 p.m. After 12 months with the intermediate license and no moving violations or curfew violations, can get full license. (beginning Sec. 32:401)
Marriage:	If under 18, must have parental consent. If under 16, must also have judge's permission. *(Sec. 1548, Children's Code 1548)*
Compulsory School Attendance Ages:	Ages 7-15 *(Sec. 17:221)*
Criminal Law:	Treated as an adult at 17. Can be transferred to adult court at 15. *(Sec. 305, Children's Code 305)*
Child Labor Law:	Under 16, 8 hours per day, 6 days per week, 40 hours per week when school not in session, 3 hours per day and 18 hours per week during school, between 7 a.m. and 7 p.m. (9 p.m. in the summer). *(beginning with Sec. 23:211)*
Curfew:	No specific statute.

MAINE

The Law:	Maine Revised Statutes Annotated. "M.R.S.A." Ignore volume numbers and look for title number.
Abortion:	Minors must have parental consent or judge' permission. *(Title 22, Sec. 2595)*
Age of Majority:	18 years old *(Title 1, Section 72)*
Driver's Licenses:	Minors must have parent's consent. At 15, can get instructional permit with driver's education class. Requires driver to be accompanied by licensed driver at least 20 years old. Can get full license after 3 months with instructional permit and proof of 35 hours of supervised driving experience. *(Title 29, Sec. 1304)*
Marriage:	If under 18, need parental consent. If under 16, must also have judge's permission. *(Title 19A, Sec. 652)*
Compulsory School Attendance Ages:	Until age 17, except if 15, and have completed the 9th grade, can withdraw with parent's permission to participate in approved work-study program or if you get the school board's permission to quit. *(Title 20A, Sec. 5001A)*
Criminal Law:	Automatically treated as adult at 18. For serious crimes, can be transferred to adult court at any age. *(beginning with Title 15, Sec. 501)*
Child Labor Law:	Generally must be 14 to work. If under 18, no more than 50 hours per week and 10 hours per day and between 5 a.m. and midnight when school not in session, 20 hours per week and 4 hours per day, between 7 a.m. and 10 p.m. when school is in session. *(beginning with Title 26, Sec. 701)*
Curfew:	No specific statute.

MARYLAND

The Law:	Annotated Code of Maryland "A.C.M."
Abortion:	Notice required unless physician waives this requirement. *(Sec. 20-103)*
Age of Majority:	18 years old *(Sec. 1-24)*
Driver's Licenses:	Get learner's permit at 15 years and 9 months, which requires supervised driving at all times. At 16 and 1 month, after 4 months with no violations, can get provisional license. If licensed under 6 months, provisional license lasts 18 months. If licensed between 6 and 12 months, provisional lasts for 12 months. If licensed between 12 and 18 months, provisional lasts for 6 months. Cannot have any moving violations. While license provisional, driving must be supervised between midnight at 5 a.m. Restrictions expire at 18. *(beginning with Sec. 16-101)*
Marriage:	If under 18, must have parental consent or be pregnant. 16 is minimum age unless 15 and expecting a child or already have one. *(Sec. 2-301 , Family Law 2-301)*
Compulsory School Attendance Ages:	Ages 5-16. *(Sec. 7-301 , Education 7-301)*
Criminal Law:	Can be transferred at 15 or younger than 15 and charged with a crime that, for adults, would be punishable by death or life in prison. *(beginning with Sec. 3-801, Courts and Judicial Proceedings 3-801)*
Child Labor Law:	If under 16, only between 7 a.m. and 8 p.m. (9 in the summer.) During school, 4 days per week and 23 hours per week, 8 hours per day and 40 hours per week when not in school. Generally cannot work if under 14. *(beginning with Sec. 3-201, Labor and Employment 3-201)*
Curfew:	No specific statute. *(Title 23A Section 2 authorizes curfews)*

MASSACHUSETTS

The Law:	Annotated Laws of Massachusetts. "A.L.M."
Abortion:	Parental consent or judge's permission. *(Title 112, Sec. 125)*
Age of Majority:	18 years old *(Title 4, Sec. 7)*
Driver's Licenses:	At 16, can get a learner's permit, which allows driving when supervised only. Between midnight and 5 a.m., the supervisor must be a parent or guardian. When have had learner's permit for 6 months and no violations, and are 16 and have had driver's education class, can get junior driver's license. For first 6 months, no passengers under 18 except immediate family unless someone over 21 also in car. No driving without parent in the car between midnight and 5 a.m. Get regular license at 18. *(Title 90, Sec. 8)*
Marriage:	If under 18, parents and judge must consent. *(Title 207, Sec. 25)*
Compulsory School Attendance Ages:	School board determines ages. Between 14 and 16, can be excused if have completed the 6th grade and are working. *(Sec. 76:1)*
Criminal Law:	Treated as an adult at 17. Can be transferred at 14 for certain crimes. *(Chapter 119)*
Child Labor Law:	If under 18, limited to 12 consecutive hours, and 48 hours per week. *(beginning with Title 149, Section 50)*
Curfew:	No specific statute.

MICHIGAN

The Law:	Michigan Statutes Annotated. "M.S.A." or Michigan Compiled Laws Annotated "M.C.L.A."
Abortion:	Parental consent or judge's permission. *(Sec. 722.903)*
Age of Majority:	18 years old *(Sec. 722.1)*
Driver's Licenses:	When taking driver's education, after 2 hours of driving experience and 10 classroom hours, get temporary driver's ed certificate, which requires supervision by parent or instructor. At 14 and 9 months, after completion of segment 1 of driver's ed, get level 1 license, which allows driving only when accompanied by licensed driver over 21. Get level 2, if have completed segment 2 of driver's ed and had not violations and 50 hours of supervised driving, 10 at night. Must spend at least 6 months on level 2. Level 2 requires supervision between midnight and 5 a.m. Then, at 17, get level 3. Must have level 3 for 12 months with no moving violations. *(beginning Sec. 257.301)*
Marriage:	If under 18, parents must consent. 16 is minimum age. *(Sec. 551.103)*
Compulsory School Attendance Ages:	Ages 6-16. *(Sec. 380.1561)*

(continued)

Criminal Law: Automatically an adult at 17. Can be transferred at 14 for serious crimes. *(Sec. 764.1f)*

Child Labor Law: Generally cannot work under 14. If under 16, 6 days per week, 8 hours per day and 48 hours per week on average, with no day longer than 10 hours, when not in school, between 7 a.m. and 9 p.m. only. During school term, 48 hours per week maximum in work and school combined. Between 16 and 18, same except hours are 6 a.m. to 10:30 p.m., 11:30 p.m. on non-school night. *(beginning with Sec. 409.101)*

Curfew: If under 12, prohibited between 10 p.m. and 6 a.m. If under 16, midnight and 6 a.m. *(beginning Sec. 722.751)*

MINNESOTA

The Law:	Minnesota Statutes Annotated. "M.S.A." Ignore volume numbers and look for section numbers.
Abortion:	Parents get 48 hours notice unless minor claims she is victim of abuse or gets judge's permission. *(Sec. 144.343)*
Age of Majority:	18 years old *(Sec. 645.451)*
Driver's Licenses:	Get instructional permit at 15 with driver's education. Allows driving only with licensed driver who is at least 21. At 16, after 6 months with no moving violation, get provisional license. Full license after 12 months with provisional license. *(beginning with Sec. 171.01)*
Marriage:	At 16, can marry with parental consent and judge's permission. *(beginning with Sec. 518.01)*
Compulsory School Attendance Ages:	At 16, can withdraw after meeting with school officials. *(Sec. 120A.22)*
Criminal Law:	At 14, can be transferred to adult court. *(Sec. 609.055)*
Child Labor Law:	If under 16, work only between 7 a.m. and 7 p.m., 8 hours per day and 40 hours per week. If under 18, cannot work after 11 p.m. on a school night or before 5 a.m. on a school day. *(beginning with Sec. 181A.01)*
Curfew:	Authorizes counties to have curfews for under 18. If do adopt, must have earlier curfew for those under 12 than for older children. *(Sec. 145A.05)*

MISSISSIPPI

The Law:	Mississippi Code Annotated 1972. "M.C."
Abortion:	Parental consent or judge's permission. *(beginning with Sec. 41-41-51)*
Age of Majority:	18 years old *(Sec. 93-19-13)*
Driver's Licenses:	At 15, get temporary driving permit, which allows driving only when supervised. When have had for 6 months with no violations, get intermediate license, which requires supervision between 10 p.m. and 6 a.m. After 6 months with no violations, get full license. *(beginning with Sec. 63-1-1)*
Marriage:	Statute says males must be 17, females 15, but minimum age can be waived by a judge. If under 21, notice of marriage license application sent to parents. (Sec. 93-1-5)
Compulsory School Attendance Ages:	Ages 6-17. *(Sec. 37-13-91)*
Criminal Law:	If guilty of felony and under 16, can do time in county jail instead of prison, after 16 in adult prison. *(Sec. 99-19-15)*
Child Labor Law:	Generally, cannot work under 14. If under 16, limited to 8 hours per day and 44 hours per week, between 6 a.m. and 7 p.m. *(beginning with Sec. 71-1-17)*
Curfew:	No specific statute.

MISSOURI

The Law:	Vernon's Annotated Missouri Statutes. "A.M.S." Ignore volume numbers and look for section numbers.
Abortion:	Minors must have parental consent or judge's permission. *(Sec. 188.028)*
Age of Majority:	18 years old *(Sec. 431.061)*
Driver's Licenses:	Get instruction permit at 15, which requires supervised driving. At 16, get an intermediate license, if you have had instruction permit for 6 months and 20 hours of supervised driving. Intermediate license required supervision between 1 a.m. and 5 a.m. Get full license at 18. *(Sec. 302.060)*
Marriage:	Under 18, must have parental consent. If under 15, must have judge's permission. *(Sec. 431.055)*
Compulsory School Attendance Ages:	Until age 16. At 14, can withdraw with superintendent's consent or judge's permission and notice to parents if you have legal, desirable employment. *(Sec. 167.031)*
Criminal Law:	Treated as an adult at 17. Transferred to adult court at 12 for felony. *(Secs. 211.071 and .041)*
Child Labor Law:	Between 14 and 16, can work only in limited occupations and not during the school term without a work permit. *(Sec. 294.024)*
Curfew:	No specific statute.

MONTANA

The Law:	Montana Code Annotated. "M.C.A." Ignore volume numbers and look for title numbers.
Abortion:	48 hours notice to parent or judge's permission. *(Sec. 50-20-201)*
Age of Majority:	18 years old *(Sec. 41-1-101)*
Driver's Licenses:	At 15, with driver's ed, can get a restricted license. (Can get at 13 if you can show a hardship). At 14 and 6 months, can get a 6 month instruction permit. Get a full license at 16. *(Sec. 61-5-101)*
Marriage:	Under 18, must have parental consent or judge's permission. Minimum age 16. *(beginning with Sec. 40-1-202)*
Compulsory School Attendance Ages:	Must be in school until later—16th birthday or completion of the 8th grade. *(beginning with Sec. 20-5-101)*
Criminal Law:	Treated as adult at 18. Transferred at 12 for serious felonies. *(beginning with Sec. 41-5-204)*
Child Labor Law:	At 14 and 15, can only work between 7 a.m. and 7 p.m. (9 p.m. on non-school night), limited to 3 hours per school day and 18 hours per school week , 8 hours per day and 40 hours per week when not in school. *(beginning with Sec. 41-2-101)*
Curfew:	Curfews allowed for minors. (Sec. 7-32-2302)

NEBRASKA

The Law:	Revised Statutes of Nebraska 1943 "R.S.N." Ignore volume numbers and look for chapter numbers.
Abortion:	Parental notification required. *(beginning with Sec. 71-6901)*
Age of Majority:	All persons under 19 are minors. *(Secs. 43-245, 43-2101)*
Driver's Licenses:	At 15, can get learner's permit. Requires licensed driver over 21 in car. Can also get at 14 if working for a school permit. The school permit allows driver to go to and from school. At 16, get provisional permit once you have had 50 hours of supervised driving. Must be supervised between midnight and 6 a.m. Full license at 18. *(Secs. 60-480, 60-4,120.01)*
Marriage:	If a minor, parents must consent. 17 is minimum age. *(Sec. 42-102)*
Compulsory School Attendance Ages:	Must attend until 16 years old. Exception for 14 year olds who have completed the 8th grade and who need to work full time to support themselves or their families. *(beginning with Sec. 79-201)*
Criminal Law:	Treated as adult at 18. Can be transferred to adult court at any age for any felony and at 16 for misdemeanors. *(Secs. 28-105.01, 43-247)*
Child Labor Law:	Under 16, maximum of 48 hours per week and 8 hours per day, between 6 a.m. and 10 p.m. if school not in session, 8 p.m. when in session. Also 8 p.m. for those under 14. *(Sec. 48-301)*
Curfew:	No specific statute.

NEVADA

The Law:	Nevada Revised Statutes Annotated. "N.R.S.A." Ignore volume numbers and look for chapter numbers.
Abortion:	Parental notice or judge's permission. *(Sec. 442.255)*
Age of Majority:	18 years old *(Sec. 129.010)*
Driver's Licenses:	At 15, get instructional permit, which allows only supervised driving. Can get regular license at 15 3/4, with driver's education class and 50 hours of supervised driving. Between 14 and 18, can also get restricted permit to drive unsupervised to and from school. *(beginning with Sec. 483.250)*
Marriage:	If under 18, parental consent needed. If under 16, judge must also consent. *(Sec. 122.020)*
Compulsory School Attendance Ages:	Ages 7 through 17. Can quit at 17 if taking GED. *(Sec. 392.040)*
Criminal Law:	Treated as adult at 18. Can be transferred to adult court at 14. *(beginning with Sec. 62.020)*
Child Labor Law:	If under 16, limited to 8 hours per day and 48 hours per week. If under 14, must have judge's permission to work. *(beginning with Sec. 609.185)*
Curfew:	No specific statute.

NEW HAMPSHIRE

The Law:	New Hampshire Statutes Annotated. "N.H.R.S.A." Ignore title numbers and look for chapter numbers.
Abortion:	No statute.
Age of Majority:	18 years old *(Sec. 21B:1)*
Driver's Licenses:	Between 16 and 18, get youth operator's license, with driver's education class. Requires supervision between 1 a.m. and 5 a.m., and must be supervised for first 90 days. *(Sec. 263:14)*
Marriage:	If under 18, parents and judge must consent. Statute says minimum age for males is 14 and females is 13. *(Secs. 457:4 and 5)*
Compulsory School Attendance Ages:	Ages 6-18, but can quit at 16 after conference with principal and with parental consent. *(Sec. 193:1)*
Criminal Law:	Treated as adult at 15. Can be transferred at 13 years old. *(Sec. 628:1)*
Child Labor Law:	If under 16, only between 7 a.m. and 9 p.m., 3 hours per day, 23 hours per week during school, 8 hours per day and 48 hours per week non-school. If under 18, maximum of 6 days per week and 30 hours per week during school and 48 hours per week non-school. *(beginning with Sec. 276-A:1)*
Curfew:	If under 16, prohibited after 9 p.m. *(Sec. 31:43C)*

NEW JERSEY

The Law:	New Jersey Statutes Annotated. "N.J.S.A." Ignore article numbers.
Abortion:	Parental notice or judge's permission required. *(beginning with Sec. 9:17A-1.1)*
Age of Majority:	18 *(Sec. 9:17B-2)*
Emancipation:	No specific statute.
Driver's Licenses:	At 16, get special learner's permit, which allows driving in presence of instructor. At 17, can get provisional license after 6 months experience with special learner's permit and completion of driver's ed. Get full license at 18. *(beginning with Sec. 39:3-13.4)*
Marriage:	If under 18, must have parental consent. If under 16, must also have judge's permission. *(Sec. 37:1-6)*
Compulsory School Attendance Ages:	Must attend until 16 years old. *(Secs.. 18A:38-25)*
Criminal Law:	At 14, can be transferred to adult court. *(beginning with Sec. 2C:4-1)*
Child Labor Law:	Under 18, maximum of 6 consecutive days per week, 8 hours per day and 40 hours per week. If under 16, only between 7 a.m. and 7 p.m. (9 p.m. in the summer). Between 16 and 18, work only between 6 a.m. and 11 p.m. (can work after 11 on non-school days and during the summer.)*(beginning with Sec. 34:2-1)*
Curfew:	If under 18, can be restricted between 10 p.m. and 6 a.m. *(Secs. 40:48-2.52)*

NEW MEXICO

The Law:	New Mexico Statutes 1978 Annotated. "N.M.S.A." Ignore volume numbers and look for chapter numbers.
Abortion:	No specific statute.
Age of Majority:	18 years old *(Sec. 28-6-1)*
Driver's Licenses:	At 15, can get instructional permit. At 15 and 6 months, with driver's education class and instructional permit for 6 months and 50 hours of supervised driving, get provisional license. At 16 and 6 months, get regular driver's license if you have had provisional for 12 months and no violations. *(Sec. 66-5-8)*
Marriage:	If under 18, need parental consent. 16 is minimum age. *(Sec. 40-1-6)*
Compulsory School Attendance Ages:	Can quit at 17 years old with permission of school board if working and parents consent. *(Sec. 22-12-1)*
Criminal Law:	Treated as adult at 18. Can be transferred at 15. *(beginning with Sec. 32A-2-1)*
Child Labor Law:	Can work under 14 with special permit, only 8 hours per day and 44 hours per week, 7 a.m. to 9 p.m. 14-18, federal regulations control. *(beginning with Sec. 50-6-1)*
Curfew:	No specific statute.

NEW YORK

The Law:	McKinney's Consolidated Laws of New York Annotated. "C.L.N.Y." Each type of code is named separately, for example the Labor code or the Education code.
Abortion:	No specific statute.
Age of Majority:	18 years old *(Sec. 3-101)*
Driver's Licenses:	Under 18, get class DJ license. This license allows driving in Suffolk and Nassau counties only when going to and from school, no driving at all in New York City. All licenses are probationary for the first 6 months. Learner's permit requires being accompanied by licensed driver at all times. Get unrestricted license at 18. *(Sec. 501, Vehicle and Traffic 501)*
Marriage:	If under 18, parents must consent. If under 16, must also have judge's permission. 14 is minimum age. *(Secs 15 and 15a, Domestic Secs. 15 and 15a)*
Compulsory School Attendance Ages:	6-16 years old. Can go part time if working. School board can require you to stay in school until 17 if you are not working. *(Sec. 3205, Education Sec. 3205)*
Criminal Law:	Treated as adult at 16 years old.
Child Labor Law:	At 14 and 15, when not in school, can work 8 hours per day, 6 days per week, 40 hours per week, between 7 a.m. and 9 p.m. When in school, 3 hours per day, 18 hours per week, 6 days per week, between 7 a.m. and 7 p.m. At 16 and 17, same as above except can work from 6 a.m. to 10 p.m. when not in school and until midnight when not in school. *(Secs. 131 and 132, Labor Secs. 131 and 132)*
Curfew:	No specific statute.

NORTH CAROLINA

The Law:	General Statutes of North Carolina "G.S.N.C." Ignore volume numbers and look for chapter numbers.
Abortion:	Parental consent or judge's permission. *(Sec. 90-21.6)*
Age of Majority:	18 years old *(Sec. 48A-2)*
Driver's Licenses:	Level 1 learner's permit license at 15 with driver's education class and school attendance. Level 2 limited provisional license at 16 after had level 1 license for at least 12 months with no violations. Level 3 full provisional license after 6 months with level 2 license and no violations. No restrictions on full provisional license, but you lose it if quit school. Full license at 18. *(Sec. 20-11)*
Marriage:	If under 18, parents must consent. 16 is minimum age. *(Sec. 51-2(a))*
Compulsory School Attendance Ages:	Ages 7-16. *(beginning with Sec. 115C-378)*
Criminal Law:	Automatically an adult at 16. Can be transferred to adult court at 13. *(beginning with Secs. 7B-1604 and 2200)*
Child Labor Law:	If under 18, work between 5 a.m. and 11 p.m. while in school. At 16 and 17, parents can consent to extra hours, if school also agrees. At 14 and 15, limited to 3 hours per day and 18 hours per week, between 7 a.m. and 7 p.m. when school in session. 8 hours per day, 40 hours per week, between 7 a.m. and 9 p.m. when it is not. *(Sec. 95-25.5)*
Curfew:	No specific statute.

NORTH DAKOTA

The Law:	North Dakota Century Code Annotated. "N.D.C.C." Ignore volume numbers and look for title numbers.
Abortion:	Parental consent or judge's permission. *(Secs. 14.02.1-03.1)*
Age of Majority:	18 years old *(Sec. 14-10-1)*
Driver's Licenses:	Instructional permit at 14, which requires supervision. Full license at 16. (Sec. 39-06-03)
Marriage:	If under 18, parental consent needed. Minimum age 16. *(Sec. 14-03-02)*
Compulsory School Attendance Ages:	Ages 7-16. Exception for children whose income is needed for family support, but only with superintendent's consent to quit. *(Sec. 15-34.1-00.1)*
Criminal Law:	Transferred at age 16 for felonies. *(Sec. 12.1-32-13)*
Child Labor Law:	If under 16, 3 hours per day and 24 hours per week during school, between 7 a.m. and 7 p.m.. When not in school, 8 hours per day and 48 hours per week, until 9 p.m. *(Sec. 34-07-15)*
Curfew:	No specific statute.

OHIO

The Law:	Page's Ohio Revised Code Annotated. "O.R.C."
Abortion:	Parental consent or judge's permission needed. *(Sec. 2919.121)*
Age of Majority:	18 years old *(Sec. 3109.01)*
Driver's Licenses:	At 15 and 6 months, get temporary instruction permit. At 16, and when have had temporary instruction permit for 6 months, get probationary license. Full license at 18. *(beginning with Sec. 4507.07)*
Marriage:	Males can marry at 18, females at 16. Minors need parental consent.
Compulsory School Attendance Ages:	Until age 18, unless graduates first. *(Sec. 3331)*
Criminal Law:	Can be transferred to adult court at 14. *(Sec. 2151.022)*
Child Labor Law:	Under 16, only work 3 hours per day and 18 hours per week during school; 8 hours per day and 40 hours per week when school not in session. Hours are 7 a.m. to 7 p.m. (9p.m. when school not in session). *(beginning with Sec. 4109)*
Curfew:	Curfews authorized; can apply to under 18 years old. (Sec. 505.89)

OKLAHOMA

The Law:	Oklahoma Statutes Annotated. "O.S.A."
Abortion:	Parental consent or judge's permission needed. *(Title 63 Sec.1-738)*
Age of Majority:	18 years old *(Sec. 15-13)*
Driver's Licenses:	License at 16 with driver's education class. Without driver's ed, can drive only during daylight hours and with only 1 passenger for six months. Then, if no violations, get full license. *(beginning with Title 47 Section 6-102)*
Marriage:	Under 18, need parental consent. Must be at least 16 unless judge gives permission because expecting a child or already a parent. *(Sec. 4303)*
Compulsory School Attendance Ages:	Ages 5-18. At 16, school and parent can agree to allow withdrawal. *(Title 570 Section 10-10)*
Criminal Law:	Generally, *automatically* and adult at 18, but for some crimes can be *automatically* transferred to adult court at 13. Any child can be transferred to adult court for certain crimes. *(Sec. 21-2152)*
Child Labor Law:	If under 16, only work 3 hours per day and 18 hours per week when in school, between 7 a.m. and 7 p.m. When not in school, 8 hours per day and 40 hours per week, between 7 a.m. and 9 p.m. *(Sec. 40-75)*
Curfew:	No specific statute.

OREGON

The Law:	Oregon Revised Statutes Annotated. "O.R.S." Ignore volume numbers and look for chapter numbers.
Abortion:	No specific statute.
Age of Majority:	18 years old *(Sec. 109.510)*
Driver's Licenses:	To get provisional license, must be 16 and have had instructional permit for 6 months, 50 hours of supervised driving, and driver's education class. Get full license at 18. *(Sec. 807.060)*
Marriage:	If under 18, must have parental consent. 17 is minimum age. *(Sec. 106.010)*
Compulsory School Attendance Ages:	Ages 7-18, except if 16 and working on GED or if emancipated. *(Sec. 339.010)*
Criminal Law:	Treated as adult at 18, but can be transferred to adult court at judge's discretion at any age. *(Sec. 419C.340)*
Child Labor Law:	If under 16, 10 hours per day, 6 days per week, between 7 a.m. and 6 p.m. *(Sec. 653.305)*
Curfew:	No specific statute.

PENNSYLVANIA

The Law:	Purdon's Pennsylvania Consolidated Statutes Annotated. "Pa.C.S.A."
Abortion:	Parental consent or judge's permission required. *(Sec. 18-3206)*
Age of Majority:	18 years old *(Sec. 23-5101)*
Driver's Licenses:	Learner's permit, which requires licensed driver in car. Learner's permit for 6 months, have 50 hours of parent supervised experience, and are at least 16 can get junior driver's license. Get full license at 17 with driver's ed and 12 months with junior license or at age 18. *(beginning with Sec. 75-1503)*
Marriage:	If under 18, need parental consent. If under 16, must also have judge's permission. *(Sec. 23-1304)*
Compulsory School Attendance Ages:	8-17 years old. At 15, can quit with approval of state's Secretary of Education or at 16 with superintendent's consent to go to trade school. *(Title 24 Sec. 13-1327)*
Criminal Law:	Automatically an adult at 18, but can be transferred to adult court for some crimes at 15. *(beginning with Sec. 42-630)*
Child Labor Law:	If under 18, 6 days a week maximum, 8 hours per day and 40 hours per week, between 7 a.m. and 7 p.m. (9 p.m. in summer). Limited to 28 hours during school week. *(beginning with Sec. 43-41)*
Curfew:	No specific statute.

RHODE ISLAND

The Law:	1988 Reenactment of the General Laws of Rhode Island 1956. "G.L.R.I." Ignore title numbers and chapter numbers and look for section numbers.
Abortion:	Parental consent or judge's approval. *(Sec. 23-4.7-6)*
Age of Majority:	18 years old *(Sec. 15-12-1)*
Driver's Licenses:	Level 1 license is a limited instruction permit and can get at 16 with driver's education class and required licensed driver in car at all times. Level 2 limited provisional license when you have had learner's permit for 6 months with no violations. Level 3 is a full license. Get at 17 with limited provisional license for 12 months and no violations. *(Sec. 31-10-6)*
Marriage:	If under 18, need parental consent. 16 is minimum age. *(beginning with Sec. 120-1-100)*
Compulsory School Attendance Ages:	5-17 years old. Exception if you have completed the 8th grade and are gainfully employed at a job needed to support yourself or others dependent on you. *(beginning with Sec. 59-65-10)*
Criminal Law:	Automatically an adult at 17 years old. Are not subject to transfer to adult court, but juvenile court can sentence you to lengthy sentence. Time served in juvenile placement until 17, then transferred to adult prison. *(Sec. 20-78-10)*
Child Labor Law:	Rules determined by state Commissioner of Labor and not by statute. *(Sec. 41-13-5)*
Curfew:	No specific statute.

SOUTH CAROLINA

The Law:	Code of Laws of South Carolina 1976 "C.L.S.C." Ignore volume numbers and look for title numbers.
Abortion:	Parental consent or judge's permission. *(Sec. 44-41-30)*
Age of Majority:	18 years old *(Sec. 15-1-320)*
Driver's Licenses:	At 15, get beginner's permit, which allows daylight driving with licensed driver. Must have for 90 days before you get full license. At 15, get provisional license when in driver's education class and had beginner's permit for 90 days. At 16, get special restricted license, which requires supervision between midnight and 6 a.m. Get full license at 17. *(Sec. 56-1-40)*
Marriage:	If under 18, need parental consent. Minimum age 16. *(Sec. 20-1-100)*
Compulsory School Attendance Ages:	5-17 years old, unless have completed the 8th grade, are gainfully employed, and the employment is needed to support you or someone dependent on you. *(beginning with Sec. 59-65-10)*
Criminal Law:	Treated as an adult at 17 years old. No transfers to adult court, but juvenile court can impose lengthy sentence and you will serve time in juvenile placement until 17, then be transferred to adult prison. *(Sec. 20-78-10)*
Child Labor Law:	Rules set by state Commissioner of Labor and not by statute. *(beginning with Sec. 41-13-5)*
Curfew:	No specific statute.

SOUTH DAKOTA

The Law:	South Dakota Codified Laws (Michie). "S.D.C.L."
Abortion:	48 hour written notice to parents unless an emergency or parental consent given or judge's permission. *(Secs. 34-23A-7 and 7.1)*
Age of Majority:	18 years old *(Sec. 26-1-1)*
Driver's Licenses:	Start with instructional permit at 14. Once you have had for 180 days, then get a restricted minor's permit, which requires supervised driving from 8 p.m. to 6 a.m. Becomes unrestricted at 16. *(Sec. 38-12-11)*
Marriage:	If under 18, must have parental consent. *(Sec. 25-1-12)*
Compulsory School Attendance Ages:	6-16 years old. *(Sec. 13-27-1)*
Criminal Law:	Can be transferred to adult court at 16 years old for serious felonies. *(beginning with Sec. 26-11-1)*
Child Labor Law:	If under 16, 4 hours per day, 20 hours per week during school, 8 hours per day and 40 hours per week when not in school, before 10 p.m. on any night that precedes a school day. If under 14, can only work in limited jobs and not after 7 p.m. *(Sec. 60-12-1)*
Curfew:	No specific statute.

TENNESSEE

The Law:	Tennessee Code Annotated "T.C.A." Ignore volume numbers and look for section numbers.
Abortion:	Must have written consent of parent or permission from judge. *(Sec. 37-10-301)*
Age of Majority:	18 years old *(Sec. 1-3-105)*
Driver's Licenses:	At 15, get learner's permit. Allows supervised driving between 6 a.m. and 10 p.m. At 16, get intermediate license when have had learner's permit for 180 days with no violations, 50 hours of supervised driving, with 10 of them at night. Full license at 18. *(Sec. 55-50-311)*
Marriage:	If under 18, need parental consent. If under 16, must also have judge's permission. *(Sec. 36-3-105)*
Compulsory School Attendance Ages:	6-18 years old. At 17, school board can allow you to withdraw if staying detrimental to others and leaving quitting benefits you. *(Sec. 49-6-3005)*
Criminal Law:	Treated as an adult at 16. Can be transferred to adult court when younger than 16 for serious felonies. *(Sec. 37-1-134)*

(continued)

Child Labor Law: At 14 and 15, work only in non-school hours between 7 a.m. and 7 p.m. on school day, 9 p.m. on non-school days. Limited to 18 hours per week and 3 hours per day during school, 40 hours per week and 8 hours per day during school. At 16 and 17, cannot work between 10 p.m. and 6 a.m. on Sunday through Thursday during school term. *(Sec. 50-5-101)*

Curfew: If under 16, cannot be out without parents from 10 p.m. on Monday through Thursday until 6 a.m. the following day, 11 p.m. until 6 a.m. Friday through Sunday. If under 18, same except can stay out until midnight Friday through Sunday. *(Sec. 39-17-1701)*

TEXAS

The Law:	Vernon's Texas Codes Annotated "V.T.C.A." and Vernon's Revised Statutes Annotated "V.R.S.A."
Abortion:	48 hours notice to parents or judge's permission. *(Sec. 33.001, Family Code 33.001)*
Age of Majority:	18 years old. *(Sec. 129.001, Civil Practice and Remedies 129.001)*
Driver's Licenses:	Get instructional permit at 15 with driver's education class. Get provisional license at 16, which requires supervision between midnight and 5 a.m. and allows only 1 passenger for the first 6 months. *(Transportation Code Chapter 521)*
Marriage:	If under 18 years old, need parental consent. Minimum age 14. *(Sec. 2.102)*
Compulsory School Attendance Ages:	6-18 years old. Can quit at 17 if taking GED and have parent's consent or court order to take GED and at 16 if part of certain programs and taking GED. *(Sec. 25.085, Education Code 25.085)*
Criminal Law:	Treated as an adult at 17 years old. Can be transferred to adult court at 14. *(Sec. 54.02, Family Code 54.02)*
Child Labor Law:	At 14 and 15, maximum 8 hours per day and 48 hours per week, between 5 a.m. and 10 p.m. only, midnight on non-school nights and during the summer. *(Sec. 51.011, Labor 51.011)*
Curfew:	No specific statute.

UTAH

The Law:	Utah Code Annotated "U.C." Ignore volume numbers and look for title numbers.
Abortion:	Parental notification and 24 hour waiting period. *(Sec. 76-7-304)*
Age of Majority:	18 years old *(Sec. 15-2-1)*
Driver's Licenses:	At 16, with driver's education class, can get license. Must also have 30 hours total experience driving; 10 hours night driving. Parent must sign to verify total hours driving experience. *(beginning with Sec. 53-3-202)*
Marriage:	If under 18, parents must consent. 15 is minimum age, and 15 requires judge's permission. *(Sec. 30-1-2)*
Compulsory School Attendance Ages:	Until age 18, although there are some exceptions for those 16 who have completed 8th grade. *(Sec. 53A-11-101)*
Criminal Law:	Can be transferred to adult court at 14 years of age for felonies. *(Sec. 78-3A-602)*
Child Labor Law:	If under 16, limited to 4 hours per day from 5 a.m. to 9:30 p.m., unless it is a non-school day. Then, allowed 8 hours per day and 40 hours per week. *(Sec. 34-23-202)*
Curfew:	No specific statute.

VERMONT

The Law:	Vermont Statutes Annotated. "V.S.A." Ignore chapter numbers and look for title numbers.
Abortion:	No specific statute.
Age of Majority:	18 years old *(Title 1 Sec.173)*
Driver's Licenses:	At 16, can get a junior driver's license with driver's education class, learner's permit for one year, and 40 hours supervised driving (10 at night) and 6 months with no violations. Regular license at 18 or at 16 with junior license for 6 months with no violations. *(beginning with Title 23 Sec. 606)*
Marriage:	Under 18, need parental consent. If under 16, judge must also consent. *(Title 18 Sec. 5141)*
Compulsory School Attendance Ages:	Ages 6-16. *(Title 16 Sec. 1121)*
Criminal Law:	Treated as an adult at 18, or 16 with a felony charge. *(Title 33 Sec. 5530)*
Child Labor Law:	If under 16, 8 hours per day, 6 days per week, between 7 a.m. and 7 p.m. (9 in summer). On school day, 3 hours per day, 18 hours per week. *(beginning with Title 21 Sec. 630)*
Curfew:	Authorizes curfews for those under 16. *(Title 24 Sec. 2151)*

VIRGINIA

The Law:	Code of Virginia 1950 Annotated "C.V." Ignore chapter numbers and look for title and section numbers.
Abortion:	Parental notification unless abuse or neglect or judge's permission. *(Sec. 16.1-241)*
Age of Majority:	18 years old *(Sec. 1-13.42)*
Driver's Licenses:	At 16 with driver's education class and school attendance. *(Sec. 46-2-234)*
Marriage:	If under 18, parents consent. 16 minimum age unless pregnant. *(Sec. 20-48)*
Compulsory School Attendance Ages:	Until 18, unless at 16, school board approves withdrawal. *(Sec. 22.1-254/5)*
Criminal Law:	Can be transferred at age 14. *(Sec. 16.1-241)*
Child Labor Law:	Federal law controls. *(beginning with Sec. 40.1-78)*
Curfew:	Cities can restrict minors between 10 p.m. and 6 a.m. *(Sec. 15.2-926)*

(continued)

WASHINGTON

The Law:	West's Revised Code of Washington Annotated "R.C.W.A."
Abortion:	Parental consent not required. *(Sec. 9.02.005)*
Age of Majority:	18 years old *(Sec. 26.28.010)*
Driver's Licenses:	At 15, get instructional permit, or at 15 with driver's education class. At 16, get intermediate license if have instructional permit for 6 months, completed driver's ed, and 50 hours of supervised driving. For first 6 months of intermediate license, no passengers under age 20. After 6 months, 3 passenger limit. Supervised between 1 a.m. and 5 a.m. After 12 months, no more passenger limits. *(beginning with Sec. 46.20.031)*
Marriage:	If under 18, parental consent. If not yet 17, must have court order. *(Sec. 26.04.010)*
Compulsory School Attendance Ages:	Ages 8-18. Can quit at 16 if working, with parents consent, or emancipated. *(Sec. 28A.225.010)*
Criminal Law:	Transfer at 15 for serious felony. *(Sec. 13.40.110)*
Child Labor Law:	Federal regulations control. *(Secs. 26.28.060, 15.04.150, 49.46.020)*
Curfew:	Authorizes cities to have curfew. *(Sec. 35.21.635)*

WEST VIRGINIA

The Law:	West Virginia Code "W.V.C." Ignore volume numbers and look for chapter numbers.
Abortion:	Parental notice or judge's permission. *(beginning with Sec. 16-2F-1)*
Age of Majority:	18 years old
Driver's Licenses:	Level 1: Age 15, drive between 5 a.m. and 11 p.m. Level 2: 16 plus 180 days with no violations with level 1 license and completion of driver's education class, supervised between 11 p.m. and 5 a.m. and 3 passenger limit. Level 3: full license at 17 with 12 months, no violations on level 2. *(Sec. 17B-2-3a)*
Marriage:	If under 18, must have parental consent. If under 16, judge must also consent. *(Sec. 48-1-1)*
Compulsory School Attendance Ages:	Ages 6-16 *(Sec. 18-1-1)*
Criminal Law:	Transfer to adult court at age 14. *(Sec. 49-5-10)*
Child Labor Law:	If under 16, 6 days per week, 40 hours per week, 8 hours per day, 5 a..m. to 8 p.m. only. *(Sec. 21-6-1)*
Curfew:	Authorizes curfew. No specifics. (Sec. 7-7-12)

WISCONSIN

The Law:	West's Wisconsin Statutes Annotated "W.S.A." Ignore chapter numbers and look for section numbers.
Abortion:	Parental consent or judge's permission. *(Sec. 48.375)*
Age of Majority:	18 years old
Driver's Licenses:	At 15 and 6 months, can get instructional permit. At 16, can drive with qualified driver and no other passengers. While under 16, can only drive with instructor or licensed driver over 21, parent's permission, and driver's ed. Get probationary license until 18. *(beginning with Sec. 343.01)*
Marriage:	If under 18, parental consent required. 16 minimum age. *(Sec. 765.02)*
Compulsory School Attendance Ages:	Ages 6-18. Can go to trade school at age 16 or take GED at age 17. *(Sec. 118.45)*
Criminal Law:	Can be transferred at age 14. *(beginning with Sec. 938.18)*
Child Labor Law:	If under 18, 8 hours per day, 40 hours per week, 6 days a week. If under 16, 24 hours per week maximum. *(beginning with Sec. 103.21)*
Curfew:	No specific statute.

WYOMING

The Law:	Wyoming Statutes Annotated. "W.S.A." Ignore volume numbers and look for title numbers.
Abortion:	Either 48 hour notification, parental consent, or judge's permission. *(Sec. 35-6-118)*
Age of Majority:	18 years old *(Sec. 8-1-102)*
Driver's Licenses:	At 15, get instructional permit. Get regular license at 16. *(beginning with Sec. 31-7-109)*
Marriage:	If under 18, parental consent required. Minimum age 16 unless judge also consents. *(Sec. 20-1-10)*
Compulsory School Attendance Ages:	Ages 7-16 or completed 10th grade. *(Sec. 21-4-101)*
Criminal Law:	Adult at 18. Can be transferred at age 14. *(beginning with Sec. 7-1-101)*
Child Labor Law:	Minimum age 14. If under 16, 8 hours per day between 5 a.m. and 10 p.m. (Midnight on a non-school night). *(beginning with Sec. 27-6-101)*
Curfew:	No specific statute.

INDEX

ABOUT THE AUTHOR

Traci Truly received her J.D. from Baylor University. She has practiced family law for more than fifteen years, which has included representing parents and grandparents in support, visitation, and custody cases. She was previously a member of the Texas Coalition for Juvenile Justice and is presently practicing law in Dallas, Texas.

SPHINX® PUBLISHING ORDER FORM

'O:			SHIP TO:		
#		Terms	F.O.B.	Chicago, IL	Ship Date

Charge my: ☐ VISA   ☐ MasterCard   ☐ American Express   ☐ **Money Order or Personal Check**

Credit Card Number   Expiration Date

✓	ISBN	Title	Retail	Qty	ISBN	Title	Retail
	SPHINX PUBLISHING NATIONAL TITLES				1-57248-220-6	Mastering the MBE	$16.95
					1-57248-167-6	Most Valuable Bus. Legal Forms You'll Ever Need (3E)	$21.95
	1-57248-148-X	Cómo Hacer su Propio Testamento	$16.95		1-57248-130-7	Most Valuable Personal Legal Forms You'll Ever Need	$24.95
	1-57248-226-5	Cómo Restablecer su propio Crédito y Renegociar sus Deudas	$21.95		1-57248-098-X	The Nanny and Domestic Help Legal Kit	$22.95
	1-57248-147-1	Cómo Solicitar su Propio Divorcio	$24.95		1-57248-089-0	Neighbor v. Neighbor (2E)	$16.95
	1-57248-238-9	The 529 College Savings Plan	$16.95		1-57248-169-2	The Power of Attorney Handbook (4E)	$19.95
	1-57248-166-8	The Complete Book of Corporate Forms	$24.95		1-57248-149-8	Repair Your Own Credit and Deal with Debt	$18.95
	1-57248-163-3	Crime Victim's Guide to Justice (2E)	$21.95		1-57248-217-6	Sexual Harassment: Your Guide to Legal Action	$18.95
	1-57248-159-5	Essential Guide to Real Estate Contracts	$18.95		1-57248-221-4	Teen Rights: A Legal Guide for Teens and the Adults in Their Lives	$22.95
	1-57248-160-9	Essential Guide to Real Estate Leases	$18.95		1-57248-168-4	The Social Security Benefits Handbook (3E)	$18.95
	1-57248-139-0	Grandparents' Rights (3E)	$24.95		1-57071-399-5	Unmarried Parents' Rights	$19.95
	1-57248-188-9	Guia de Inmigración a Estados Unidos (3E)	$24.95		1-57071-354-5	U.S.A. Immigration Guide (3E)	$19.95
	1-57248-187-0	Guia de Justicia para Victimas del Crimen	$21.95		1-57248-192-7	The Visitation Handbook	$18.95
	1-57248-103-X	Help Your Lawyer Win Your Case (2E)	$14.95		1-57248-225-7	Win Your Unemployment Compensation Claim (2E)	$21.95
	1-57248-164-1	How to Buy a Condominium or Townhome (2E)	$19.95		1-57248-138-2	Winning Your Personal Injury Claim (2E)	$24.95
	1-57248-191-9	How to File Your Own Bankruptcy (5E)	$21.95		1-57248-162-5	Your Right to Child Custody, Visitation, and Support (2E)	$24.95
	1-57248-132-3	How to File Your Own Divorce (4E)	$24.95		1-57248-157-9	Your Rights When You Owe Too Much	$16.95
	1-57248-100-5	How to Form a DE Corporation from Any State	$24.95			**CALIFORNIA TITLES**	
	1-57248-083-1	How to Form a Limited Liability Company	$22.95		1-57248-150-1	CA Power of Attorney Handbook (2E)	$18.95
	1-57248-099-8	How to Form a Nonprofit Corporation	$24.95		1-57248-151-X	How to File for Divorce in CA (3E)	$26.95
	1-57248-133-1	How to Form Your Own Corporation (3E)	$24.95		1-57071-356-1	How to Make a CA Will	$16.95
	1-57248-224-9	How to Form Your Own Partnership (2E)	$24.95		1-57248-145-5	How to Probate and Settle an Estate in CA	$26.95
	1-57248-232-X	How to Make Your Own Simple Will (3E)	$18.95		1-57248-146-3	How to Start a Business in CA	$18.95
	1-57248-200-1	How to Register Your Own Copyright (4E)	$24.95		1-57248-194-3	How to Win in Small Claims Court in CA (2E)	$18.95
	1-57248-104-8	How to Register Your Own Trademark (3E)	$21.95		1-57248-196-X	The Landlord's Legal Guide in CA	$24.95
	1-57248-118-8	How to Write Your Own Living Will (2E)	$16.95			**FLORIDA TITLES**	
	1-57248-156-0	How to Write Your Own Premarital Agreement (3E)	$24.95		1-57071-363-4	Florida Power of Attorney Handbook (2E)	$16.95
	1-57248-158-7	Incorporate in Nevada from Any State	$24.95		1-57248-176-5	How to File for Divorce in FL (7E)	$26.95
	1-57071-333-2	Jurors' Rights (2E)	$12.95		1-57248-177-3	How to Form a Corporation in FL (5E)	$24.95
	1-57248-223-0	Legal Research Made Easy (3E)	$21.95		1-57248-203-6	How to Form a Limited Liability Co. in FL (2E)	$24.95
	1-57248-165-X	Living Trusts and Other Ways to Avoid Probate (3E)	$24.95		1-57071-401-0	How to Form a Partnership in FL	$22.95
	1-57248-186-2	Manual de Beneficios para el Seguro Social	$18.95		*Form Continued on Following Page*		**Subtotal** _____

Find more legal information at: www.SphinxLegal.com

Qty	ISBN	Title	Retail
		FLORIDA TITLES (CONT'D)	
_____	1-57248-113-7	How to Make a FL Will (6E)	$16.95
_____	1-57248-088-2	How to Modify Your FL Divorce Judgment (4E)	$24.95
_____	1-57248-144-7	How to Probate and Settle an Estate in FL (4E)	$26.95
_____	1-57248-081-5	How to Start a Business in FL (5E)	$16.95
_____	1-57248-204-4	How to Win in Small Claims Court in FL (7E)	$18.95
_____	1-57248-202-8	Land Trusts in Florida (6E)	$29.95
_____	1-57248-123-4	Landlords' Rights and Duties in FL (8E)	$21.95
		GEORGIA TITLES	
_____	1-57248-137-4	How to File for Divorce in GA (4E)	$21.95
_____	1-57248-180-3	How to Make a GA Will (4E)	$21.95
_____	1-57248-140-4	How to Start Business in GA (2E)	$16.95
		ILLINOIS TITLES	
_____	1-57071-405-3	How to File for Divorce in IL (2E)	$21.95
_____	1-57248-170-6	How to Make an IL Will (3E)	$16.95
_____	1-57071-416-9	How to Start a Business in IL (2E)	$18.95
_____	1-57248-078-5	Landlords' Rights & Duties in IL	$21.95
		MASSACHUSETTS TITLES	
_____	1-57248-128-5	How to File for Divorce in MA (3E)	$24.95
_____	1-57248-115-3	How to Form a Corporation in MA	$24.95
_____	1-57248-108-0	How to Make a MA Will (2E)	$16.95
_____	1-57248-106-4	How to Start a Business in MA (2E)	$18.95
_____	1-57248-209-5	The Landlord's Legal Guide in MA	$24.95
		MICHIGAN TITLES	
_____	1-57248-215-X	How to File for Divorce in MI (3E)	$24.95
_____	1-57248-182-X	How to Make a MI Will (3E)	$16.95
_____	1-57248-183-8	How to Start a Business in MI (3E)	$18.95
		MINNESOTA TITLES	
_____	1-57248-142-0	How to File for Divorce in MN	$21.95
_____	1-57248-179-X	How to Form a Corporation in MN	$24.95
_____	1-57248-178-1	How to Make a MN Will (2E)	$16.95
		NEW YORK TITLES	
_____	1-57248-193-5	Child Custody, Visitation and Support in New York	$26.95
_____	1-57248-141-2	How to File for Divorce in NY (2E)	$26.95
_____	1-57248-105-6	How to Form a Corporation in NY	$24.95
_____	1-57248-095-5	How to Make a NY Will (2E)	$16.95
_____	1-57248-199-4	How to Start a Business in NY (2E)	$18.95

Qty	ISBN	Title	Rets
_____	1-57248-198-6	How to Win in Small Claims Court in NY (2E)	$18
_____	1-57248-197-8	Landlords' Legal Guide in NY	$24
_____	1-57071-188-7	New York Power of Attorney Handbook	$19
_____	1-57248-122-6	Tenants' Rights in New York	$21
		NORTH CAROLINA TITLES	
_____	1-57248-185-4	How to File for Divorce in NC (3E)	$22
_____	1-57248-129-3	How to Make a NC Will (3E)	$16
_____	1-57248-184-6	How to Start a Business in NC (3E)	$18
_____	1-57248-091-2	Landlords' Rights & Duties in NC	$21
		OHIO TITLES	
_____	1-57248-190-0	How to File for Divorce in OH (2E)	$24
_____	1-57248-174-9	How to Form a Corporation in OH	$24
_____	1-57248-173-0	How to Make an OH Will	$16
		PENNSYLVANIA TITLES	
_____	1-57248-211-7	How to File for Divorce in PA (3E)	$24
_____	1-57248-094-7	How to Make a PA Will (2E)	$1
_____	1-57248-112-9	How to Start a Business in PA (2E)	$1
_____	1-57071-179-8	Landlords' Rights and Duties in PA	$1
		TEXAS TITLES	
_____	1-57248-171-4	Child Custody, Visitation, and Support in TX	$2
_____	1-57248-172-2	How to File for Divorce in TX (3E)	$2
_____	1-57248-114-5	How to Form a Corporation in TX (2E)	$2
_____	1-57071-417-7	How to Make a TX Will (2E)	$1
_____	1-57248-214-1	How to Probate and Settle an Estate in TX (3E)	$2
_____	1-57248-228-1	How to Start a Business in TX (3E)	$1
_____	1-57248-111-0	How to Win in Small Claims Court in TX (2E)	$1
_____	1-57248-110-2	Landlords' Rights and Duties in TX (2E)	$2

SUBTOTAL THIS PAGE _____

SUBTOTAL PREVIOUS PAGE _____

Shipping — $5.00 for 1st book, $1.00 each additional _____

Illinois residents add 6.75% sales tax _____

Connecticut residents add 6.00% sales tax _____

TOTAL _____

Find more legal information at: www.SphinxLegal.com